Tomorrow's Universities:
A Worldwide Look
at Educational Change

Also of Interest

Research in the Age of the Steady-State University, edited by Don I. Phillips and Benjamin S. Shen

Rural Education in Urbanized Nations: Issues and Innovations, edited by Jonathan P. Sher

**Legal Handbook for Educators*, Patricia A. Hollander

*Education in Rural America: A Reassessment of Conventional Wisdom, edited by Jonathan P. Sher

*Going to College: The Study of Students and the Student Experience, James R. Davis

*Teaching Strategies for the College Classroom, James R. Davis

Women and Minorities in Science: Strategies for Increasing Participation, edited by Sheila M. Humphreys

***Rural Education: In Search of a Better Way*, edited by Paul Nachtigal

Science and Technology in a Changing International Order: The United Nations Conference on Science and Technology for Development, edited by Volker Rittberger

***Women and Technological Change in Developing Countries*, edited by Roslyn Dauber and Melinda L. Cain

*Available in softcover only.
**Available in hardcover and paperback.

Westview Special Studies in Education

Tomorrow's Universities:
A Worldwide Look at Educational Change
W. Werner Prange, David Jowett, and Barbara Fogel

In this book the authors present a unique synthesis of materials that evolved from the World Conference on Innovative Higher Education, which brought together the heads of universities from over thirty countries, along with other prominent men and women concerned with higher education, to share information on education innovation and change. Much more than simply a conference report, the book addresses the fundamental issues of change in higher education and how change works and where it is leading, and looks at the ways in which innovations meet changing needs.

Dr. W. Werner Prange is professor of creative communication and former vice-chancellor of the University of Wisconsin-Green Bay. He is also chairman of the Task Force on International Education/Council for Interinstitutional Leadership in Washington, D.C. Dr. David Jowett is professor of science and environmental change at the University of Wisconsin-Green Bay. Barbara Fogel is a consultant in education and former director of higher education for development at the International Council for Educational Development.

Tomorrow's Universities: A Worldwide Look at Educational Change

W. Werner Prange,
David Jowett, and Barbara Fogel

Westview Press / Boulder, Colorado

Westview Special Studies in Education

Copyright © 1982 by Westview Press, Inc.

Published in 1982 in the United States of America by
    Westview Press, Inc.
    5500 Central Avenue
    Boulder, Colorado 80301
    Frederick A. Praeger, President and Publisher

Library of Congress Catalog Card Number: 82-060045
ISBN 0-86531-410-1

Composition for this book was provided by the authors.
Printed and bound in the United States of America.

To Farhad Riahi and the late Abelardo Samonte

Contents

Tables and Figures

Foreword

TOMORROW'S UNIVERSITIES: A WORLDWIDE LOOK AT
EDUCATIONAL CHANGE is an important contribution to higher
education and to the understanding of university innovations throughout the world. The authors of this volume
have provided a much-needed, authoritative, and comprehensive account of the practical as well as the philosophical reasons for global university innovation at the
beginning of the 1980s.

While the title of the book seems to emphasize
universities, the content of the book and its implications are broader, encompassing higher education in the
world today as modified by university innovation.

The period of rapid university change and adaptation
(from the early 1960s to the mid-1970s) seems to have
moderated. By contrast the present is a period of re-
examination of roles, ends, and means of traditional and
nontraditional institutions--a period of assessment and
consolidation. Traditional institutions and values still
stand, but they now stand alongside nontraditional institutions and values. Between them an uneasy truce
prevails, with misunderstanding its chief component, as
other problems demand top priority.

In the more developed countries, higher education now
faces recessionary economies, a shrinking pool of
students, diminishing budgets, and escalating costs. A
reduction of public confidence clouds the horizon because
of institutional inflexibility, rising costs, suspected
lowering of quality, and the power of faculty and professionals to frustrate needed change.

In less developed countries, higher education is
pinched by severe economic conditions, an inadequate
supply of qualified students from seriously underdeveloped lower schools, dependence upon inappropriate
models for higher education, and the lack of indigenous
models. Higher education faculties, often a blend of
foreign and national professionals with allegiances to

models developed elsewhere, sometimes seem at cross
purposes with needs, problems, and aspirations at home.
No wonder there is uncertainty regarding universities'
ends and means and the motives for change.

Yet, as this volume clearly indicates, a strong
intellectual commitment to the reform of higher
education in developed and underdeveloped countries still
continues. Innovation is now quieter, less visibly
radical, and more assessment oriented. It is a time of
healthy hiatus.

In 1977 Roy Niblett observed that "innovation in
higher education is endangered not only by a lack of
money but by a deeper deficiency--the lack of unifying
philosophy capable of drawing together the innovative
efforts."* The appearance of TOMORROW'S UNIVERSITIES at
this time is fortuitous.

The authors of this volume, W. Werner Prange and
David Jowett of the University of Wisconsin-Green Bay,
and Barbara Fogel, formerly with the Academy for
Educational Development, are widely experienced in international higher education and university innovation.
They have based their work in this volume on the proceedings of a 1978 conference at Wingspread (the S.C.
Johnson Foundation conference center in Racine,
Wisconsin). The Wingspread conference provided a forum
for a world assessment of innovation in higher education.
Although the authors were seminal leaders in planning and
carrying out the Wingspread conference, their book is
much more than a report of a significant conference.

Prange, Jowett, and Fogel have presented the
intellectual yields of the Wingspread conference in a
unique way. The reader of their book experiences the
conference as it would have been if he had attended every
meeting, taped and reviewed every address, questioned all
the speakers, read every background paper, checked all
references, analyzed every contribution, compared and
contrasted every viewpoint, probed each case study and
statistic, and then in continuing debate, patiently
evolved a synthesis of the whole that is more than the
sum of the separate conference activities.

The process used in preparing this book calls to mind
what Lewis Thomas said about the Delphi Technique: "We
pass the word around; we ponder how the case is put by
different people; we read the poetry; we meditate over
the literature; we play the music; we change our minds;
we reach understanding. Society evolves this way, not by
shouting each other down, but by the unique capacity of

_____
* W. Roy Niblett. "Innovation," INTERNATIONAL
ENCYCLOPEDIA OF HIGHER EDUCATION. (Asa S. Knowles,
editor) San Francisco: Jossey-Bass, 1977, Vol. 5,
p. 2169.

unique, individual human beings to comprehend each other."* This is the process that led to TOMORROW'S UNIVERSITIES.

What was said and debated at the Wingspread conference has been painstakingly analyzed and organized according to theme, concerns, and goals of the conference. In addition, current and relevant background literature on innovation in higher education has been woven into the text to flesh out areas touched on only lightly or not at all, even in so comprehensive a conference. The spontaneity of conference give and take, touches of warmth and flashes of humor as well as the drama of disagreement have all somehow been preserved.

Part I of TOMORROW'S UNIVERSITIES presents the problems that throughout the world have forced higher education into new roles, ends, and means: access, relevance, flexibility, and efficiency. In Part II, innovative institutional responses to solve these problems are presented: delivery systems, new clienteles, innovations in the land-grant tradition, comprehensive higher education, interdisciplinarity and problem focus, extension and national development, research, the management of innovation, and new challenges/new responsibilities.

The text is liberally peppered with case studies supplied by distinguished conference participants personally familiar with each innovation. The innovations are discussed in the context of their origin and development and are candidly assessed. The contributions of developed and developing countries are examined. Similarities and differences are noted, and the effects of culture, economics, socio-political situations, and educational tradition are probed.

A strong theme of attention to the indigenous culture emerges as the hallmark of effective innovation. World leaders of higher education--whether conservative, liberal, or radical--express their views and assess the future of university innovation in higher education.

TOMORROW'S UNIVERSITIES will help all readers concerned about higher education to understand the current world state of higher education as universities adjust, adapt, innovate, hold fast, reach out for new values, and wrestle with the global questions that are shaping the universities of tomorrow.

---

* Lewis Thomas, THE MEDUSA AND THE SNAIL. New York: The Viking Press, 1979, p. 39.

No final, unifying philosophy of innovation emerged from the Wingspread conference. Nevertheless, if such a philosophy is ever to emerge, the present volume offers a substantial base for its development.

--Charles A. Wedemeyer
Madison, Wisconsin

Introduction

In May 1978 the heads of universities from over thirty countries, along with other prominent men and women concerned with higher education, met to compare notes on educational innovation and change. The meeting grew out of the friendship of several leading educators from separate continents, all of whom actively promote and participate in educational change; notably Rector Hans Meijer of Linköping University in Sweden, Chancellor Farhad Riahi of Bu-Ali Sina University in Iran, and Chancellor Edward W. Weidner of the University of Wisconsin-Green Bay. With the support and encouragement of the then Shahbanu of Iran and of the Johnson Foundation of Racine, Wisconsin they brought together a group of change-minded men and women in higher education. Their host was the Johnson Foundation, which has for many years been active in promoting education, environmental concerns, and international amity through meetings at their superb conference center at Wingspread.

The building Frank Lloyd Wright designed and called Wingspread, situated on a rolling prairie site north of Racine, Wisconsin, was built in 1938 as a residence for the Johnson family. In 1960, through the gift of Mr. and Mrs. H.F. Johnson, it became the headquarters of the Johnson Foundation and began its career as an educational conference center.

In the years since, it has been the setting for many conferences dealing with subjects of regional, national, and international interest. It is the hope and belief of the foundation's trustees that Wingspread will take its place increasingly as a national institution devoted to the free exchange of ideas among people.

The rolling expanse of the Midwestern prairies was considered a natural setting for Wingspread. In the limitless earth the architect envisioned a freedom and movement. The name Wingspread was an expression of the nature of the building, reflecting aspiration through spread wings--a symbol of soaring inspiration, and in more recent years, the free expression of ideas.

Without the financial support of the Johnson Foundation, neither the conference nor this volume would have been possible. But the foundation gave much more than money. In particular, the unfailing enthusiasm of Leslie Paffrath, president of the Johnson Foundation, and of Henry Halsted, vice president-programming, were essential both in planning stages and during the course of the conference. A Wingspread conference is perhaps the closest thing to an English country house weekend of the Edwardian era that the world today provides. Only superb organizational skills can provide such comfort, while maintaining an atmosphere of vigorous intellectual exchange.

Among the many other people who contributed to the success of the conference, foremost was Chancellor Edward W. Weidner of the University of Wisconsin-Green Bay. As Fred Harvey Harrington, former president of the University of Wisconsin, said in a letter to the Johnson Foundation:

It was Chancellor Weidner who proposed this conference to the Johnson Foundation in 1974, and it was his concept of what was needed that gave the meeting its breadth of view and its high standard of quality.

This is not surprising. International education and innovative education are two of the forces that have revolutionized the universities in the past generation. Ed Weidner stands high in both of these fields, and he has brought together the two approaches in his career and in this Wingspread venture. It is thanks to such as he that tomorrow's universities, here and abroad, will always feel the need for world approaches and for innovation.

It has been my good fortune to be associated with Ed Weidner for twenty years, and to have had the opportunity to see how effectively he has championed both innovative and international education. We first met when he was Vice Chancellor of the East-West Center and was bringing out his now classic book on THE WORLD ROLE OF UNIVERSITIES. Later we served together on a United States government educational mission to Mexico (Ed was the key to the success of that mission). Then, in 1966-67, when he was in charge of innovation and change at the University of Kentucky--another of his interesting assignments--I was able to persuade him to join us in Wisconsin as chancellor of the not-yet opened Green Bay campus of the University of Wisconsin. What interested him was

the opportunity to innovate from the planning stage
onward, to introduce interdisciplinary and broad
environmental approaches, and allow students and
faculty to experiment and grow together.

Despite the problems of the seventies, the University
of Wisconsin-Green Bay has been a success, and its
success is Ed Weidner's success. Small though it is,
the Green Bay campus is known far beyond the boundaries of Wisconsin. I have heard it talked about
during the last decade in Europe, in Africa, in the
Middle East, and in South and Southeast Asia, as well
as in all parts of the United States. So, Ed has had
an impact on this innovative front. And meantime, he
has continued his international contacts, as in
serving on the Council of the United Nations
University.

We are all indebted to Edward W. Weidner.

Those who gathered at Wingspread for The World
Conference on Innovative Higher Education were also
seeking imaginative ways to respond to their
environments. Although their countries and conditions
differ greatly--developing countries need leaders,
experts, and techniques for bringing growing populations
out of poverty, while developed countries have falling
enrollments and generally need a firmer link between jobs
and education--many societies face similar pressures for
change. These pressures include:

. New groups demanding access to higher education. As
  people continue to see the university as a way to a
  better life, more individuals and groups seek its
  benefits. Women, ethnic minorities, and working
  adults are joining the traditional young undergraduate in applying for admission.

. A new awareness of what one educator described as a
  "lack of fit between the products of the education
  system and what countries really require."

. New demands that higher education pull its own
  weight; that the money spent on it should prove
  itself productive.

The purpose of the conference was twofold. First, it
sought to provide a forum for the exchange of experiences
and for mutual encouragement among those actively engaged
in promoting educational change. The second purpose was
to bring together representatives of a wide range of
nations and to avoid the national parochialism that too
often obscures the significance of individual experience.

Funds were available to pay the travel expenses of many people, particularly from the Third World, who otherwise would not have been able to attend.

To form a representative group of innovators, small enough to share ideas, the conference organizers had to make difficult decisions about who was to participate. It was, unhappily, not possible to invite more than a sample of educators and, consequently, many able innovators were absent.

Everett Kleinjans, president of Hawaii's East-West Center, began the conference with a keynote address entitled "Contextual Innovation." It was the only formal event. Subsequent sessions centered on themes and were each presided over by conference participants. Not infrequently the moderators selected colleagues as inter-venors to stimulate and direct the discussion.*

James Perkins, director of the International Council for Educational Development, moderated the first session entitled "The Cultural Context of Educational Change." Chancellor Edward W. Weidner of the University of Wisconsin-Green Bay presided over the second session on "The Emerging Curriculum." Responsibility for the third session, "The System of Delivery," was in the hands of Mulugeta Wodajo of The World Bank (formerly vice president of Addis Ababa University in Ethiopia). The fourth session, entitled "The Role of Research," was led by Rector Hans Meijer of Linköping University, Sweden. And Chancellor Farhad Riahi of Bu-Ali Sina University in Iran acted as moderator for the last session, entitled "Problems of Articulation and Administration."

The division of the conference into these five sessions was the decision of the organizing committee, which also developed for each session a series of suggested themes and questions. These proved somewhat superfluous. The participants were forthright, eloquent, and more than capable of developing their own themes and questions. The organizers felt, however, that the conference should consist of free-form discussion rather than the presentation of formal papers. Conference proceedings too often are a series of prepared speeches that could as easily be read as heard, and the organizers hoped for more informal and practical discussion. Indeed, the format of Wingspread conferences and the layout of the superb conference center are deliberately designed to facilitate such informality. The organizers of the World Conference suggested that participants prepare themselves principally for open and vigorous debate, bringing written reports for their colleagues if they chose to do so. Copying facilities were available, and a large number of papers were quickly passed around. Discussion was the core of the conference.

---

* See Appendix

While the sessions helped to structure the
discussions, the authors of this volume have chosen to
put these discussions in a larger framework. In
particular, they have used the primary literature to
describe and develop ideas that permeated the conference
discussions. For example, the Open University was not
represented, nor was there any formal discussion of the
American land-grant tradition. But both, in their
separate ways, were clearly so integral to the thinking
of many of those present that an account of the conference that failed to describe them would not be
complete. Furthermore, many of the thoughts expressed by
participants reflect opinions of other scholars, and
indeed were so acknowledged in the conference
discussions. The authors have gone to some trouble to
identify and report from the original sources, but have
clearly indicated by attribution where they have done so.
The first four chapters present themes that permeated the
conference and are central to change in higher education
as a whole. The remaining chapters deal with the ways
(illustrated with case histories) in which innovators are
responding to the problems of higher education.

The first chapter deals with access. Higher
education has, characteristically, restricted admissions
to a lucky few. But as the barriers of class, money, and
even intelligence have fallen, enrollments have expanded
worldwide. At the same time, higher education has shown
a growing concern for lifelong learning and service to
nontraditional students. The parts of the Third World
that can afford higher education for only a small
minority seek rather to ensure that the, minority is
chosen fairly and that the privileged few repay their
debt by service to society.

The second chapter is concerned with curricular
relevance: What is the most useful kind of learning?
How can higher education best prepare its students for
today's world? What is relevant in one place may be
irrelevant in another; what is relevant today may not be
relevant tomorrow. The search for relevance has forced
institutions to redefine their purposes. Do they seek to
provide job training, problem analysis, examination of
social and personal values; the application of knowledge
to economic development, pure research, extension, or
individual enrichment?

All participants agreed that the university must
accommodate itself to the circumstances in which it
exists. Such factors as stage of economic development
and national traditions impose a requirement for flexible
response on the part of higher education. What this
response can be and how one brings about change are the
subjects of the third chapter.

The fourth chapter deals with questions of cost and
efficiency. How does one afford better quality and more

x

services? What is the most efficient way to manage educational change? How does the university organize to fit its new nature and goals?

Chapters 5 through 9 are concerned with specific models for innovation and depend heavily on case histories. The models are the Open University, the organization of education to serve new clienteles, the American land-grant tradition, the broadening of the concept of the university to incorporate all facets of higher education (which we have termed the comprehensive university), and the idea of problem focus and interdisciplinarity as a novel organizing principle. While most of the case studies describe institutions represented at the conference, again we have on two or three occasions described other institutions by consulting sources in the literature because they illustrate vividly views introduced by conference participants. As has been pointed out, the format of the conference permitted only a sample of educators to be invited. Discussion of institutions not represented at Wingspread in the report of the proceedings is an attempt to rectify in part errors of omission in drawing up the conference schedule.

Chapters 10 and 11 deal with the university as a provider of services other than teaching. Essentially, these services are extension and research. The university holds no monopoly on either of these functions. Nevertheless, many, if not most, educators regard them as essential, both to serve better the wider community and to maintain the university as a vital and informed center of intellectual excellence.

Chapter 12 deals with the problems of management, particularly as they affect the process of innovation and change. Most participants at the conference were administrators or had administrative experience. The last chapter attempts a summary of the current status of innovation in higher education as it emerged at Wingspread.

The message of the conference and of this book is unfashionably optimistic: Innovation in higher education is alive and well. In the 60s and early 70s, while new ideas emerged and innovation was in the air, many observers felt that nothing much was actually happening. The tale at Wingspread, however, was of the manner in which change is indeed creeping through the doors and windows of higher education, perhaps not to revolutionize the old, but certainly to augment it with new goals, new methods, new purposes, and new institutions. In the words of Arthur Hugh Clough, whom Winston Churchill quoted to such good effect in 1941:

For while the tired waves, vainly breaking
Seem here no painful inch to gain,
Far back through creeks and inlets making,
Comes silent, flooding of the main....

The book that follows is a hybrid beast. It is based on, and quotes extensively from, speeches and statements recorded at the conference. The ideas that permeate the book are those of the men and women who were at Wingspread, and many of these ideas evolved synergistically throughout the course of the discussions. But the book also draws from the written material participants brought with them and from other accounts of the institutions represented. It is an attempt by the authors to provide a picture of the current status of innovation in higher education worldwide, illuminated by statements from those most intimately involved--the innovators themselves. Any shortcomings are the responsibility of the authors alone. Any value the book may have lies in the work and the clear descriptions of that work provided by the many dedicated people who participated in the Wingspread conference and who are listed in the appendix.

We would be remiss, however, if we failed to acknowledge a special debt to Chuck Wedemeyer for his encouragement and support; to Jackie Maki for her untiring editorial aid; and to Sharon (Bisely) Gutowski for her patience in typing the manuscript through several drafts.

W.W.P.

D. J.

B. F.

1
Access:
Who Should Get in?

Who should go to the world's colleges and universities? As more people see higher education as the door to success, wealth, power, happiness, or even survival, the question has become more pressing and more politically urgent.

In almost all countries, developing as well as developed, public demand has put pressures on universities and governments for wider and more equal access to the benefits of higher education. But such pressures have raised difficult questions. How many students can and should be admitted to higher education? By what criteria should they be selected? Does raising numbers mean lowering educational quality? How can educational opportunity truly become equal?

How these questions are answered depends, as the Wingspread conference made clear, on a society's goals, on its priorities, on its stage of development, and on its interpretation of social equality. The university everywhere has been affected by world currents of change. Technology continues to propagate at a dizzying rate, and higher education is expected in many places not only to produce people who can put the new tools to use, but also to transform society. As the image of the university as an isolated ivory tower gives way to higher education's acknowledged role as a force for national development, the concept of higher education as a privilege for the few transforms into the belief in higher education as a right for everyone.

These changing concepts have brought about a revolution in higher education. The walls once enclosing only the elite must now expand to include more and more people; higher education must fulfill the traditional purposes of the university while at the same time meeting a sometimes bewildering range of national needs and personal goals. The educational process has changed so much that educators now talk of "delivery systems" in higher education as though it were a bottling business or a

1

postal service. Indeed, some recent forms of higher education have used manufacturing methods and the mail to produce and deliver education. A large number of the innovations discussed at Wingspread deal with these problems of widening access.

Webster's dictionary defines access as "permission, liberty, or ability to enter...or to make use of." In discussing access, the Wingspread conference focused on three questions:

1. Who should have the permission or liberty to enter higher education? Few--an elite? Many--those who can be helped through social policy to meet a minimum standard of admission? Or everyone who wishes higher education--young and old, rich and poor, those who have educational credentials and those who do not?

2. If only some are selected for admission, how will their abilities or qualifications be determined? By tests and school records only? By consideration of nonacademic factors, such as job experience? By an evaluation of their chances of success? By a combination of criteria?

3. As more people enter higher education, how can the quality (and value) of education be maintained? Is excellence best preserved through a diverse system that provides alternatives to fit a wide variety of needs? Or is a uniform system that offers everyone the same subject matter and level of instruction more desirable?

Higher education has a different history in each of the countries represented at Wingspread, but educational development tends to fall on a scale roughly character-ized by three stages. These three stages are sometimes described as elite or selective, mass, and universal; and they are generally, but not always, distinguished by corresponding stages of economic and social development. Each country will answer the above questions differently, depending on what point it has reached in its own development.

Selecting the Few

Traditionally, and in many countries and universities still, higher education serves an elite group although this elite may be variously defined. Juan Muñoz, rector of the University of the Andes in Colombia, expressed the traditional view that people selected for the university are people of intellectually high standards in society and that these people generally come from the middle-high and high classes of the country. While some universities have had experience in choosing people from the lower intellectual classes, the results have been poor because the intellectual instrument is not good.*

F.J. Willett, vice chancellor of Griffith University in Australia, disagreed, saying that at Griffith 15 percent of the places are reserved for men and women over 25, who compete for entry not on the basis of scholastic record, but on the basis of what they have done in their lives. Many are deficient in formal schooling, but they have high motivation and they have done very well. In rejoinder, however, Dr. Muñoz pointed out that while 15 percent of the students are selected in some nontraditional way, they are nevertheless selected, so they still represent an elite.

Dr. Muñoz' point is a valid one. There are intellectual as well as social and economic elites, just as there are political and cultural elites. Entry to the university has traditionally been considered a privilege of family or talent, and only recently have most countries sought to expand the group that qualifies for entry.

But poorer countries still simply cannot provide for all. Available resources severely limit university places, and tests must select students for higher education who are most likely to become the countries' leaders and managers. Educators must find the most able young people and train them to take charge.

Nevertheless, like their more developed counterparts, developing nations cannot ignore the demands for greater social equality nor the need to develop in more of their people urgently needed technical and scientific skills. The difficulty, said Muñoz, is knowing how to select the students. Once examinations are as good as they can be, he said, and loans or grants are made available for all university costs--for study abroad, as well as at home--then justice lies in choosing only those people who intellectually deserve to go to the university.

Widening the Pool

Equal opportunity, however, has in many countries turned out to mean more than subsidized tuition or even examinations to test ability. It no longer seems enough to find those rare children of poverty who can compete intellectually with their more advantaged peers and to provide university tuition for them, worthy as that might be. Long before the point of admission, a child's

---

* Throughout the book, statements or opinions attributed to individuals without footnotes are derived from the transcript of the Wingspread conference. Footnotes refer to material derived from publications, whether or not they were distributed at the conference by participants.

ability may be stunted or hidden by having too little to eat, by poor teaching and overcrowded classrooms, and by little incentive from family or surroundings. Such a child simply cannot compete fairly for hard-to-reach places on the ladder to higher education. In developing countries, where three quarters of the population lives in rural villages, the student in the village primary school is already far behind the city child. Few boys and even fewer girls finish more than a few years of basic studies. High school is unattainable to most. In Zambia merely having been to school already qualifies one as a member of the elite, said Jacob Mwanza, vice chancellor of the University of Zambia. And Varaphorn Bovornsiri of Thailand declared that equal opportunity in higher education can be achieved only if primary and secondary education have more support.

That equal opportunity requires intervention in the primary and secondary schools is a relatively new idea, characteristic of a gradual shift throughout the world from the "elite" stage of education toward the "mass" stage. Under the older, elitist view, intelligence is regarded as innate and measurable by tests and by school performance. Equal opportunity then simply means admitting qualified applicants regardless of their background or ability to pay.

In the past thirty years, however, there has been a growing belief in many countries that intelligence is influenced by the environment; it can be tested but is subject to change.[1] If children are to have an equal chance for higher education, therefore, they must be compensated for previous disadvantages over which they have had no control and which may have obscured their real ability. Thus, there has been a transition to a new interpretation of equal opportunity in which society is expected to take responsibility for removing environmental handicaps to learning.[*]

* Neave[2] discusses three idealized educational styles, calling them elitist, socially oriented, and individual centered, respectively. He suggests that the elitist concept informs to a degree the Robbins Report on higher education in Britain, indicating perhaps the status of higher education in that country in the early 1960s. On the other hand, the socially oriented approach has characterized many of the educational reforms in Western Europe, including the establishment of polytechnics as degree-granting institutions in Britain. The third style, equivalent to the notion of education permanente, may be taking form in Sweden and the United States, he says. Some evidence of this trend comes from a 1977 UNESCO report[3] which urges member states to make the university more accessible to women and to inhabitants of rural areas.

How can those from lower educational levels be brought up to the required standards for university admission, asked H.R. Arakeri, vice chancellor of the Indian University of Agricultural Sciences. Other Wingspread participants reported on efforts to bring children up to acceptable achievement levels. In Venezuela, for example, poor students are admitted to the university through a formula that recognizes not only test scores, but also the potential student's native region, educational preparation, parents' education, and other factors. Malaysia identifies bright students in the last year of primary school and encourages them to go to secondary schools, where they are helped and guided by university personnel. Yarmouk University in Jordan admits top high school graduates from each province, regardless of the level of education their schools have provided, and then gives remedial assistance as required.

In the Philippines a program has been set up to find poor but able children from rural areas and to help them with scholarships, guidance, and special tutoring. Efforts are being made at the University of the Philippines to assist children of poor families to raise their education levels to equal those of the more well-to-do. Unequal abilities, said this university's Chancellor Abelardo Samonte, can commonly result from differences in nutrition and early schooling. Bu-Ali Sina University in Iran also evaluates the social and economic backgrounds of applicants and gives priority to students from rural areas.[4]

Despite these laudable efforts toward equal access and the sharp increase in enrollments, in poor as well as in industrialized countries, the kinds of people who can hope to receive higher education in many countries tend to stay much the same as they have always been. Primary and secondary schools act as screens, eliminating all but an elite from the race for university openings. Few children get even to primary and secondary schools, and of those, higher education continues to select students who give evidence of the highest ability and best preparation--under 5 percent of all 20 to 24 year olds in developing countries.[5] Between 60 and 70 percent of the students at the University of the Philippines still come from metropolitan Manila and upper income families, and other universities have a similarly high proportion of socially and economically privileged students. In most societies those so privileged fail to include adequate numbers either of racial and ethnic minorities or of women. Speaking about Asian societies a few years ago, the noted Asian scholar Tarlok Singh warned that higher education might indeed operate as an agent not merely of growth and change, but also of greater inequality.[6] Regrettably, not only Asian nations but many others as

well are currently enacting the inequities of this
scenario through their higher educational programs.

Taking the Next Step

Mass access is defined rather arbitrarily at the
point where 15 percent or more of the college-going age
group is enrolled in postsecondary education.[7] Europe,
the USSR, and North America have reached this point. In
developed countries as a whole, enrollment rose from 12
percent in 1960 to 24 percent in 1970,[8] with Sweden and
the United States now reaching almost half of the
designated age group. (In the United States 75 percent
of the population finishes high school and 60 percent of
those graduates continue with postsecondary education.[9])
There are other characteristics of this transition
from elite to mass access. As more people continue their
education past secondary school, the kinds of programs
available tend to multiply. Countries moving to broader
access also show changed attitudes toward higher
education and begin to modify admissions criteria.
J.W. Burkett has commented upon college admissions
procedures as follows:

Ironically, admission procedures are designed and
used traditionally not to facilitate access to
learning but to withhold it. If hospitals operated
in a similar fashion, they would insist that no one
be admitted who might embarrass them by failure to
emerge in good health, thus increasing the already
high standards of the healthfulness of clients
emerging from the system. Institutions of higher
education must concentrate on the quality of their
instruction and the quality control of their finished
product, not on the selection of those who cannot
fail, regardless of what the institution may or may
not contribute to the achievement of their educational goals.[10]

The view that all individuals should have the right
to pursue their educational goals as far as they wish has
gained popular support in the last two decades in a few
of the more developed countries. These societies
especially have sought new means to bring more young
people and, more recently, older adults as well into
higher education. They have looked for ways to improve
and equalize schooling and to compensate for social and
economic handicaps with more student aid, government
programs, and anti-discrimination legislation. There
have been a number of reasons for this continuing search
for better ways to broaden access:

1. As more jobs require higher education, more people demand it;

2. Equality of educational opportunity has come to mean a right to higher education;

3. Institutions of higher education in some developed countries now face empty seats and classrooms.

   This third reason has become evident only recently. Higher education expanded after World War II to meet large increases in population and increases in demand. Now the birthrate has stopped climbing, fewer children are entering primary schools, and secondary and post-secondary institutions, struggling to make places for the students who now crowd their classrooms, will have too many places in a few years.
   Demography, in fact, is one of the most difficult problems facing German universities, said Siegfried Grosse of the University of Bochum in West Germany. Despite the establishment of twenty new universities in the last twelve years, places will still not be available to accommodate the peak age class in 1985 when there will be 27 percent more students demanding places than there were in 1975. On the other hand, the rapid decline in the number of school-age children after 1985 will bring about empty schoolrooms, and there will be few openings for teachers, who make up a large proportion of German university graduates.   Consequently, the universities over the next few years will be training teachers who will not be needed.
   Yngvar Løchen, rector of the University of Tromsö in Norway, gave another reason for the decreasing number of students: The university is no longer the only respect-able place to get an education.   "In my country," he said, "other avenues to education are now being well developed, and they lead to a job for a smaller expen-diture than a costly and time-consuming university degree.   This means that the university is losing its market."
   If the young coming from secondary schools will not fill college and university buildings, perhaps these institutions can open their doors to other groups--former dropouts or working adults, for example--in accordance with the social ideals of equal opportunity for all. In a time of social change and technological growth, more people in jobs and professions find they need additional continuing education to help them to keep up with their responsibilities and to pursue personal goals, and they may respond eagerly to invitations to return to the classroom.
   Perhaps this in part explains why, in the United States, the long anticipated decline in enrollments has

still failed to materialize. While in 1976-77 there were 9 percent fewer students in colleges or universities than there had been the year before,[11] enrollments climbed again up to the year 1981. Rather than experiencing diminished demand, American colleges and universities are struggling to accommodate more students, while budgets suffer erosion through inflation.

In conclusion, then, the search for new students is worldwide and is encouraged by several trends: a demand for equal educational opportunity; the need in many developing countries for more highly trained men and women; and, in the developed world, a decreasing number of students and a growth of alternatives to the universities. Innovators have looked both for new means of extending paths of entry and for ways of modifying old rules of admission. Wingspread participants spoke about broadening access to education for people who live in remote areas, people who must work, people who missed the chance to apply to a college or university when they left secondary school, or people who may not have finished secondary school and who do not qualify for university entrance under traditional rules.

Geography

"We have discovered that physical distance is one obstacle to equality of opportunity," said Claudio Gutierrez, rector of the University of Costa Rica. "Most people cannot travel long distances for education." So that education can come to the students who cannot come to the university, Costa Rica has established off-campus university centers. Similarly, Norway has built district colleges, and Finland has established new universities throughout its thinly populated northern areas so that each region can have an equal ratio of student places to population. Chitta Mitra, director of the Birla Institute of Technology and Sciences in India, suggested that in developing countries, more than convenience may be involved in a decision to attend the university. Students admitted to the university from the villages, he said, traditionally have no wish to go back to the farms. It may be better, then, to take education to the people rather than people to education, thus helping to distribute expertise where it is most needed.

In the United States, State universities such as the University of Wisconsin have developed institutions throughout their states' geographical regions. One such campus, the University of Wisconsin-Whitewater, has set up centers staffed with its own faculty to serve the area within a specific radius. Edwin Speir, the University of Wisconsin-Whitewater's vice chancellor, said one result has been that many faculty have begun to treat their students as clients; they consult with them about

specific needs and develop courses around those needs.
In this way, the university reaches out more responsively
to part-time adult students to provide what is often a
first exposure to university education.

Age: The Mature Student

Adult students appear in increasing numbers on many
campuses. "We are now thinking about including groups
other than 18 to 24 year olds," said J.F.M.C. Aarts of
the Catholic University in Nijmegen, Holland, "and we are
working on all stages of continuing education for all
people."
In a number of countries and institutions, continuing
education has grown up alongside, but separate from, the
degree program of the university. Luis Garibay, rector
of the Autonomous University of Guadalajara, described
two such university programs in Mexico.[12] The Center of
Continuing Education in the University of Mexico's
College of Engineering serves engineers who wish to
change their speciality or occupation, or who need to
update their knowledge and skills. It maintains close
contact with industry and other employers of engineers.
Also, the Autonomous University of Guadalajara has had a
division of continuing education since 1974 and offers
courses for practicing professionals in architecture,
medicine, engineering, administration, economics, and the
chemical sciences.
While other campuses have also made room for this
kind of continuing or adult education, only recently have
adults been admitted into the mainstream of the university through flexible admission policies and programs.
The University of Wisconsin-Whitewater, said Edwin Speir,
in taking the university to the people, is seeking to
discover what kinds of outside experience and informal
learning can be awarded university credit. Potential
students are encouraged to translate what they have
learned by experience into degree credit. This translation of experience into credit, explained Speir, is
potentially the most radical aspect of the university's
current program.
Sweden also has tried to base admissions on real,
rather than on merely formal, competence. Several years
ago it began a pilot program called the 25-5 Rule,
specifying that adults aged 25 or over with at least 5
years of working experience had the right to enroll in
certain fields of study at the universities.[13] The
number of students admitted according to the 25-5 Rule
has steadily increased during the 1970s, to 17,500 in
1976. Almost half of these 25-5 students were over 35

years old, and a considerable number were over 45.[14]
There were almost equal numbers of men and women.*

In Sweden, although working experience under the 25-5
Rule could include both child care and military service,
the proportion of students with backgrounds as manual
workers has been almost the same among 25-5 students as
among traditional students.[16] The University of
Paris-Vincennes in France, however, according to Guy
Berger, tries to avoid being only a second chance for the
middle class by offering an opportunity to nontraditional
groups--foreigners, minorities, workers, housewives, and
others--to exchange views and to discuss and analyze
their working and life experiences, whether they are
working towards a diploma or merely taking individual
courses to satisfy special interests or career
aspirations. Professor Berger, from the Department of
Education at the University of Paris-Vincennes, said the
French government created Vincennes after the 1968
student riots as an experimental university to serve a
new population of students, some of whom do not have a
high school degree and many of whom are already
established in jobs or careers. Students there range in
age from 18 to 60 and represent 107 countries,
exemplifying certainly a diversity of backgrounds and
educational needs. Many of these "walk-in" students come
to the university primarily to widen their knowledge
rather than to achieve a degree, itself a radical departure from French tradition.

Another means of widening access to adults is by
promoting part-time study. By allowing adults with jobs
or other responsibilities to work for a degree, some
colleges and universities provide alternatives to those
who, for some reason, could not or did not enroll in
full-time higher education. In Sweden only a fifth of
the students entering higher education under the 25-5
Rule intend to pursue a full degree when they begin.[17]
In Canada and the United States there has been a heavy
demand among adults for part-time programs leading to

---

* Neither the United States nor Sweden, however, requires
work experience for university admission. Unlike China,
where until recently work experience in farms and fac-
tories after secondary school had been compulsory for
entrance to higher education, Sweden and the U.S. allow
credit for work experience but do not demand it. The
University of Dar es Salaam in Tanzania, on the other
hand, has combined both policies: Prospective students
spend at least a year working before entering the
university. But Dar es Salaam, like countries much
closer to mass education, also admits some older students
under a "mature age entry" program and a "special entry"
scheme, both designed to give those with unconventional
educational preparations a second chance.[15]

better jobs in business, health, and social work.
Malaysia, too, has instituted off-campus courses mainly
for those who seek higher salaries through better
qualifications. Part-time Malaysian students, however,
must be qualified for university entrance and must have
spent a year within the university as full-time students.
In England some feel that it has been at least partly the
lack of part-time programs in the existing traditional
universities that has led to the success of the Open
University.[18]

General Delivery

Most radical and imaginative in its departure from
traditional university admissions procedures, the Open
University is perhaps the logical outcome of the belief
that all individuals, whatever their ability and previous
schooling, should have access to whatever knowledge and
instruction they seek. Walter Perry,[19] vice chancellor
of the British Open University, has described the
university's origins as follows:

> Since the concept of the Open University was largely
> based on the premise that there should be more egali-
> tarianism in higher education, the planning committee
> determined that access would be made easy for all who
> wished to take advantage of the new institution.
> Poverty would not serve as a barrier to entry, which
> meant that fees must be kept low. Full-time study
> would not be required because students would continue
> working at jobs and careers. This, in turn, required
> that education be taken to the student wherever he or
> she might live, rather than bringing the student to
> education....Finally, entry would not depend on
> academic qualifications; it would be open to all
> students who wished to try.

Everyman's University in Israel was modeled on
England's Open University, explained Max Rowe, Everyman's
vice chancellor, who described his institution's policy
to Wingspread participants. There are no entrance
requirements. Courses are first advertised in the newspapers, and prospective students write for the special
sample material of the course they are considering.
Students judge from this material whether the course
meets their needs and whether they are competent to
complete it. If they believe they can, they then
register and pay one half the fee; the second half is
payable several weeks after the course has begun.
Eighty-five percent of those who pay the first half also
pay the second half of the fees.
The course for which students sign up at Everyman's
University lasts about four months, and the student gains

one credit after successfully completing assignments and passing an examination. The majority of students, said Rowe, are those who are not qualified for conventional universities, or who live far away from universities, or who failed in their first encounter with higher education. He went on to say that the era of mass education has arrived, and there is no way back to the methods of elite training. The present challenge is to evolve educational methods that will provide some form of individualized guidance, stimulate individual creativity, and achieve high educational standards.

Quantity vs. Quality

As more people enter postsecondary education, concern grows over how to achieve and maintain such high standards. Higher education is, and must remain, involved in the pursuit of excellence. "A university's commitment to intellectual excellence is its primary and most significant contribution to a developing nation," said a report of Asian university administrators.[20] The ideal of equal rights must, therefore, somehow be reconciled with the ideal of individual merit and with the quality and value of a degree. Educators and public policy makers must address the dilemma of how to protect what Ashby calls the "thin clear stream of excellence" while at the same time providing opportunities for the less qualified. In Brand Blandshard's phrase, "Quantity is at war with quality."

Those who wish to restrict access to higher education argue that unlimited access creates an educated body of unemployed, that only a limited group--perhaps 10 to 15 percent--has the talent necessary for higher studies, and that expanding higher education will water it down, lowering all to the intellectual caliber of the least common denominator.

From its start, Walter Perry defended the Open University against such charges.[21] To those who argued that the Open University was a threat to higher scholarship, he replied that while we must do all we can to nurture Ashby's "thin clear stream of excellence," we must not neglect the wide and muddy river of ability. That is, we must also recognize other kinds of excellence; namely, those found among people...who want to do things rather than just to study things.

Can a society do both? The university rectors and vice chancellors at Wingspread differed as to whether wider access and high standards could best be achieved by uniformity (making all programs as alike as possible) or diversity within any one system of education.

Claudio Gutierrez of Costa Rica supported diversity. In order to offer equal opportunity to each individual, the educational system must address itself to different needs. To meet these needs, education must provide diversity in professional fields, in geographic location, and in educational level, with opportunities both for early graduation on the one hand and for complete graduate programs on the other. Diversity implies giving many more people the opportunity for higher education.

Both Eduardo Gonzalez-Reyes of the Organization of American States and Phasook Kullavanijaya, rector of Prince of Songkla University in Thailand, agreed. Gonzalez spoke of his belief in the coexistence of various forms of higher education while Phasook maintained that the demand for equal opportunity, together with the fact of students' unequal capabilities, requires that the university create diversified curricula and programs, as well as provide new methods of learning. Emphasis should be directed not only to the regular traditional four-year program leading to a college degree, but also to shorter programs, diploma or otherwise. Adnan Badran of Jordan said that the developing countries, which can seldom afford more than one institution, need a multipurpose university to encompass various kinds of education--community colleges, sandwich courses, and extension service, among others.

Farhad Riahi of Iran, however, disagreed. If the new system is better, he asked, why keep the traditional model? He feared that if two systems tried to live together, then one would become a system for the poor while the other would be for the wealthy, with the wealthy adopting the traditional system.

In fact, in a number of countries, a variety of postsecondary institutions with different admissions policies do exist side by side, and several administrators at Wingspread said they believed that different kinds of institutions supplement rather than compete with one another. F.J. Willett felt there was an advantage in the existence of several kinds of universities in Australia--it created a choice. When Griffith University was established, the previous existence of conventional programs made possible the assumption that students who wanted traditional programs would be able to find them elsewhere. Griffith was consequently free to experiment.

The British system of higher education includes the polytechnics, both new and old universities, and the Open University. In the United States, the best efforts to classify the three thousand existing institutions reveal no less than a dozen or more categories, taking into account extensive differences among the hundreds of places now called universities, the still greater number called colleges, and the one thousand community colleges.[22] Charles Wedemeyer, professor emeritus of the University of Wisconsin-Madison, pointed out that we already live with many systems and will continue to do so. People of different ages will use different parts of these systems at different periods in their lives; and because motivation varies with sex, age, and interest, many different mechanisms and modes for teaching and learning are required of the higher education establishment.

Versions of the Open University are being planted among the more stately trees of higher education in both developed and developing countries, those with predominantly elite systems as well as those reaching the mass stage; besides England and Israel, Wingspread participants mentioned Holland, Finland, Canada, Thailand, Colombia, Costa Rica, Mexico, Venezuela, and Saudi Arabia as countries pursuing open learning. Most of these programs are intended for adult students who do not meet the usual entrance requirements. Indeed, Dr. Badran of Jordan said he believed that the open university is a supplementary rather than an alternative tool of learning, a more appropriate mechanism for providing specialized knowledge when the student has reached maturity.

Nevertheless, Chancellor Riahi's concern that institutions garner different status and prestige depending upon the stringency of their admissions policies was not easily dismissed. Chitta Mitra of India agreed that the open university, in addition to offering an alternative to traditional universities, might unintentionally be creating a caste system. However, the answer perhaps is to incorporate the alternative into the mainstream of academia. Max Rowe of Israel said, "If open learning remains on the margin of higher education, it would be a failure. If it is a success, it should be incorporated into the traditional university."

Perhaps the basic issue is whether the traditional university is able to assume the new task of educating many more students with widely different qualifications and talents or whether new institutions are needed. As Max Rowe observed, there is no regressing from mass education; the challenge is to find ways to reconcile excellence with larger numbers. Clark[23] maintains that no single form, no one type of institution, will suffice in mass higher education. The United States has been luckier than Europe, he believes, because no single form dominates the American system. In Europe, on the other hand, the assumption grew that genuine and respectable higher education meant university education. Where only the nationally supported public university is legitimate as a reputable place to study, to introduce other forms of mass education is difficult. As a result, Clark points out, since 1960 this dominant form in Europe—the national public university—has been greatly overloaded, with large numbers of students and faculty making increasingly heterogeneous demands. Differentiation of form in this situation might both relieve the burden on traditional institutions and provide new opportunities for a new clientele.

Higher Education for All

Asked to describe the university of the future, Varaphorn Bovornsiri of Thailand replied that it should be a lifelong educational center promoting education for everyone, a place where the emphasis is on knowledge rather than on credentials. She was thus looking ahead to a third stage, beyond mass access, sometimes referred to as universal access.

As we have seen, few countries have reached that point usually considered a condition of mass access, where more than 15 percent of the 18 to 24 age group are in some form of higher education. In countries that have reached this point there have been increasing efforts both to include more classes of people--such as working adults, women, the handicapped, and various racial, linguistic, and ethnic groups--and to provide a variety of alternative forms and programs of higher education for different abilities and needs.

Nations approaching mass access have also sought to improve lower-level schooling and to widen the pool of potential candidates for higher education by making it possible for all young people to attend secondary schools. In Sweden, for example, almost half--and in the United States three quarters--of all 18 year olds remain in school. In the more selective systems, such as West Germany and England, all but a relatively small group (a quarter or less) are filtered out of the educational system well before they reach 18.[24]

College and university places almost everywhere are limited by resources and jobs. If higher education is a right, however, access to it cannot depend on the student's ability to pay. On the other hand, most countries cannot afford the costs of supporting large numbers of students. How can the individual's right to education be weighed fairly against the right of society to balance its allocation of resources among competing needs? Of necessity, most nations limit or expand student access to higher education according to manpower requirements. Developing countries especially must consciously decide how many people should be admitted to postsecondary education and what kinds of studies the nation most needs.

But countries' needs differ. African countries need more professionals while Latin America generally has a surplus of doctors and lawyers. Developed countries, too, are concerned that they may educate people for whom there will be no jobs. A UNESCO report[25] noted that

several participants feared that wider access to the
university might aggravate the overproduction and
unemployment of graduates. "Should the number of
graduates be adjusted to the number of jobs available?"
asked Pierre Merlin, president of the University of
Paris-Vincennes.

Germany, for example, sets a ceiling on the number of
college and university places in some fields of study,
and students with the highest grades compete for these
places. Which fields to limit and which to open has been
the subject of hot debate.[26] Even in the United States,
where student demand usually determines how many enter
any field of higher study, the Federal Government
recently announced a policy of limiting medical school
places by cutting support for medical school expansion
and by using government funds to support students
entering family medicine rather than surgery.

Universal access has been described as a condition
where (1) all college age persons are financially able to
attend college if they otherwise wish to do so; and (2)
places are available for them.[27] Such access, though, is
only possible in the most affluent countries. In certain
parts of the United States where high school graduation
alone qualifies students for some form of higher
education, several alternative educational opportunities
are available. Only in such areas are more than half of
the 18 to 24 age group enrolled--one sign of transition
to universal access.

If higher education is to be a right, should not the
individual then have more freedom of choice about where
and when and how to be educated? The open university,
perhaps more than any other single innovation, has shown
how education can be designed so that the user, rather
than the institution, does such choosing. It may be some
time yet before higher education is a universal right.
As nations begin to solve problems of costs, dispel
threats to scholarly excellence, and abolish discrimination for reasons of sex, race, social class, age, and
previous schooling, though, they will begin to approach
universal accessibility to higher education.

2
Relevance:
What Should They Learn?

The traditional university has been under attack everywhere for not being "relevant" to social needs. In the poorer countries of the world people urgently need food, housing, better health care, jobs, and ways to lift themselves up out of poverty and despair. They need teachers, doctors, economists, agricultural experts, and political leaders with vision, knowledge, and understanding. The university seemed to promise help in solving problems of development by giving people the required skills and training so they could see what ought to be done and then do it.

But the universities in developing countries, copied largely from traditional European models, have sometimes seemed remote from and unresponsive to the needs of the people. The doctors they trained have left for well-equipped hospitals in wealthier countries or have established practices in the cities, rather than treating disease within the villages. Agricultural experts, too, have sought laboratories and government positions away from the countryside.

Young men and women who, it was hoped, would lead their countries to prosperity showed little interest in learning about the needs of struggling villages and cities. For example, Chitta Mitra has said that there is no tangible evidence of any impact by the educational system on the prosperity of India or on the improvement of its quality of life.[1]

Developed countries have also worried about how effectively higher education serves society. As more people have entered colleges and universities with a wide variety of personal goals and expectations, many have begun to insist that traditional courses are not preparing them for life. Large numbers of graduating students, in fact, have unmarketable skills and cannot find jobs. At the same time, too few graduates seem prepared or willing to tackle the most difficult social problems--problems involving justice, equity, energy,

17

poverty, or environment--and, like graduates in
developing countries, they avoid placement where they are
most needed.

Many of the changes in higher education reported at
Wingspread have grown out of demands for relevance to
real-life experiences and needs. Participants at
Wingspread agreed, however, that one could talk of
"relevance" only if one had a clear picture of the goals
of higher education. Max Rowe of Everyman's University
in Israel observed this:

> We are constantly being urged to be relevant and to
> serve the needs of the community. We are fully
> conscious of this requirement, but it is not easy to
> translate it into practice. The needs of society
> vary from place to place and from time to time;
> moreover, they depend very much on one's philosophy.

Lewis Mughogho, principal of Bunda College of
Agriculture at the University of Malawi, expressed
similar reservations about too facile demands for
relevance:

> In Africa, universities are themselves innovations
> because they are not a part of our culture. They
> are expected to serve the special purposes of
> development. But what is relevant today may not be
> relevant tomorrow.

The search for relevance has thus forced institutions
of higher education to redefine their purposes. Are they
looking for relevance to the needs of society or to the
concerns of the individual? Should the university try to
solve current social problems, or should it give students
the skills and training with which they may some day
solve new problems? Should it match training with job
openings or concentrate on producing leaders? Should it
respond to the popular will and the ever-changing needs
of society, or should the university follow the advice of
Alan Pifer[2] and be "independent of society, self-
directed, slow to respond to the fashions and currents of
the day, housed in a set of unique, selective institutions whose sole purpose is to foster the highest levels
of intellectual development and achievement?" How can
higher education provide both immediate and long-range
benefits to individuals and society and still reconcile
old virtues with new needs?

The Wingspread participants had different answers to
these questions and different views of the university's
role. According to varying views, the university was
seen as most relevant when it performs the following
diverse functions:

- Trains men and women, through practical courses, to fill available jobs and manpower needs;

- Gives students an understanding of "real" world issues and trains them to analyze and solve actual problems;

- Examines values;

- Applies knowledge to solve current development problems;

- Engages in pure and free research;

- Interrelates teaching, research, and extension;

- Develops the mind and personality of the individual;

- Reckons with new needs and experience.

Each purpose and combination of purposes has produced distinctive new institutions and programs. Higher education can certainly contribute to national development by providing training, understanding, advice, and methods for putting theory into practice; it can also contribute to wider social purpose by conducting pure research, encouraging individual growth, and providing more opportunities for more people. The mixture of ends and means that makes the most sense for a particular institution, though, as Max Rowe pointed out, varies with time and place.

Training: Manpower or Citizens?

While Lewis Mughogho of Malawi was concerned with ways to educate the few most relevantly, Pierre Merlin of France and H.R. Arakeri of India worried about creating more manpower than their countries could use. All agreed, however, that the modern university must function primarily to train men and women to do its country's work; it cannot be simply a repository of culture or an idyllic haven for reflection and research.

Wingspread educators were divided on the most appropriate role for higher education in training. One group felt that institutions of higher education should first and foremost produce enough technical, scientific, and professionally trained people to meet the nation's requirements—teachers, engineers, physicians, farm managers and agriculturists; others argued that higher education makes its most important contribution by training young people, not as specialists, but as generalists, who are willing and able to respond to

change and to serve the community as citizens and
leaders. Some participants felt that the university
should combine the two roles, but others wondered whether
there were not other institutions or other less expensive
ways to prepare people for available jobs.

These differences hinged partly on the dilemma of
whether higher education is responsible to the individual
or to the community. Should higher education prepare
students to fill job slots, or should it seek to develop
the mind and personality of the individual? How can
colleges and universities serve each individual's own
goals and interests and, at the same time, prepare and
inspire men and women to meet community needs?

The need to train more people for jobs is perhaps
most urgent in developing countries, especially in the
new nations of Africa. N.O.H. Setidisho, rector of the
University of Botswana and Swaziland, was emphatic that
for a developing country with a small university, an
essential educational service is to provide manpower.
Vice Chancellor Mwanza of Zambia agreed that there is an
acute shortage of high-level manpower. Furthermore, he
pointed out that in developing countries there are so
many priorities that competition for limited resources is
high; hard decisions must be made on spending. Even in
Saudi Arabia, where money is more abundant (Saudi Arabia
added $100 million to its university budget between 1970
and 1977), the country, said Dean Mohamed Zayyan Omar of
King Abdul Aziz University, depends more on manpower than
on oil. "There is now no question whether higher education in a developing country should be involved in social
development," said Phasook Kullavanijaya of Thailand.
"The question is rather how higher education can satisfy
the changing needs for trained manpower."

These participants advocated what a recent U.S.
report called advancing the human capability of society
at large.[3] Such capability, however, may depend as much
on an understanding of human and social needs, on the
ability to respond to new situations, and on the recognition of values and attitudes, as it depends on special
skills and knowledge.

Understanding Problems

How can higher education improve the student's grasp
of pressing issues? One way is to bring together the
separate disciplines in a common effort to shed light on
broad problems. For example, Griffith University in
Australia has designed its entire program of undergraduate instruction to demonstrate the relevance of academic
analytic training to real world issues. It has oriented
its curriculum to the understanding of human adjustment
to changing physical, social, and intellectual

environments, and its four schools--Australian
Environmental Studies, Modern Asian Studies, Humanities,
and Science--focus on different aspects of these
problems.

Similarly, to integrate knowledge and allow more
undergraduate contact with research, the University of
Linköping has built its research program around four
problems or themes: Public Health, Human Communication,
Technology and Social Change, and Water in Nature and
Society. Denmark has also established two university
centers with interdisciplinary and problem-oriented
programs. The University of Campinas in Brazil has
established an interdisciplinary problem-focused program
of teaching and research. And Bu-Ali Sina University in
Iran centered its curriculum and each of its fields of
activity on a major problem of the surrounding rural
community. In the University of the Philippines,
although the formal academic structure has not been
reorganized along interdisciplinary lines, departments
frequently cooperate in a common curriculum.

Problem orientation, however, is difficult to define
so that it applies to all programs. There are two kinds
of problem-oriented education, said Chancellor Weidner of
the University of Wisconsin-Green Bay. One kind tries to
train people to solve specific problems, and the other
exposes students to problems as a focus for liberal
education. The first kind seeks primarily to develop
skills; the second to further liberal learning. As technology changes, required skills also change, and those
whose education primarily emphasizes skill acquisition
return to the university every few years. On the other
hand, if one learns to analyze problems and develop
alternative solutions, one can apply that ability to a
variety of situations, even as conditions change.

One further difficulty with tying higher education's
programs to specific problems, said Chancellor Weidner,
is that the designated learning methods may prescribe
solutions. Some students in Europe especially, he said,
espouse what they call "project-oriented" education for
political purposes. They feel they know the conclusions
before they begin and then undertake study and research
simply to justify those conclusions.

Problem-oriented education should not prescribe
action for society, said the Wisconsin chancellor.
Instead, it should concentrate on diagnosing problems and
on developing alternative solutions to them, encouraging
students to work with people of different backgrounds and
views. The university is in this way distinguished from
a political party or government agency. This kind of
nonprescriptive approach, as a matter of fact, has been
part of the American educational scene for many years in
the land-grant colleges, said Chancellor Weidner. These
agricultural colleges are truly problem oriented and

22

truly interdisciplinary, but their philosophy has seldom
been applied to problems other than agriculture. The
University of Wisconsin-Green Bay is an example of an
institution trying to apply this college of agriculture
tradition to other arenas of American life.

Several university heads at the conference spoke of
difficulties inherent in these views and in the interdisciplinary study of real world problems. Not the least
of these difficulties is that raised by Rector Løchen of
Tromsö:

> Who defines social problems? If we are to cooperate
> with groups in seeking solutions to societal
> problems, who defines which groups we will cooperate
> with? The notion behind this process is that
> something can be solved if we only develop the right
> skills and define the right problem.

Siegfried Grosse of Germany spoke about how hard it
is to define the subject matter of interdisciplinary
study. There is, he said, a demand for interdisciplinary
teaching and research just at the time when disciplines
are becoming more specialized, focusing on an ever-
narrowing array of subject matter. Is it possible, he
asked, to teach in an interdisciplinary fashion when
students do not yet know the basic subjects well? People
from psychology, sociology, and linguistics, for example,
have difficulties in finding common ground in psycho-
linguistics and socio-linguistics. They try to meet on
the hyphen, quipped Grosse, without knowing the two
sides.

Mohamed Zayyan Omar took vigorous exception to the
concept of education that does not prescribe for society.
The university is subsidized by the state, he said, to
work toward specific goals; therefore, it is unrealistic
to expect it to operate apart from the government. It is
the job of the university, he said, to train the people
needed by both government and the private sector.

But the nature of problem orientation leads to
further confusion. The essential definition of problem
orientation was questioned by Rector Sven Caspersen of
Aalborg University Center in Denmark. Is it a pedagogical trick to keep doing what we are now doing, or is it a
way to relate study to the world of work? In a fast-
changing society, he continued, it is important to teach
students to combine disciplines, to identify problems,
and to understand the values of the culture.

Social Values

The values of the culture, as the preceding debates
suggest, affect both the university's means and its ends.
Such values determine whether higher education prescribes

or does not, whether it establishes responsibility to the individual or to society, whether it promulgates political dogma or the search for truth. They determine what problems are chosen for study, methods for defining such problems, and the very level of urgency associated with solving them. The only thing you cannot do with values, said Vice Chancellor Willett of Australia, is to ignore them. Perhaps a skill can be value free, but a problem certainly cannot.

The university can help to clarify and examine social values, potential as well as existing ones. There must be a search for national principles, said Botswana's Rector Setidisho while Rector Caspersen of Denmark was equally insistent that education should provide something to live for, as well as to live with.

Most of the programs discussed at Wingspread seek to influence student values as well as learning. Most accept the need identified by Everett Kleinjans, president of the East-West Center in Hawaii, to train people for a world different from the world of academia. But, Kleinjans asked, how does one teach cooperation in a milieu where students compete for grades, faculty compete for students, and institutions compete for money--where the most exciting game man has devised is war?

Problem-oriented, interdisciplinary programs try to make the student aware of how problems are interrelated and of the need for group and individual cooperation to solve them. In the Philippines, said Chancellor Samonte, the university also tries in its teaching and research to counteract the Southeast Asian aversion to manual labor. Programs in which students provide service to the community are designed thus not only to improve community conditions, but also to give students a sense of connection to their less educated countrymen and countrywomen, to encourage them to serve at home rather than abroad, and to bring their training and expertise to poor and backward areas. Above all, as Chancellor Weidner pointed out, success of the problem-oriented method depends primarily on an attitude whereby both student and teacher feel obligated to do something about problems.

Solving the Problems

Educators in developing countries agreed that the university must help to identify the problems of society and train people to solve them. They worried less about fine distinctions of role than about specific mechanisms by which the university could take direct action on problems. Rector Setidisho explained this concern:

We in the Third World have a common objective for establishing a university: to promote development of the country. The curriculum is designed so that

we can certify that the individual who has gone
through the university has acquired the skills to
identify and solve problems. Unless the individual
has reached that stage, we don't consider him good
for anything.

Lewis Mughogho of Malawi, among others, concurred with
the view that the university should try to solve current
development problems, and he went on to point out certain
consequences. Not the least of these consequences is
that in order to solve such problems, some developing
countries' universities have broken in several ways with
the traditional university model they inherited from
Europe. More of these Third World institutions now focus
their training and research on local problems, and many
seek to extend the benefits of the university as far as
possible into their nations' complex and demanding
circumstances.
     For most, the first step in this pragmatic approach
is the training of developers. Since the demand for
equal educational opportunity cannot be met in most
developing countries, said Dr. Mughogho, the task is to
ensure that the few be educated most relevantly. One
approach to this task is to back up teaching with local
development research, to build up a body of knowledge
about the country--its geography, history, demography,
natural resources, economics, and health problems.
Another way to fit training to social needs is to mix
theory with practice, encouraging students to discover
for themselves what should be done.
     This approach--fitting theory to local need--was
described by Chitta Mitra of the Birla Institute of
Technology:

     In looking at the possibilities of applied research,
     our university found it was affecting both teaching
     and its relationship with the community. Solar
     energy research, for example, was at first considered
     too trivial for the university. But the subject was
     more complex than had been thought. Designing solar
     devices for a rural setting requires an excellent
     knowledge of physics, and using local materials
     requires engineering know-how. We often found that
     excellent academic researchers fell on their faces
     with local problems while imaginative people who were
     willing to tackle local problems found plenty of
     material to publish in academic journals. In the
     villages around us were new opportunities for
     acquiring new knowledge and for disseminating it.
     The villager was living in a situation where science
     was manifest. Students began to learn research
     techniques and at the same time to see how they could
     be used. In designing a solar device or a water

pump, we were both conducting research and applying
it.

Universities in developing countries have thus tried
to join more closely the three commonly acknowledged
functions of the university--teaching, research, and
service. Firsthand knowledge acquired in the villages
has enlivened classroom learning and brought students in
touch with community problems. "We must devote most of
our time to teaching and applied research that can be
used," said Vice Chancellor Mwanza. "We want to be sure
that research will help design a curriculum that will
prepare students to affect the community. The cost of
education must have a return." Dr. Zeferino Vaz of
Brazil concurred, "Research and teaching cannot be
separated. The university has responsibility for the
community--to break the vicious circle of poverty and bad
health in developing countries."
Some universities have sought a more direct impact on
their communities, bringing university teachers and
students to the fields and villages to improve as well as
to study local conditions. The university of development, said Chancellor Riahi of Bu-Ali Sina University in
Iran, is characterized first by its services to the
surrounding community.[4] Such services are especially
urgent in developing countries. In Botswana, for
example, explained Rector Setidisho, almost everyone is a
cattle farmer. If the farmer could be helped to improve
his stock and become aware of available markets, his life
could improve. The university should play a role at this
basic level, providing programs that could improve the
quality of primary education, agriculture, and small
business in rural areas.
The best of these outreach and service programs not
only deliver services, they also feed acquired knowledge
back into research and curriculum. Dr. Luis Garibay,
rector of the Autonomous University of Guadalajara,
described the evolution of one such program. Ten years
ago, he said, the university began an extension program
in health services that in the most recent years had been
formally applied to medical training. Students and professors working in the local community as part of this
program came to realize that medical care was impersonal
and dehumanizing and that doctors were not serving where
they were most needed.
In response, the university took a new look at its
medical training. Medical students had been spending
their first year in the classroom, separated from contact
with patients. The university changed this approach,
however, to include community experience from the start,
and it further revised the curriculum to draw on several
disciplines and focus more directly on actual community
problems. Students learned that medical care was related

to housing, nutrition, farming methods, and water supply,
and that solving health problems requires more than one
kind of expertise.

As a result of this program's success, said Garibay,
sixteen of the twenty faculties in the university now
work in similar fashion. Contact with the community, he
said, has changed the way students think and feel about
both their education and their future careers, and it is
changing their capacity to link theory and practice.
They are also more likely than they were to go to areas
that need them after graduation.

"Research, teaching, and extension must complement
one another in the university," said Abelardo Samonte.
"The student and the community can learn from one
another. At the University of the Philippines, extension
work off campus is part of instruction." Similarly, in
Bu-Ali Sina University in Iran local craftsmen taught in
university workshops, and students were apprenticed on
local farms.[5] And Puey Ungphakorn, former rector of
Thammasat University in Thailand, has said that while we
have been taught that the primary duty of students is to
study in order to render service to society, in fact,
service itself has become study par excellence. The
simple truth is that a circle exists--study for service
for study.[6]

Basic Research

Not everyone was convinced that the university best
serves society by applied research and extension programs, and some university heads felt that, with the
above approach, they might be sacrificing long-range
needs for immediate benefits.

Politicans who ask for relevance of research and are
impatient to see results threaten the pure and free
research which is a major contribution of the university
to society, said Siegfried Grosse. When scholars are
forced to devote their efforts exclusively to immediate
problems, society loses the chance to pursue paths to new
knowledge. Relevance is a magic word, said Grosse, but
we cannot find out what is applicable to social needs
without traveling some dead-end roads. There are
fashions in research as there are in other fields, and
many of the currently fashionable subjects will lead
nowhere.

In Germany, research is traditionally connected only
narrowly with teaching. Once a rather sacrosanct
academic pursuit, research now faces several dangers.
The sharp increase in enrollments has put pressures on
the universities to devote faculty time to instruction
rather than to research; research funds are increasingly
scarce; new administrative tasks take time away from

potential research; and, as academic unemployment grows, graduate students shun the research role for more secure jobs.

In Finland, too, the opportunity for research has worsened as the government puts increasing emphasis on teaching, said Osmo Ikola, rector of the University of Turku. And in the United States, Jerome B. Wiesner, president of the Massachusetts Institute of Technology, warned recently that dwindling support for research and increasing government constraints have diminished the capacities of the university to address the nation's problems. Two of the implications of this reduced support are an inadequate reservoir of young scientists (because universities cannot offer young researchers new positions) and a notable shift in attention from basic to applied research. Scientists have argued, said Wiesner, that while fundamental research is often riskier, it is also ultimately more conducive to scientific discovery and invention than is the safer and more predictable realm of applied science.[7]

In a similar vein, Rector Løchen of Norway wondered who would take up the more creative intellectual tasks of inquiry if the university becomes too practical. He went on to say that there is a very unclear relationship between theory and practice, and we have not yet developed effective techniques to attain our goals. Thailand evidences similar concerns. Because of pressures from governments and society, said Sippanondha Ketudat, the scholars in the university may be forced to devote their research efforts to immediate problems. But even in a developing country, he said, basic fundamental research must be carried out, for this in the long run may be more important to public needs. A university's commitment to intellectual excellence is its primary and most significant contribution to a developing nation.[8]

Higher education, most participants felt, must balance basic research against applied research just as it must balance research against teaching and teaching against extension or community service. Even basic research, moreover, can enrich rather than detract from teaching. A university setting provides the world's most creative environment, said Wiesner, when it involves the interplay of bright, fresh minds with those of the world's great scholars. While one can easily claim that the student is learning, the professor is just as surely learning, too; and their joint goal is new knowledge.[9]

For Rector Meijer of Linköping University in Sweden, the issue is one of social priorities. Although priorities clearly vary from culture to culture and from society to society, developing countries may be especially tempted to concentrate on using other countries' existing knowledge; Meijer warned, however, that unforeseen cultural shock may result from buying

knowledge from another culture. A ratio should be
established between basic and applied research, with some
allowance for flexibility, said Adnan Badran of Jordan.
In balancing local priorities against international
concerns, he suggested that a developing country's
university establish links with a university in the
developed world.

Hamdan Tahir, vice chancellor of the University of
Science in Malaysia, described another way to balance
basic and applied research:

> When the government supports research, you are always
> expected to do something for government. We solve
> the problem by establishing both short-term and long-
> term programs. We have set up a center of policy
> research to look at a variety of problems. If the
> government wants research, it goes to the center
> rather than to the faculties. The university and not
> the government, for example, monitors countrywide
> drug abuse.

The issue is not whether research should be
fundamental or applied, said Chitta Mitra, but rather why
both fundamental and applied research cannot be done on
problems which are of critical importance to the
country.[10] Farhad Riahi also suggested that basic and
applied research might not, after all, be so far apart.
He assured the conference that pursuing practical
research does not necessarily mean being provincial.
Relevant training will not only assure the student a job,
but also can lead from research in specific practical
problems to involvement in complex, interdisciplinary
problems.

How Relevant is Relevance?

When the university becomes a development tool used
primarily to solve social problems, does it move away
from its true purpose? Max Rowe, vice chancellor of
Everyman's University in Israel, thought it might,
suggesting that the main strength of the university
should lie in the making of the individual. Universities
today, he went on to say, have neglected the basic
function of training the leader in society, the individual who can lead or innovate. They will not establish
relevance or legitimacy through responding to all manner
of short-term problems or through attempting to undertake
assignments for which they are not equipped. While the
choice of academic subjects that a university offers must
have a distinct relation to the time and needs of
society, the role of the university remains what it has
always been; namely, to help students acquire knowledge,
a disciplined mind, a power of independent thinking, and

a competence in their respective academic areas. In Rowe's view, the universities should revert to their prime function--to qualify men and women to play successful roles in society. The relevance for which one clamors, said Rowe, would then come from these men and women, through their ingenuity and their urge for achievement.

U.S. sociologist Nathan Glazer has also suggested that while concentrating on the world as it exists and how to act in such a world is on the whole a healthy attitude, it is also narrowing and deadening. Larger perspectives are generally provided by the disciplines and bring in air and light.[11]

Nevertheless, as the conversations of the Wingspread participants revealed, both curriculum and research are responding to public demands for change, and educators everywhere are seeking ways to make these academic elements more meaningful and to link them more closely to the life of the community. Interdisciplinary curriculum, problem-oriented research, and the emphasis on service are all evidence of this trend.

Initial or Continuing Learning?

Perhaps, though, the particular content of higher education may have less effect on academia's future service to society than will the sequential timetable by which that content may be acquired. One can no longer amass before the age of 25 all the skills and technical knowledge needed for a lifetime. The explosion of knowledge has meant that young people must spend more and more time preparing for jobs and careers, only to have both careers and education become obsolete during their working lifetimes.

"I believe that there must be a ruthless pruning of the content and length of initial education together with a concurrent provision of continuing education," said Walter Perry,[12] vice chancellor of Great Britain's Open University. "We must not try to keep pace with the rapid acquisitions of new knowledge by expanding and lengthening the curriculum of initial education, for that will only prove futile."

The demand for continuing or lifelong education has already meant a change in the nature of higher education in many parts of the world. As we have seen, universities in Holland, Mexico, Sweden, Malaysia, Israel, and the United States, among others, have loosened restrictions on admission or offered part-time courses for adults who may want to qualify for better jobs, change careers, become better citizens, or perhaps just learn something they always wanted to know. In the United States, reports Alan Pifer,[13] there are 3.6 million

people past the age of 24 enrolled in colleges and
universities--over one third of the total enrollment.

A UNESCO meeting in 1977 favored extensive use of the
university for lifelong education as a way to place it
at the service of the whole people.[14] Placing the university at the service of the whole people, however,
requires radical changes in higher education, including
changes in its teaching and curriculum. For one thing,
older students returning to the classroom are not like
students coming straight from secondary schools. The
older students, said Pierre Merlin, president of the
University of Paris-Vincennes, tend to be more mature,
more experienced, and more motivated; therefore instruction for them must be more rigorous and more concrete.
Universities must reckon with the new needs and
experience of these older groups, added J.F.M.C. Aarts of
the Catholic University of Holland.

In some cases, perhaps, existing universities neither
can nor should change. Walter Perry has suggested that
the Open University offers a new and relatively inexpen-
sive system of continuing education--an alternative to
the initial education system that avoids concurrent
reductions in funding for established institutions of
higher learning.[15] Similarly, at Everyman's University
in Israel, which also combines distance learning with
self-paced instruction, almost 80 percent of the students
are over 24, and more than a third are over 34.

Whether new institutional models like the Open
University supply the burgeoning demand for learning over
a lifespan, or whether established colleges and universities make room for new groups of older students,
relevant higher education must increasingly provide high-
level instruction wherever and whenever individuals
require it. In responding to social needs, higher education must address not only changes in knowledge, but also
changes in student populations and in their modes of
learning. It must prepare individuals to define and
solve new problems, as well as to manage the complex of
human activities we so glibly term "society."

3
Flexibility:
Where Does Change Take Hold?

A student on a U.S. college campus was overheard complaining to a companion, "I wouldn't mind if they were hostile in a sensible way." The eavesdropper never learned who "they" were, but they might have been educational reformers, bent on innovation. When considering the sweeping changes proposed for the ends and means of higher education, many educators share the student's querulousness. If only higher education could change sensibly, without pain and without the buzz and sting of angry opposition.

Major change, however, is almost never painless. As higher education everywhere struggles to equalize opportunity, to prepare people to serve their societies, and to satisfy a wide spectrum of individual needs, faculties fear for their jobs and status, students worry about whether employers will accept their training and their credentials, and both groups are understandably skeptical about the improvements promised by the reforms.

Higher education must, of course, respond to the new knowledge exploding into today's world, but changes in higher education have certainly involved more than revising textbooks or lecture notes. Most innovations discussed at Wingspread address the domineering presence of change itself. How can the college or university prepare students to deal constantly with the new? How can students learn methods of solving problems when the facts or "givens" differ from day to day? If students must understand and live with rapid change, educators must in turn remodel curriculum and institutional structure to complement radical changes in the student body, in the relationship between education and society, and in the philosophy of higher education. The learner, rather than the subject matter, must become the focus of special concern; methods must be devised to help students acquire knowledge and competence whenever and wherever they need them.

31

How does one bring about these changes? "We tried to
move from a teaching to a learning society," said Albert
Badre, president of Beirut University College, "but there
has been little change; the new kind of education is
still a slogan. The problem is how to reach our
objective."
Wingspread participants agreed on both the need for
and the pain of change. They agreed, too, with an OECD
conclusion[1] that innovators require more insight into the
process of innovation before they can improve the management of it. Is it easier to innovate when changes are
made gradually or suddenly? As Everett Kleinjans vividly
characterized the question, should one tear off the
bandage tape hair by hair or in one shrieking rip?

Belief in Alternatives

Unfortunately, there seems no one way to close
permanently the gap between what higher education is and
what it might be. Most educators at Wingspread saw no
"one shrieking rip" that would do the job, but looked
rather for ways to sustain a high rate of change and
innovation in education to meet corresponding changes in
the world at large. The future-oriented university is in
its infancy, said Chancellor Riahi of Iran, and still has
a long way to go before claiming the right to supersede
conventional universities. We are only proposing courage
and a will to innovate.[2]
"A new circumstance has to be created that encourages
innovation and experimentation to discover alternative
models that will make education purposeful and responsive
to the needs of society," said Chitta Mitra of India.[3]
"It is not necessary to wait for a D-Day of social
transformation."
Innovation takes many forms. As far as higher
education is concerned, it means a purposeful attempt to
alter the nature of the educational process, usually in
response to changing societal goals, or to reach a new
clientele or to better serve existing students. As we
said in the Introduction, innovation does not always
produce significant change because it should involve the
risk of failure. Not all experiments succeed. It may
involve change in an existing institution, or a new
institution attempting to break with regional or national
educational traditions. Consequently, an innovation in
one nation may be standard practice in another. However,
innovation is seldom imported unchanged from place to
place. Adaptation always occurs, and not infrequently
innovations are not attempts to borrow from a single
tradition, but rather to take the best features of
several modes of education with the goal of achieving a
new synthesis suited to local needs.

Successful innovation thus requires first a state of mind: courage, the will to innovate, and a belief that the continuing ferment of alternatives is the only way to keep higher education on its toes. For some of us, said Guy Berger from Paris-Vincennes' Department of Education, innovation is purpose; for some it is a means for increasing efficiency; and for some it is a way of life. Innovation, he said, may be considered as a value in itself, as a way to fight against the permanent trend toward apathy and repetition. The problem is how to maintain this attitude of innovation, to avoid losing enthusiasm and participation, and to maintain effective democracy in function.

Change Agents

An atmosphere of experiment and innovation encourages new ideas, but it takes a strong and purposeful person to ignite change. Reform needs a reformer, or as Rector Phasook of Thailand put it, innovation needs someone to do it. Almost anyone can qualify as the spark--teacher, administrator, student, or an outside consultant--as long as he or she has the imagination and energy necessary to synthesize and effect a new idea. Lyman Glenny describes typical faculty innovators as young, nontenured, not influential within inner faculty circles, and more inclined to student welfare than to faculty politics.[4] Nevertheless, some of the most far-reaching educational changes have been started by older, established leaders or administrators. In Australia, for example, new institutions were planned by senior staff from established universities.[5]

In developing countries, innovative educators have often studied abroad where they have encountered ideas and methods that stimulated their own thinking. In developed countries, too, the innovator is likely to bring ideas in from the outside, whether as a newly appointed department head with a curriculum proposal, for example, or as a student who seeks a change in procedures. On the other hand, Chitta Mitra reported he had found that M.I.T. graduates who had returned to India were the greatest opponents of change.

No matter how worthy and innovative the proposals, though, they are likely to die at birth unless they can attract support from the top. The key to successful innovation, said Sippanondha of Thailand, is in the hands of the university's leaders.[6]

Why does a faculty member in one place start educational reform while one at another institution produces no new ideas? The problem, said Phasook, is how to train people to be innovative, to get academicians (physicists, agriculturists, economists, and other specialists) to become educators with a university view.

People seek to effect change for a wide variety of reasons; and an innovator, like anyone else, may be motivated by a complicated assortment of pressures, desires, and fears. Ideals certainly are important spurs to action: A person honestly believes that a new goal is worth pursuing or that a new method will improve results. As Yngvar Løchen of Norway put it, nobody would travel to Tromsö in northern Norway, where the snow lies until May, to work in a new university if it had been established as a traditional institution. Reformers generally care deeply about the reforms they propose and are willing to fight even frigid weather for their adoption.

The potential return on an undertaking, however, must be worth the risk. To encourage people within higher education to originate new ideas and techniques, one must either increase the possible rewards or minimize the risks. Introducing personnel to a world view, as Phasook suggested, or exposing them to new ideas abroad are only first steps.

Present reward systems in most academic settings effectively stifle the majority of efforts to change education. Successful innovators are unlikely to find power and prestige awaiting them. Even if one can charm suspicious colleagues to a new way of thinking and persuade department heads, chancellors, and government officials that the proposed change will cost nothing but reap great benefits, professional advancement still usually depends on one's research reputation and publication record, not on one's contributions to curriculum reform. Inner satisfaction and a sense of usefulness alone must sustain most innovators, for few other rewards ensue.

On the other hand, there are substantial risks. For example, innovators may lose their places on the career ladder while they take time to plan problem-centered learning. Colleagues are likely to be apathetic if not hostile, superiors remain passive or obdurate, and leisure time disintegrates. Finally, even successful innovative proposals too rarely confer status on the proposer.

High risks and low rewards discourage risk-takers and encourage faculty members to be cautious rather than imaginative. It is important, said Vice Chancellor Willett of Australia, to have reward systems that reinforce the search for better ways to do things. The nutritive requirements for innovation, says Lieberman, are flexibility and risk taking.[7] At a minimum, it would seem that risk-taking innovators should have some hope for gain--at least in job satisfaction, in increased personal competence, and in security from loss of job and status.

The Climate for Change

Like individuals, institutions respond cautiously
according to the law of risk and return and generally
must have an overwhelming reason to break with
established ways. The climate for change is, in fact,
most often determined by a sense of crisis: urgency
often engenders innovation.

Outside pressures for change may be powerful enough
to offset internal risks. Desperate conditions in
developing countries certainly motivate higher education
to be more responsive to development needs. Campus
unrest in the 1960s led to the universities' concern with
social relevance. Changes in social attitudes and law
are prompting new admission policies. And new groups of
students admitted under these policies (women,
minorities, older adults) stimulate new educational
approaches by bringing new needs, experiences, and
interests to the campus.

Institutions embark on new programs also as a means
to ensure their own survival. Many of the innovations we
have talked about, said Rector Løchen of Norway, aim at
an increase in the number of students or an expansion of
the concept of student. This concern, plus our need to
justify our budget and activities are, to some extent,
responsible for our great interest in innovations.

Thus, innovation may stem from the social and
economic conditions of the nation or from immediate educational or institutional distress. Dropping (or
soaring) enrollments and changes in the composition of
the student body have occasioned interdisciplinary
programs; poor employment prospects for graduates have
led to training that better integrates theory and
practice.

The need for funds, too, can stimulate new kinds of
research. The Birla Institute of Technology and Science
in India began to look for more concrete research topics
to attract government grants. Curriculum and teaching at
the university had previously been heavily oriented to
individual disciplines, reported Chitta Mitra, its
director. As a result of the search for funds, the
university began to transform itself from a traditional
university to a more vital, relevant one.

Deliberate efforts from outside higher education to
evoke innovation from within have not generally been
successful. In Great Britain, the Nuffield Foundation
initiated a scheme of matching grants to encourage institutions to support promising change, but according to a
recent analysis of Britain's higher education, the grants
have so far not succeeded in creating any real shift in
institutional priorities.[8] In the United States as
well, innovative programs sponsored by government funds
have often vanished when the funding ceased.

Timing is important, observed Everett Kleinjans. As
the social and cultural context changes so does the
opportunity--the historical moment so to speak--for
innovation. At any given time there must be the right
combination of individual and climate, of leadership and
flexible regulation, of ideas and resources.

Barriers to Change

One can never be fully ready for change, just as one
is never fully ready for independence, said Chitta Mitra.
Crises subside and others rise to take their places, but
one's devotion to a needed change must transcend the
relatively ephemeral urgencies of a university's day-to-
day operations. Chancellor Weidner of Wisconsin agreed
that it takes a lot of work to keep innovating. Sooner
or later resistance builds up. Such resistance may come
from all sides--from faculty and students, from prospective employers, and even from other institutions that are
skeptical about the value of nontraditional programs.
Established faculties may see radical changes in
curriculum, departmental structure, or teaching methods
as a threat to academic standards or to their own carefully guarded interests. They may fear that they will
lose a particularly prized course or will have to sacrifice funds or facilities to new programs in which they
will have little part. Not surprisingly, most faculty
members also oppose innovations requiring them to modify
or even replace personal values or attitudes. "The fact
that educational operations are carried out by persons as
instruments of change, rather than through the use of
physical technology (tools, machines, operating
processes)," explains Huberman, "makes it necessary to
change basic attitudes when we change behaviors or
skills. 'Things' or 'information' are easier to cope
with than changes in practice, attitudes, or values."[9]
Even new institutions that start with new faculties
have trouble, according to Wingspread reports. For
instance, the most difficult problem at Yarmouk
University in Jordan, admitted its president Adnan
Badran, has been attracting faculty. Faculty members are
not willing to risk their reputations in a "second best"
university.
The new University of Paris-Vincennes was able to
recruit faculty in 1968, but later faced other problems.
Most of those who initially applied were young and
enthusiastic, some already well-known but not compatible
with the old patterns of other universities, according to
Pierre Merlin, president of Vincennes. At first these
new faculty members participated enthusiastically in
discussions, committee meetings, and general assemblies
where problems were considered. But later, in their
forties, many have become tired and complacent, no longer

as imaginative or innovative as they once were; and many even want to transfer back to the traditional universities. After its hopeful start, Vincennes is left with inadequate money to recruit a replacement faculty of young, dynamic, and open-minded individuals.

Faculty members, though, are less likely to lose interest or to resist changes when they themselves influence and enact new programs. When they design and plan, they have a greater stake in the success of the change. They may also have legitimate questions about the value of proposed changes and must be convinced that high academic standards are not threatened by conscientious innovation.

University heads at Wingspread spoke of some of the ways they enlist faculty support. Yarmouk University now competes successfully for faculty, said President Badran, by offering salaries and fringe benefits to faculty members who wish to do research abroad. Several universities reported on special training sessions for their personnel to advance their understanding of new educational ideas and to give them the competence to apply such innovations. The nature of change, said Chitta Mitra, depends on how the individual perceives his role--as the object or subject of change.

Just as reward systems (salary, leaves, promotion policies, and status) can encourage ideas to sprout within higher education, so can they also determine whether the seeds take root. New approaches--such as an instructional focus on problems, interdisciplinary planning, distance learning, and work study programs--often serve the self-interest of neither their practitioners nor their creators, and without added incentives, may hamper their own acceptance among the academic community. The extramural program at the University of the Philippines at Los Baños, for example, involved traveling for professors, said Chancellor Samonte. Faculty resented the time and inconvenience and didn't see this program as a way to advance their careers; consequently, the program was discontinued.

As another example, to expect academics to commit themselves to a package of interdisciplinary teaching, according to British educator Brian MacArthur, is to ask them to act as missionaries in a foreign land from which return home is difficult if not impossible; to ask them to abandon research in favor of teaching is to ask them to take a substantial cut in their chances of career mobility. "Many academics are prepared to do these things," says MacArthur, "and it is to their credit; but until the system of career currency in higher education changes, or is changed, it must remain unsurprising that new institutions based on the abandonment of traditional subject boundaries will gradually, if surreptitiously, revert to the discipline-based norm."[10]

The Wingspread participants had experienced these difficulties firsthand and appealed for suggestions about how to deal with them. Establishing a problem orientation is heavy, unfamiliar work and challenges traditional career patterns, said Vice Chancellor Willett. Such curriculum revision needs constant care and reinforcement, and the faculty need to be adequately compensated for the new, unpredictable demands upon their energies. No one at Wingspread, though, claimed satisfactory answers as to how such innovations could be most effectively reinforced and how old reward systems could be altered accordingly.

Tenure policies, for example, have become an obstacle at Everyman's University in Israel. Faculty are engaged in producing up-to-date instructional materials, said Max Rowe. For that task, he lamented, we need people who remain young forever. If the university awards tenure, it may not be able to keep the right kind of faculty. Are long-term contracts perhaps one answer?

Just as faculty can either promote or block change, students also figure critically in attempts at innovation. As consumers of higher education, they can demand or reject new courses; they can provide a market for some subjects and not for others. Their resistance to innovation, however, is often based on the anticipated value of their degree. Several Wingspread participants reported that they had to convince students, as well as faculty, that innovation had not--and would not--threaten high standards. Students who want jobs when they leave the university, observed Rector Løchen, would object if the university too obviously departed from the traditional. In developing countries, added Abelardo Samonte, one constraint on innovation is the belief that the formal degree is more important than the actual learning one acquires.

An innovative institution must persuade not only faculty and students but also older colleges and universities, employers, and government that it maintains high academic standards and produces competent, employable graduates. "When we switched from the British to the American marking system," said Chitta Mitra, "our greatest problem and disappointment was the reaction of other universities; Delhi University would not accept our students for admission." Chancellor Weidner elaborated on the problems of acceptance, "With other institutions, Green Bay is in a kind of vise: The traditional university looks down on the innovative university as second class, but at the same time, every other university thinks of itself as just as innovative as we are."

An OECD report[11] has pointed out that much of the opposition to change derives from fear of the unknown. Plans are intangible things, and it is essential to be able to show in a practical form the outcome of the

change if people are to be persuaded to accept it. The
Aalborg University Center in Denmark sought a solution to
such resistance through exposure. It set up exchange
programs for students and faculty in older institutions
both in Denmark and abroad; Rector Caspersen described
the advantages of having staff go to other universities
where they find themselves "selling" their own. Aalborg
has also established cooperative boards with people outside the university--employers, trade unions, city
governments, public agencies, and cultural institutions.
University people talk about what they are doing, why
they are doing it, and how they might do it better,
providing an avenue for the university to work with the
community.

The problem of employment opportunities for graduates
of the new university was one of the hardest to solve,
said Chancellor Riahi.[12]   F.J. Willett had faced the
same problem in Australia where, he suggests, that while
employers say they want problem-solving specialists, they
actually abandon such professed interest in interdisciplinarity to hire, for example, an "economist."

To convince Iran's biggest employer, the government,
that its graduates were well prepared, Bu-Ali Sina
University cooperated with the government in establishing
community service networks in the university area and
alternating classroom and field experience for its
students. The university agreed to study and participate
in regional development projects, and the government,
according to usual Iranian practice, agreed to be the
employer of last resort for graduates. Rector Phasook of
Thailand also emphasized the need to involve other agencies and individuals in projects from the beginning. He
suggested seeking ways to integrate the university's work
with that of local government and industry, thus
increasing not only community service but also graduates'
employability.

Building New Institutions or Changing Old Ones

The advantages of diversity within a system of higher
education have been discussed earlier. There is another
question, however: Is a new institution the best or only
way to bring about significant educational change? One
point of view was offered by F.J. Willett of Griffith
University. While defining and maintaining a problem
orientation is always difficult, he said, it is possible
if an institution starts from scratch as Griffith
University did. It is very difficult, if not impossible,
though, to attempt to graft a problem orientation onto an
otherwise developed institution. Adnan Badran of Jordan
agreed, saying that when a new university is established,
it needn't be bound by old ways.

In most countries it has, indeed, been easier to
create new institutions than to change old ones, easier
to start or expand programs than to close them down.
Furthermore, as Everett Kleinjans pointed out, new
institutions supply a need for diversity and different
perspectives. In the United States, especially, new
institutions have tended to spring up in response to new
needs and new demands. Such institutions have created a
range of alternatives and even challenged older institutions to revise and initiate new programs, in many cases
to compete for students.

New kinds of institutions, such as the East-West
Center in Honolulu (a learning center that does not award
degrees), have advantages in being less tied to tradition
and freer to explore new ways to organize education.
Similarly, when Griffith University was created by the
government, it had the opportunity (indeed, the mission)
to do something different; Vice Chancellor Willett
directed its search for fields of inquiry towards those
in which the traditional university had not experienced
much success.

New institutions may also become models, offering
more traditional colleges and universities a source of
new ideas from which they can select. Such new models,
too, can increase the purposes and diversify the methods
of higher education without eliminating the benefits of
older ways. In developing countries, Chancellor Riahi
has said, original university research for promoting
socio-economic development is indispensable, and this
research can only be fully achieved in a university of
development.[13]

New needs require new institutions, said the report
of the Commission on Postsecondary Education in
Ontario.[14] However, in summarizing the report, a
Canadian educator pointed out that attention to the
numerous demands of a community, however legitimate,
could distract a university from its major academic
objectives.[15] Diversity among institutions is perhaps,
then, the answer. In the long run, said an OECD report,
education will need a wide range of policies and instruments for sustaining a high rate of change and
innovation, just as these elements have proved necessary
in industry.[16]

New institutions, however, can unintentionally become
dangerous. They may become ivory towers of their own
where innovators blithely apply new methods and devise
new forms of higher education without having to
demonstrate accountability to established faculties and
administrators. Older institutions can, in turn, ease
their constricted consciences by persuading themselves
that students and faculty who want the new can find it
elsewhere; and some established universities further
relish the opportunity to shed troublesome reformers onto

more experimental campuses. The French government, said
Pierre Merlin, has tended to use Vincennes as a showcase
to prove its liberal spirit, an action which may be
complimentary but is itself a distortion of the role
innovative institutions should play in higher education.
    Despite the need for diversity, an innovative
institution should not be an excuse for academia to rest
on its laurels and should not by its concentration of
innovators in one place widen the gulf between the new
and the old. Either a university's innovations are
adopted and generalized by other universities, said
Merlin, or it is condemned to an aging and hardening
process.
    Another danger is that new institutions, in their
efforts to acquire standing among faculty and students,
become carbon copies of their established sisters. As
noted before, they fear a loss of prestige if they do not
conform to traditional standards. For example, except
for the Open University, some educators cite the new
British universities as less bold than they might have
been.
    In some cases, new institutions have little choice;
they must conform. Regulation from the top cuts down on
diversity but may have the inverse advantage of spreading
new ideas more evenly within the system. According to
Burton Clark, however, monopoly of power--while it can be
a useful instrument of change--soon becomes a great
source of rigidity.[17] In India, for instance, an un-
yielding syllabus and examination system makes it almost
impossible for those with new educational perspectives to
strike out in new directions. A number of Indian educators have suggested establishing a greater number of
autonomous colleges as the only way to improve Indian
higher education.[18] President Albert Badre agrees that
autonomy is precious. Apart from being accountable to
the New York State Board of Regents, which licenses the
university's degrees, said Badre, Beirut University is
not accountable to government and is free and flexible.
    Constructive change certainly requires tension
between the impetus of the new and the resistance of the
old. Obviously not all change is improvement, and
faculty or administrators reluctant to give up old values
can provide a steadying force. Falling popularity of
Greek and Latin study may not be a sufficient reason to
abolish the classics, for example, and science professors
who resisted a bias against science in the 1960s are not
necessarily obstacles to progress.[19] In short, employer
demand for "widget turners" should not always elicit new
programs. "There is a tendency to create an illusion of
innovation," said Rector Løchen, "or innovations that are
unrelated to their real purposes."
    Older universities are themselves reminders of
traditional purposes and may sometimes be testing grounds

for new aims. Some have spurred innovation by
diversifying within their own gates. Alternative means of
access, new patterns of study, and new kinds of degrees
can all attract new students to established institutions.
With a diverse student population, institutions must
design innovative programs to meet various needs. Many
of the traditional universities have, in fact, become
very different places in the past twenty years. (Four
older universites represented at Wingspread, for example,
had instituted or were planning major change: community
work-study programs in the University of the Philippines;
continuing education at the Catholic University of
Nijmegen, Holland; an open university program at the
University of Turku in Finland; and a new focus on the
learner at Lebanon's Beirut University College.)

New Orthodoxies

Whatever the nature of the change and whatever the
kind of institution (new or old, innovative or
traditional) most institutions' representatives at
Wingspread admitted to a common problem. F.J. Willett
of Australia stated it early in the conference, calling
for special care to ensure that today's unorthodoxy does
not too easily become tomorrow's orthodoxy.
Once accepted, innovation is no longer innovative.
In time, the radically different goal or method becomes
habit and the accepted way. "A prerequisite for change,"
said Mulugeta Wodajo, "is that people are not happy with
what they have." It follows that once they are happy
with a given change, they will hold on to it. Thus,
those who once originated changes resist any new changes
that seem contrary to the original idea, said Chancellor
Weidner. Vice Chancellor Willett observed that while it
is too early to know what will happen at his young
university, it is already clear that certain questions of
policy, which used to incite ferocious battles, now are
no longer argued. Models have been developed that work
relatively well and now tend to be accepted.
This conservative characteristic of groups and
institutions serves, as already noted, as a healthy
mechanism to stablilize change. Why then continue to
rock the boat? The answer lies partly in Chitta Mitra's
assertion that knowledge is not absolute. Instead, as he
observed, a dynamic theory creates new practice which in
turn leads to new theory. As a result, innovation
involves risks, but it also creates excitement. Only by
seeking alternatives to what "is" can higher education
approach what "ought to be," said Mitra.
Apparently people are more likely to come up with new
ideas when they have been exposed to other institutions'
innovations and when they are encouraged by better
systems of reward. Also important, said Rector Løchen,

is a clear definition of your goal. It is not enough to
start with a notion that seems good; it is also necessary
to ask tough intellectual questions. When you want to
introduce change, you have to be sure about the changes
you want, confirmed Eduardo Gonzalez-Reyes of the
Organization of American States.

The philosophy and goals of higher education vary
with a country's social values, its economic needs, and
its way of seeing the individual in relation to society.
Changes needed in one place may be useless or
unacceptable somewhere else. "We have common problems,"
said Chancellor Riahi, "but we must each solve them
according to our own special circumstances." This sentiment was echoed by Chitta Mitra, who said that innovation
cannot be copied from abroad. Our task when we leave
here, he said, is not to copy each other, but to respect
innovation wherever it occurs. Familiarity with each
other's diverse innovations, then, will certainly promote
the essential flexibility demanded of tomorrow's
universities.

4
Efficiency: How
Do We Set a Price on Progress?

Old ways of running higher education do not seem to
fit the new demands being made on it. The college or
university opening its doors to new groups of students,
seeking better ways to serve national purpose, and
designing programs of lifelong learning ultimately finds
that it needs new styles of management. At the same
time, as higher education competes with other needs,
society demands that its money be well spent. It wants
to see results.

Higher education is efficient when its quality is
high in relation to its costs. Wingspread participants
were looking for ways in which administration,
technology, and involvement of faculty could more effectively support better education without raising its
price. In seeking to cut waste while reaching new educational goals, many of the institutions represented at
Wingspread had tried giving students a voice in university affairs, changing department structure, training
staff, and adapting open university techniques. One of
their biggest difficulties amid these attempts was
measuring how well they were doing.

The traditional university has, over several
centuries, nurtured departments, faculties, and schools
loosely bound together by a system of relationships. The
evolution of such an institution has been determined more
by the need to conserve than by the desire to initiate.
Deans, presidents, and vice chancellors disturb these
traditional structural connections at their own peril,
and in most traditional universities, innovation
languishes. Faculty members, John Millett has said, are
bright with ideas about how to change society but sadly
deficient in ideas about how to change colleges and
universities.[1]

Mulugeta Wodajo of the World Bank addressed these conservative tendencies of traditional systems of governance:

> We have inherited the decision-making machinery of metropolitan universities with their senates and councils and other democratic governance mechanisms. This is a cumbersome method of making decisions. If bright ideas come from young, bright staff members, it takes two or three years to get these ideas into operation. I suggest that in developing countries, the traditional decision-making machinery is not appropriate if we are to achieve the efficiency we need.

Developed, as well as developing, countries have trouble making the academic machine serve new purposes. Siegfried Grosse from the University of Bochum in Germany said the academic structure is unwieldy, and it takes a long while for an idea to find its way through the organizational labyrinth. There is a great gap between the present acceleration of life and the measured pace of the university.

Other characteristics of the conventional university also make its administration difficult, said Rector Løchen of Norway. For instance, membership in the university is not clearly defined; people come and go continuously. The university is traditionally separated into parts—faculties, institutes, disciplines, students, teachers, and other factions—which are not correlated according to some common plan; furthermore, these parts have interests that are often conflicting. And the value placed on academic freedom also works against the administrative system. Real innovations are consequently difficult to bring about, even when they are well-founded and well-presented. Such difficulties are direct outgrowths of the peculiar nature of the university structure.

New Management

One question confronted at Wingspread, then, was how to organize the university to fit its new nature and goals. Several participants spoke of efforts to set up a different administrative structure, but many of the new designs brought along their own problems. "We have avoided departments but have clusters," said Chancellor Riahi of Iran. "The administration lacks backbone." Rector Løchen echoed this sentiment: "We tried to restructure the power system within the institution, but there were clear tendencies to fall back to systems where the faculty could be on their own."

Like several other institutions, the ten year old
University of Paris-Vincennes tried to give more people
at the university a hand in running it--seeking a
democratic process of university management.   Pierre
Merlin, its president, described it as follows:

Under French law, the university is managed by a
council composed of faculty, students, and staff,
which also elects the president.   Administrators
serve part time when they are elected, continuing
to teach as well.   To enlarge the political base of
the decision-making process, Vincennes decided to
create advisory committees in each category:
pedagogy, faculty, budget, lifelong education, and so
forth.   Each department sends representatives to the
committees, and meetings are public so faculty and
students can hear the reasons for each decision.

But this system is very fragile.   People get tired of
spending a lot of time in meetings.   Also, this so-
called democratic management in fact tends to be
elitist because the same people always have the key
roles, and the same people are thus always in
control.   After ten years, only about 10 percent of
the faculty plays an effective role in the management
of the university.

Rector Ikola of Finland reported a similar experience
in an older, more traditional university:

Radical demands by students for participation in
university decision making have resulted in a
tripartite administration: faculty, other staff,
and students.   Only 30 percent of the students
actually participate and don't represent all student
groups.   Most students are not as interested as they
thought they would be, so they don't often come to
meetings.   When students are elected politically,
they are more active in the university council, but
they take directives from the political parties.

The University of Turku has become more innovative
since this reform, and student participation in the
university is important.   But I wonder whether the
students have enough expertise in administration.
The new system has advantages--there is more feeling
of being part of the university--but its disadvantage
is that it wastes time.

Others were more optimistic about the role of
students in management.   Vice Chancellor Willett pointed
out that student participation in governance is not new

48

in Australia. Every Australian university since the
1920s has had 10 percent of its governing body made up of
students; Griffith University has gone further, to 30
percent. Yarmouk University also has students who are
elected to the governing council every year. President
Badran finds this healthy. Students tend to think of
administrators as arbitrary, he said. On the council,
though, they hear things discussed and find out how the
administration really works.

In addition to administrative structural reforms, a
number of institutions have also experimented with
academic structure. Those centering their academic
programs on a few comprehensive issues--Griffith
(Australia), Linköping (Sweden), Aalborg (Denmark),
Campinas (Brazil), Bu-Ali Sina (Iran), and the University
of the Philippines--for example, have established schools
or divisions which each accommodate several interrelated
disciplines. Thus, their academic structure reflects
their philosophical problem focus.

On the whole, it has been easier to start such new
structures in a new institution rather than to reorganize
traditional departments in an older one. At the Birla
Institute of Science and Technology in India, however,
the structure was modified indirectly by strengthening
the core curriculum and thus weakening departmental
power. "We now have divisions in which academic functions cut across the university," said the institute's
director. "Faculty and students can associate with
whichever division they choose."

The challenge is how to get interdisciplinary
organization to meet human needs, said Chancellor Samonte
of the University of the Philippines. We need a mechanism for establishing task forces to work on special
problems, he said. Action requires interaction between
professors, government representatives, business people,
and community leaders. Representatives of all these
groups should meet to define issues, set policy, and then
follow up the study by discussing its results.

New structures have also been devised to include a
variety of degree levels under the umbrella of one
institution. The newly established Yarmouk University in
Jordan, for instance, has a two-year polytechnic program
as well as traditional bachelor's and master's degree
programs. Yarmouk's President Badran described this
blend of programs:

In the developing countries, the university ends up
with too many white collar graduates and no one to do
the job. We estimate that one engineer, for example,
needs five technicians to assist him. At Yarmouk we
are concerned with all levels of postsecondary
school: two-year programs, many in the sciences;
schools of medicine, dentistry, public health and

nursing; and technical diploma programs in every
discipline. The variety of programs allows more
people with different backgrounds to enroll in the
university.

Diversity

Some of the advantages of diversity have already been
discussed. A range of subjects, educational levels,
locations, professional fields, and entrance policies
gives more people the opportunity for higher education
and prepares these people to serve more of society's
needs. A range of alternatives encourages, too, a growth
of imaginative ideas for improving the learning process.
Good management also appears to require diversity.
As higher education moves from an elite to a mass access
system and is expected to perform a growing number of
tasks, it needs what Burton Clark describes as the capacity to face simultaneously in different directions with
contradictory reactions to contradictory demands.[2]
A unilateral system, where every institution has
virtually the same program and admissions policies, cannot easily demonstrate such a capacity. Nor do individual institutions in such a system have many incentives to
improve management efficiency. In Sweden, says Swedish
educator Bertil Östergren, there is little competition
for students among institutions and thus little of the
pressure for change characteristic of a system that
offers more of an array of alternatives.[3]
Östergren concludes that there is a need for more
local institutional freedom, and Alan Pifer, president of
the Carnegie Corporation of New York, agrees. He considers that academic institutions, by their very nature,
do tend to perform best if given as much freedom as
possible by the societies they serve.[4]
Neither diversity nor autonomy, of course, guarantees
efficiency; indeed, separate educational institutions may
waste resources by duplicating one another's programs and
appealing to the same interests or clienteles. How many
different institutions may exist without too much dupli-
cation and overlapping activity depends on the social and
economic forces within the educational system and within
the country.
In the United States, as educational costs have risen
and enrollment has fallen, a number of small independent
colleges have no longer been able to attract enough
students and have had to close their doors. On the other
hand, the multicampus systems of the individual states
now include more than 552 publicly controlled 4-year
institutions.[5] The University of Wisconsin, as an
example, has 13 4-year campuses together with 14 2-year
centers or community colleges. Wisconsin students

can also attend 17 publicly controlled 2-year technical institutes.* Students in Wisconsin, consequently, have many alternatives in postsecondary education, and Chancellor Weidner of the University of Wisconsin-Green Bay finds that, indeed, one problem is explaining to them the advantages of so many innovations.

Dr. Badran of Jordan believes that developing countries cannot afford this choice. Rather, they need to know what approach to education can make the best use of limited resources. England can expand its polytechnic colleges, he said; the United States can support its land-grant colleges and now community colleges along with the more traditional universities. But developing countries can't provide such a variety of institutions. Because the university is expensive, a more economical center of higher education should be established that can design a curriculum to meet social needs. If social or employment needs change, the student should be able to switch courses within the core curriculum.

Such program diversity requires careful planning and coordination, said Rector Gutierrez of the University of Costa Rica, who proposed establishing a national office for higher education to coordinate the planning of the country's different universities. A single five-year plan could then be proposed to each university board, which would be free to adopt or not to adopt the plan or could amend it in an effort to reach consensus. What is important, said James Perkins, chairman of the board of the International Council for Educational Development, is that each country develop a management system that will protect the autonomy of the university while ensuring diversity and service to the national purpose.

Improving the People

Efficient management of any of the forms of innovative higher education already described also requires special teaching and administrative skills. Since staff salaries represent 60 to 80 percent of the costs of education, the competence of faculty and administrators will affect both performance and results--the ways in which problem-centered and inter-disciplinary programs, for example, are carried out and their effects on student preparation or national development. Determining how best to use staff and student time is the really significant efficiency problem, a Swedish educator has said.[7]

---

* Community college enrollment in the U.S. has greatly expanded. Public 2-year institutions which enrolled 10 percent of the 2.7 million U.S. degree credit students in 1955, accounted for a quarter of the 9.7 million degree credit enrollments in 1975.[6]

The emphasis that most innovative higher education places on teaching leads to special difficulties. Many innovative programs are based on new views of learning and of the ways teacher and student should interact. The student is no longer the empty vessel which the teacher must fill, says a University of Costa Rica administrator in an explanation of teaching policies at his university. The teacher consequently is no longer a complete depository of wisdom, but like the student, he or she is a being with a certain degree of knowledge and the possibility of acquiring even more.[8]

Interdisciplinary programs require new ways of thinking. Faculty members traditionally tend to focus exclusively on their own fields. With few interdisciplinary curriculum models, many university teachers are unclear about how the different disciplines are connected; furthermore, they are wary of sharing program responsibilities with those in other fields.

While most faculty members are not prepared for these new philosophies of education, sometimes they are expected to jump into the deep waters of interdisciplinary planning or problem-centered teaching without knowing how to swim. Teachers in innovative programs often did not have the qualifications that an educational experiment requires, said an Aalborg University Center report.[9] Similarly, Chancellor Riahi of Bu-Ali Sina University has found that faculty training in conventional institutions falls short of preparing them for many teaching challenges. Zayyan Omar of Saudi Arabia also shared doubts about professors' preparations for effective teaching.

Most Wingspread participants agreed that better management requires a revision in staff training. "Primary and secondary school teachers," said Mulugeta Wodajo, "receive specific training in teaching methodology, but university teachers are regarded as adequately trained if they are qualified in their specialty. I believe," he continued, "that improvement in university teaching will require that we devise adequate training programs for faculty." Vice Chancellor Hamdan Tahir of Malaysia agreed that academicians do not know enough about how to teach effectively. There is a need to train faculty for both teaching and administration, he said, since administrators are drawn from faculty ranks.

Training faculty for new roles in innovative programs, however, raised at least one demur. Rector Phasook of Thailand expressed concern that such in-service training might mean the demise of academic rigor. He asked if it was good to loosen people from strict academic training and lead them to expediency? Interdisciplinarity often means no discipline, he cautioned.

There is a need for structure if only to handle interdisciplinary projects.

Cost Effectiveness

Administrators are considering tight budgets as well as better education when they look for ways to improve performance and to use faculty time more effectively. Most Wingspread participants wanted to know more about how higher education can get the most for its money.

A serious effort should be made, said Thailand's Rector Phasook, to find effective and less costly methods of teaching and learning. Phasook urged giving special attention to new ideas such as the open university, characterized by campus and by students' independent learning with minimal, but effective, assistance from teachers.

In the open university concept, a small number of teachers direct from a distance the study of a large number of students. To Wingspread participants, an open university seemed to promise resources for increasing numbers of students, and several administrators with open university experience claimed that its costs were lower than those for traditional education. Max Rowe pointed to a World Bank report on Everyman's University which concluded that, in comparison with traditional universities in Israel, the cost at Everyman's University (both capital cost and annual operations) theoretically should be less than half that at the traditional universities. Max Rowe hastened to add, however, that the conclusions of the World Bank experts were based on certain assumptions regarding projected numbers of students and degrees awarded annually. There is still an uphill struggle ahead, he said, before these numbers are reached and such favorable cost comparisons with traditional universities achieved.

Charles Wedemeyer, William Lighty professor of education emeritus at the University of Wisconsin-Madison, described the problem of cost comparison as follows:

> The problem is to find the point at which the unit cost falls below that of the traditional university. The British estimated that the Open University would have to open to 25,000 students to return a lower per unit cost than traditional university education. This enrollment was intended to accommodate about a 30 percent possible attrition rate. In fact, the per unit costs fell further below the conventional university than anticipated; they could have made it with 9,000 students.

The start-up costs for the Open University were about $17 million. It would have cost $80 million to start up a conventional university to serve the same number of students. The three costs are the start-up costs, operating costs, and maintenance costs. Operation and maintenance of an open university course are hard to figure for a number of reasons: Changes in individual courses may cost more than changes in the traditional university course, but if the cost is figured over the period of use of course materials and the number of students, the per unit cost tends to be less. Most accountants don't know how to figure these differences and you have to get someone who knows how to show true cost-benefit ratios.

Evaluation

In weighing the benefits of an open university or any other educational innovation in terms of its costs, one must have standards of success. The cost of education must have a return, said Vice Chancellor Mwanza of Zambia. But what kind of return--social, economic, or individual? And how much progress realistically can be expected?

Rector Løchen of Norway spoke of the difficulties at the University of Tromsö in defining success:

We find it difficult to state clearly and precisely when it is that we are successful. Is it when we have produced many students, even of low quality? Or is it when we have published a few but extremely good books? Or when we have managed in some mysterious way to fulfill a politically defined purpose? When a group from the university has been able to improve the health of some underprivileged group? It may be so difficult to define the criteria of success because it is so difficult to define our product. What are we working for? Without a clear idea of a product we don't know the process of creating it.

Educators everywhere have difficulty in defining success and in judging progress toward it. But innovators more than others are expected to justify new ends and means and to convince the doubters. Tradition has the advantage of general acceptance; people are far less likely to ask why they should continue what they have been doing than to ask why they should change. The University of Wisconsin-Green Bay, for example, spends more money on evaluation than do all other branches of the University of Wisconsin combined, said Chancellor Weidner, because one of the burdens of an innovative institution is having to prove the worth of its achievements.

Three questions seem to describe the evaluation issue: (1) What do innovators expect to accomplish? (2) How does an institution devise indicators for evaluating progress? and (3) Who decides whether higher education is accomplishing what it should?

Aims have already been discussed. For example, Wingspread participants sought ways to produce leaders, to clarify and solve social and economic problems, to provide better access for more students, to offer a wider choice of programs, to meet society's needs for trained personnel, and to extend knowledge and research. These are broad goals, however. Innovators must also have a clear idea of the specific aims of the program: what skills it seeks to foster, what new attitudes or behavior it seeks to effect, and what impact it hopes to have on society. The more precise the goal, the easier it is, then, to devise means for reaching it and to measure the results.

Nevertheless, even when programs seek concrete social benefits (less disease or more crops, for example) other influences may obscure the outcome. Place, time, and social and political events affect results as much as do the educational methods. A report on the four year old Aalborg University Center observed, for instance, that judging the center's effect on North Jutland and its development problems is complicated by the current tensions and conflicts of Danish society. The authors of the report ask whether failures resulted from the experiments being too advanced, or from their having been conducted in a period of crisis and depression, or--even more fundamentally--from their having been conducted in North Jutland.[10]

Evaluators of higher education have often confused ends and means. Both educators and the public too often measure education by the processes or means for achieving quality--buildings, student/faculty ratios, library books, and faculty degrees--rather than by the results. One might as well judge a work of art by adding up the number of hours the artist spent on the painting or sculpture, together with the dollars spent on paint and canvas or marble. Money and effort do not inherently produce a thing of beauty.

In judging the efficiency of higher education, says Howard Bowen, the only valid outcomes are changes in persons and changes in society as a consequence of higher education.[11] A recent U.S. study on the accreditation of nontraditional education programs by the Council on Postsecondary Accreditation also recommended that educators should give greater weight to measures of educational accomplishment and performance than to the traditional assessments of educational form and process.[12] In essence, how well are the students learning? Just how competent are they? The study panel further suggested that learning could be measured by comparing students' entrance test scores with later scores, by examining graduates' performance in graduate schools, and by taking a long-range look at alumni achievements. Chancellor Samonte of the Philippines agreed. New programs should be constantly evaluated, he said, to find out whether graduates do better under the new system than under the old. What, for example, are the results of problem-oriented research in terms of new ideas?

Either insiders or outsiders can evaluate new education enterprises. Chancellor Weidner said that at the University of Wisconsin-Green Bay, evaluations are conducted by colleagues. In Australia, said Vice Chancellor Willett, Griffith University established the Center for the Advancement of Learning and Teaching to encourage careful attention to course design at all levels of the university. The center is concerned with design, not methodology--with the relationship of assessment to defining problems. That is, the university works through the center to develop a capacity for assessing its own teaching effectiveness.

Another kind of assessment necessarily accompanies interdisciplinary programs. "If you become involved in interdisciplinary work," said Rector Løchen, "you will immediately have referees coming in from all kinds of fields. This complicates matters and to some extent changes authority and power relations."

In evaluating its open university methods of instruction, Everyman's University in Israel has gathered information on all applicants (by age, sex, education, and occupation), on the numbers who actually achieve a degree, and on the costs per student. The World Bank report on Everyman's also looked at per student costs from the perspective of the national economy, including the recurrent costs of teaching, capital expenditures, and incomes that students forego because of their studies. (At a conventional university, the student's total unemployment might be two and a half years; at Everyman's, about one year.)[13]

Outside evaluations, such as the World Bank's assessment of comparative costs at Everyman's University, can provide detachment and perhaps a wider perspective than a university's evaluation of itself. Such reports may not always be more persuasive to policy makers, though. President Merlin of Vincennes reported that a team of government experts sent to evaluate the university's experience found the results so successful that they recommended applying Vincenne's widened access to other universities. However, Merlin indicated that

56

the government refused to adopt the recommendations of
its own experts.
   While higher education (both innovative and
traditional) needs to define better links between costs
and benefits, statistical tools should be used with
caution. Equating the benefits of higher education with
individual earnings or gross national product, for
example, can be misleading. In the first place, it is
difficult to isolate the cause of economic advantage. Do
individual earnings differ because of education or
because of other factors, such as natural ability, family
background, sex, occupation, and location? Secondly, not
all the benefits of education, to the individual or to
society, can be measured in terms of money. Higher education has a potentially powerful impact on the values,
political structure, and culture of a society as well as
on its economics. (So convinced of this impact was a
Danish trade union that it demanded "research and
teaching for the people and not for profit" from Aalborg
University Center.[14])
   The principal economic products of higher education
are educated talent, knowledge and technology, creative
competence and works of art, continuing education, and
educational justice, affirms John Millett. Furthermore,
he admits knowing of no way to fix an appropriate price
for each of these products.[15] At Wingspread, Chitta
Mitra echoed this same sentiment with the rhetorical
challenge, "What is the cost/benefit of bringing science
to the people or of training people to solve problems?"

Who Judges?

   Finally, to whom is higher education responsible--its
student clientele, prospective employers, the educational
system, government, or society as a whole? And who
should decide whether any given change helps an institution fulfill its responsibilities to any of these groups?
   The college or university exists essentially for its
students and, thus, ultimately must be most accountable
to them. Students worry about getting into college,
paying for it, and learning what they need to know for a
satisfying life and career. Increased access has brought
with it an increased variety of student needs.
Consequently, student demands for better ways to meet
their needs have inspired changes in college and university programs and teaching techniques, as well as changes
toward more diversity of programs and institutions.
   Education must be individualistic, said Chancellor
Weidner, because of the great variety of people it
serves. The success of an academic institution or of a
particular innovative program is measured ultimately by
how well all of its customers fare.

How they fare depends in part on the value of the credentials the institution confers, since a degree has become one's passport to graduate school, to a job, or to a special place in society. Some institutions in the United States that tried to eliminate grades other than "pass" or "fail" had to return to traditional As, Bs, Cs, Ds, and Fs because students' records lacked credibility and hence "market value." Graduate schools and employers thus affect programs by their admission policies or job requirements. They back their approval of new programs by their willingness to accept graduates. On the other hand, the connection between jobs and specific programs is not always clear. "If bad teachers leave the university and teach badly in the schools," said Siegfried Grosse of Germany, "no one says, 'What is the matter with the university?'"

Government may have expectations and goals for higher education which differ from those of both students and employers. Government is concerned with access, manpower training, research, and cost effectiveness. It may also oppose, as it does in the U.S., discrimination for reasons of sex or race, and it may look to the college or university for advice on social or economic issues. Its values may sometimes even conflict with those of the institution. One Wingspread participant, an educator from a developing country, maintained that his government wished to keep people ignorant about certain topics for political advantage while the university, on the other hand, was concerned with overcoming ignorance. In a different example of conflicting values, a U.S. administrator noted that a shortage of city funds, not educational policy, put an end to open admission in the City University of New York.

Citizens of any society certainly have a legitimate interest in what higher education is or is not achieving for the money spent, but they rarely agree on what higher education should achieve. The range of groups interested in the outcomes of higher education, says Lyman Glenny, is exceeded only by the number of ways the many constituencies of higher education expect the institutions to be accountable and efficient.[16]

It is the educators, however--and administrators, in particular--who usually must decide whether new educational enterprises are worth their cost. If the educators cannot confidently assess the results of changes, says Howard Bowen, neither accountability nor efficiency have any significant meaning, and rational management becomes virtually impossible. Indeed, he notes that every educator has sat in meetings of faculty or governing boards where sober and spirited discussions of educational policy take place without anyone having a solid knowledge of what difference one decision or another would make in the students' cognitive or personal

5
Delivery Systems

The British Open University

No development in recent times has so caught the imagination of the academic community as has the British Open University, and at Wingspread there was much discussion of the ways in which its techniques could be adapted. Besides its evident success in attracting large numbers of students, there are two other major reasons for its appeal. The first is the apparent cost advantages, at least at its present scale of operation. The second is its ability to attract students from a broad cross-section of the social, economic, and educational spectrum.

True cost/benefit ratios are difficult to estimate and depend on a clear understanding of start-up costs, operating costs, and maintenance costs. Comparisons require assumptions regarding numbers of students and of degrees awarded annually, as well as estimates of the functional life span of course materials. Nevertheless, at this stage the open university concept appears to offer savings. Britain's Open University presently estimates that its cost of educating a student is no more than 40 percent of a comparable education in a conventional British university. As already stated, the World Bank report on Everyman's University, Israel's version of an open university, concludes that in comparison with traditional Israeli universities, Everyman's per student cost should be less than half. This projection, however, must yet be verified in actual practice.

Whether the British Open University has been successful in attracting students from lower socioeconomic groups has been open to question. In fact, only 10 percent of the Open University students are manual workers.[1] However, 10 percent of the enrollment of 60,000 is 6,000 students, the population of a fair-sized British university. Furthermore, the parents of two-thirds of the Open University students belong to the lower socio-economic groups from which the conventional university draws only a small percentage of its students.[2]

Leading proponents of the Open University may be disappointed, though, that one-third of its students are already qualified schoolteachers seeking their first formal degree. (The British educational system awards an immediate and appreciable salary increase to teachers who obtain a baccalaureate.) The Open University's proportion of teachers has led to the gibe that it has become a cheap mechanism for turning Britain's teaching profession into an all-graduate body. So it is, but the converse reality is also significant: Two-thirds of Open University students are not teachers.

The dropout rate of the Open University has also been criticized as undesirably high; two-thirds of the students fail to complete a degree. Again, though, this must be viewed in perspective. The Open University has made no concessions on quality. Consequently, students face a remarkably difficult program in a society that offers relatively few alternatives for serious part-time students, as compared with the United States, for example. In Britain, nothing like the United States' system of junior colleges and community colleges exists. The high dropout rate, therefore, may reflect not so much the weaknesses of the Open University, but rather a need for other educational options for certification at a level less than the full bachelor's degree.

A crucial decision of the Open University was to develop a credit system. This represented a radical departure from the usual system of the English university and a move towards the American, although the Open University's particular credit system probably parallels the traditional Scottish system more than any other. Under the conventional British system, general education is assumed complete prior to university entrance. Characteristically, the last two years of secondary education involve the study of only three disciplines; and only two of these will be continued at the university, with perhaps one or two additional courses supportive of the major. Thus, for example, a traditional university student may study botany and zoology, with a minor in chemistry; or history, with minors in economics and literature.

The Open University system of foundation courses is a clear break with this tradition, enabling it to accept students who do not meet formal entrance qualifications. Beyond the foundation courses, students select subsequent courses (or half courses--not all courses carry a whole credit) with some restrictions, until they have accumulated sufficient credit for a degree. Some skeptics see this freedom to choose as a step towards the American "cafeteria system," but a strong disciplinary emphasis remains an element of the study program. The Open University thus remains essentially faithful to its national traditions.

A second critical innovation has occurred in the development of the courses themselves. Correspondence study is not in itself new; for a century and a half it has been possible in Britain to read the necessary books and present oneself for examination by the University of London. However, the average textbook is not designed for self-study; it is designed as an adjunct to conventional classroom study. The achievement of the Open University has been to produce programmed packages to facilitate self-study. It was expected that mediated instruction, especially that involving broadcast delivery systems, would play a central role; in fact, the original title was the University of the Air. However, the written word still remains the primary mode of communication and study, although it has been significantly augmented by radio and television and by the development of study centers.

In summary, it is probably true that mediated instruction delivered via radio, television, cassette tapes, and other technological packages, has been less important than originally envisaged while the written word has been more important. But the programmed packaging of the written word to facilitate self-study has been itself a major innovation. Less significantly, the study centers where students can gather with a tutor to watch, listen, and discuss their coursework seem almost to have been a superfluous afterthought. They are used by only about 50 percent of the students, but are nevertheless highly valued by those who do use them.

The development of kits for home experiment in the sciences is a further innovation and represents a technological breakthrough for science instruction. The absence of laboratory experience has always presented an almost insuperable obstacle to the distance study of science. Overcoming this obstacle is one of the Open University's achievements, well described by Perry.[3]

The extent to which the success of the Open University will prove transferable to other countries remains problematic. Unlike other European nations, Britain has never made any pretense of providing higher education for all who are qualified. Entrance to British universities has been and remains an essentially competitive process. When the available places are filled, students are turned away. As late as 1961-62, British postsecondary enrollments totaled only 192,000 students, both full time and part time; and only a minority were full-time university students. Most were full-time students in teacher training colleges or part-time students in technical colleges. By 1971-72, this number had risen to 463,000 and by 1974-75, to 546,000.[4]

But even considering the highest figure, the state of Wisconsin, with a population less than 10 percent that of the United Kingdom, has at least one-third as many students in higher education. In 1974-75 the University of Wisconsin System alone, quite separately from institutions in the private sector, enrolled 144,000 students. Some caution is necessary in comparing raw numbers of students in this way and calling them all university students. In Britain, the usual level of preparation among entering university students is considerably higher than it is in the United States. Nevertheless, students in British colleges of education (enrollments totaling about 122,000) have required preparation comparable to their United States counterparts; and students at British polytechnics may be only slightly better prepared than United States high school graduates. However, it seems likely that the pool of eager, intellectually capable students who have been denied the chance of a university education, and who form the Open University's main clientele, may not be available in most other developed nations. Even so, the cost benefits of the Open University may still provide an important lesson for other nations. The budget of the University of Wisconsin, for example, is a billion dollars and rising steadily, and the problem of reducing costs is critical almost everywhere.

Everyman's University, Israel

Of the institutions directly represented at Wingspread, the closest in structure and function to the Open University is Everyman's University of Israel. Max Rowe described it at Wingspread:

Everyman's University began operations in the fall of 1976 with 2,300 students and now in the fourth term of operation has 8,000. The main focus is upon traditional courses, but there are some vocational courses and what are called second-chance courses. There are no entrance requirements and in fact, 30 percent of the students have not matriculated.

We begin by advertising a course in a newspaper. Prospective students receive sample material which enables them to judge whether the course is what they need and whether they are competent to complete it. If the student is satisfied, then he registers and pays half the fee, with the second half due half-way through the course. About 90 percent of the students get that far. The basic unit of study is a course consisting of twelve units—each unit taking about fifteen hours to complete; and the course lasts about four months. Evaluation is by examination, and one credit accrues to the student for each successfully completed course. Eighteen credits constitute a baccalaureate.

We have a very small nucleus of staff--at present about fifteen. The courses provide specially written textbooks to the students, prepared by academics from all over the country. It takes about two years to prepare the written material for one course, and we remain convinced that the written text is the most cost-effective and educationally effective method of delivery. Equipment is provided for science students, and a pocket calculator for mathematicians. Audio-cassettes are available for language students, and for geography and Jewish studies there are guided tours of the country. We also have a little radio and TV work.

We have twenty-five study centers established around the country, with a tutor in attendance /at each/. The tutor does not deliver lectures, but answers questions and can be reached by telephone. The students attend every three weeks, but our experience is similar to that of the British; namely, that only 40 to 50 percent of the students avail themselves of the opportunity. However, science students must attend the laboratory sessions, which are also given about once every three weeks. For the nonacademic courses, particularly electronics and electricity, we provide a major home laboratory that must be returned at the end of the course.

Evaluation is through computer graded assignments and a final exam. The student is given considerable freedom of choice in the courses to be taken, but not total freedom. We call it a modular system. We have three levels--introductory, intermediate, and advanced--and no more than six credits can be taken at the introductory level, and a minimum of four must be taken at the advanced level. Students of science are encouraged to take some courses in the humanities, and so forth.

The response has been greater than we expected, and perhaps even greater than we desired. We expected to get a larger response from teachers, but they only make up 20 percent of our student body. The majority of students are those not qualified for universities, or who live far away from universities, or those who failed in their first encounter with higher education. We have a much higher percentage of the disadvantaged groups than /do/ traditional universities.

    Everyman's University is both like and unlike the
Open University of Great Britain. Both offer bachelor's
degrees, but Everyman's University also offers vocational
courses, currently in electricity and electronics, and
regards continuing education for adults as a primary
purpose. The Open University, in effect, also offers
continuing education on a large scale to the two-thirds
of its students who fail to complete a degree; almost
certainly many Open University students undertake single
courses for vocational development in such fields as
electronics or computing.
    Everyman's welcomes teachers and considers the
development of a wholly graduate teaching profession a
worthy aim, while the number of teachers in Open
University programs is more often cited as a criticism;
evidence of its marginal utility, so to speak. There is,
however, no reason to believe that the staff of the Open
University feels that teaching teachers is a second-rate
activity. What may be true is that the Open University
is publicizing a narrow mandate to avoid potentially
damaging comparisons with conventional universities in
Britain, while in practice it is accepting the broader
mandate that Everyman's can openly espouse.
    Everyman's has adopted the credit system, but 18
rather than 6 credits are required for a degree.
Consequently, the curriculum of Everyman's is more
fragmented, closer to the American system of semester-
length 3-credit courses, than is the Open University's.
The requirements of a course are 12 study units, each
unit requiring 12 to 18 hours of work per week.[5] Perry
calculates an investment of about 390 hours of work
necessary to earn each Open University credit,[6]
approximately the same as that needed at Everyman's or
even at Scottish universities, which are well respected
in Britain.
    Both the Open University and Everyman's depend mainly
on the written word--on correspondence instruction, with
radio and television occupying a significant but secondary instructional role. Both institutions are keenly
aware of the need to design courses, not simply to write
material; indeed, Everyman's acknowledges its debt to the
Open University for the development of this technique of
structural course building. Both have found value in
tutorial centers with local part-time tutors, but both
find that only about half the students use these centers.
Finally, both in slightly different ways have devised the
foundation course concept as a bridge to the university
for those lacking conventional entrance qualifications.
    Just as the Open University is criticized, not least
by itself, for not reaching enough manual workers,
Everyman's has problems reaching the Oriental Jewish
immigrants into Israel. They form a comparable
underclass and make up only 20 percent of Everyman's

8,000 students. A dispassionate observer might caution both institutions against interpreting relative success as failure, simply because success has not yet come up to expectations. Max Rowe quotes the wisdom of Solomon: Those who have some knowledge seek more; those who have little seek none. The ingrained habits of centuries will not be overcome overnight. It will take time for sectors of the public unaccustomed to having access to a university education to take full advantage of their relatively new opportunity.

The Israeli experience closely parallels the British. The significance of Everyman's University on the international scene might be that, in a small nation that has not neglected higher education, there may be a substantial pool of eager and able students not served by more conventional universities. The fact that an important innovation can be replicated does not mean that it is universally applicable. It does mean, though, that it is of more than local significance.

Perspectives on Distance Learning

It must be clear to even the casual observer of the educational scene that distance or open learning is a concept whose time has come. Seemingly, scarcely a nation exists that is not vigorously pursuing its own scheme or expanding an already healthy system of nontraditional higher education for off-campus clienteles. Besides the obvious reasons of social need and reduced cost, it seems likely that the enthusiasm in part lies in the successful technological mix of programmed texts, quality media productions (i.e., not merely televising a professor in front of a blackboard), learning centers and tutors, science kits, and other such modes of instruction. The achievement lies in the mix rather than in the separate elements, all of which have had their proponents and successes in the past. In spite of the appeal of distance learning, however, uncertainties remain, and the Wingspread participants were not universally enthusiastic on the subject.

Joseph Aarts of the Netherlands raised the question of the cost-effectiveness of an open university. Max Rowe replied by quoting from the World Bank report on Everyman's University. He said that taking steady state costs, which should be reached 5 years from now, the cost of a first degree (including capital costs) would be $5,600 at Everyman's, as compared with $11,000-$12,000 at a traditional Israeli university. With regard to capital costs, the report concluded that to establish Everyman's, provide the few buildings needed, and develop the 120 courses planned will require about $20 million, or about $100,000 per course. On the other hand, the cost of a new traditional university would be about $40 to $50 million.

Charles Wedemeyer expanded on this:

It is important to cost out at the steady state. Small universities may be educationally successful but fail because there are too few students to make the institution economical. In our initial study for the Open University, we decided that a minimum of 25,000 students was necessary to allow saving over the regular university costs. It turned out that 19,000 students would have been sufficient.

There are three categories of costs involved: start-up costs, operational costs, and maintenance costs. The balance of these is quite different in the Open University when compared with a conventional university. Start-up costs are not higher. It was believed that the cost of starting a conventional university, which would serve 25,000 students on its opening day, would be $80 million, whereas the cost of the Open University was only $17 million. Operational costs of the Open University are only about 40 to 50 percent of the conventional. Maintenance costs are the toughest to estimate because they contain factors not found in conventional practice. If you develop a mediated course that you expect to have a life of three years, and then find that you have to make changes before then, the cost of pulling out old units and inserting new ones is much greater than having a regular professor simply alter his mode of presentation.

A more severe problem is that we have been accustomed to amortize our costs over an annual period, whereas the costs for Open University course work need to be spread over a longer period. If difficulties of accounting practice can be overcome, there is no doubt in my mind that cost-benefit ratios will be less than those of regular institutions.

Despite the success of the Open University and the eagerness with which the model has been greeted elsewhere, it should not be regarded as a panacea for the problems involved in the extension of university education. Other types of innovation have equally promising roles to play. Furthermore, as has already been pointed out, many people at Wingspread had reservations about open universities. Gonzalez-Reyes of Venezuela stated that while in the face of great resistance a clause was inserted into the Venezuelan law to permit such experimentation in higher education, the concept is

still not firmly established in Latin America. While
there are one or two notable exceptions, such as the
University of the Andes in Bogotá and the Autonomous
University of Guadalajara in Mexico, he said that
generally tradition is strong among students, faculty,
and the population at large. Gonzalez-Reyes does
believe, however, that the open university idea addresses
real educational needs. He espoused the search for technology that will enhance the capacity of people to
transfer knowledge from man to man. But he also said
that countries that lack long-standing traditions of
instruction and learning may have difficulties in
adopting the open university system. He suggested a need
to develop new materials within the indigenous cultural
context of such countries and then to use existing communication networks to facilitate the diffusion of this
material. But he warned that in many countries such communication networks simply do not exist or are extremely
inefficient.

Luis Garibay confirmed that so far there has been
little interest in open universities in Latin America,
though there are some experiments--in Mexico at the
National University and at the Monterey Technical
Institute, and in Colombia, Venezuela, and Costa Rica
where international cooperation has been initiated. He
felt that one problem was the open system's failure, as
yet, to generate necessary motivation among the students,
a lack which he thought may be attributable to a cultural
attitude common in Latin America.

Garibay also pointed out that a second problem has
been a concerted attack on the open university idea by
traditional universities. Such problems are not, of
course, restricted to Latin America. A continued, almost
obsessive need to avoid becoming a second class institution pervades Perry's account of the development of the
Open University in Britain, where rank ordering of institutions of all kinds approaches a national vice.

Institutionalization of distance studies in the
Federal Republic of Germany has had to cope with similar
problems. Despite the conviction of proponents such as
Dohmen[7] that distance learning should concern itself, at
least in part, with those prevented by circumstance from
undertaking regular university study, West German educational tradition demands that degree students be conventionally qualified for university admission and be
prepared for the same State-administered examinations as
regular students. Dohmen acknowledges that distance
learning should, in the short term, attempt to relieve
the pressure on admissions noted by Siegfried Grosse in
Wingspread discussions. However, in the longer term
Dohmen proposes that such off-campus educational programs
assume the responsibility for lifelong learning and take
up the challenge of serving the nontraditional students.

He suggests that this would do more than simply expand
opportunities for adult education. Such "opening up" of
the university to nontraditional learning/distance
studies might make academic study both less schoolish and
more scholarly, bringing it into closer contact with real
life.

Because university education is a responsibility of
State governments in the Federal Republic, a nationwide
open university has not been feasible. The "Deutsches
Institut für Fernstudien" in Tübingen, built up by
Dohmen, studies and develops courses and modules for
distance studies and offers them to universities and
other institutions for further learning in the Federal
Republic of Germany. It coordinates the endeavor to
bring in more and more elements of "angeleitetes selbst
studium" into higher education, but the most ambitious
single project has been the Fernuniversität, established
in 1975 by North Rhine Westphalia and described by
Peters.[8] This new university accepts full-time students
as well as part-time adult students qualified for university admission, and it prepares them for State
examinations. Its methods are essentially those of the
Open University and of Everyman's--specially commissioned
textual materials programmed for self-study and augmented
by tutors, study centers, and some educational media
packages. Also significant is the acceptance by the
Fernuniversität of adults who wish to qualify for credentials in special areas through one-semester or one-year
courses. This innovation represents an adventurous
departure from convention in West Germany; and while the
number of students now reached is small relative to the
population, the future of such educational alternatives
in Germany is sure to attract growing attention.

From another perspective, Hamdan Tahir suggested that
a study of the open university concept indicated that it
is not a justifiable option for Malaysia in the face of
its present economic strictures. On the other hand, off-
campus courses have been initiated at the University of
Science in Malaysia (USM) for those who need to upgrade
their professional qualifications. Of the 3,200 students
enrolled, Tahir indicated that about one quarter are
attending off-campus instruction. He went on to say
that, while not neglecting the humanities, Malaysia has
recognized a pressing need for more scientists.
Therefore, although as in Britain and Israel, many of
USM's off-campus students are teachers improving their
qualifications to warrant higher salaries, this situation
is welcomed in Malaysia as one way to fill the need for
more and better science teachers.

In a similar vein, Mohamed Omar pointed out that
Saudi Arabia is adopting an open door policy for
students:

Within 5 years we have achieved the figure of 5,000
external students, chosen according to their
geographic distribution in the Kingdom. The same
requirements are placed upon these students as for
regular students. They use the same textbooks and
are examined by the same professors. We are
following closely the model of the Open University in
England, setting up regional centers and utilizing
radio and TV. We find that the cost is only 10 percent of that for regular students.

Both the Malaysian and the Saudi programs are more in
the nature of external degree programs rather than true
open university programs. The technological mix that
characterizes the Open University is not yet present.
There are other differences, too. The Malaysian program
does not entail open admissions, demanding comparable
entrance qualifications for internal and external
students. And in Malaysia, said Hamdan Tahir, external
students spend their final year in residence, to enable
them to experience "the life of comradeship in the
university."
The successes claimed for the open university model,
both in Britain and Israel, in terms of cost effectiveness and educational achievement, inevitably lead to
questions about the role of the traditional university.
After all, if large numbers of people can be educated,
essentially in their spare time, to a level comparable
with traditional university students at only 40 percent
of the cost, should not all students be educated in this
way? As Adnan Badran of Jordan put it, is an open university an adequate alternative for 18 year olds or is it
simply an alternative for returning older adults? Does
it compete satisfactorily with the traditional freshman
and sophomore year experiences, which provide contact
between student and faculty, work in laboratory and
library, and participation in campus life? Badran
suggested that an open university is better regarded not
as an educational alternative but as a supplement, which
might follow junior college, for example, and permit
study in a specialized subject.
Max Rowe of Everyman's replied to Badran's
observation initially with statistics which neatly sum-
marize the current status of the two most successful
examples of the open university. The British Open
University at first had fixed a minimum enrollment age of
21, to avoid competition with conventional universities,
but it is now developing a separate program for the 17
to 21 year old group. In contrast, the average age at
Everyman's University is 32, but there is no minimum age.
Nine percent are in the age group up to 20, 23 percent
are 21 to 26, and 40 percent are 27 to 35 years old.
Rowe went on to suggest that experience with this system

indicates that motivation is the main factor, and that enthusiasm for learning may occur at any age. With regard to contact among students, and between students and faculty, he said:

> I think we can all agree that if we could provide everybody with education on the Harvard or Oxbridge models, that would be best. But it is not possible, except for the elite, and we are in a period of mass education. The study centers provide some opportunities for relationships with tutors and with other students. But we are seeking an alternative to the elitist system and that leads us to technology as a means of delivery.

As we have noted in the section on access, Chancellor Riahi of Iran and Chitta Mitra of India delivered the most trenchant attacks on the open university concept. "I suggest that there cannot be two systems, or one is bound to be a second-class system for the poor," Riahi noted. And Mitra echoed the criticism: "I have this concern about the Open University, that it may be creating a caste system." These are by no means marginal comments about the role and the future of higher education. An open university may, indeed, provide comparable intellectual accomplishment to that acquired in conventional universities. There may even be, as Wedemeyer suggested, greater congruence between the goals of students in an open university and the goals of educators because of the self-selection of this option by students. But questions remain in many minds as to whether these less traditionally educated graduates will be able to climb career ladders in fair competition with the conventionally educated, and whether the socializing function of higher education can be achieved, or perhaps even effectively dispensed with, through an open university experience.

There are at least two possible responses to such questions. Charles Wedemeyer, while admitting that the conventional system is a powerful cultural artifact, suggested that it no longer serves the needs of society. There is now a need for more knowledge, all of which cannot be acquired in youth, leading to a demand for life-long learning:

> There has always been a plurality of systems, and alternatives today are not viewed with hostility. I think that in the future, we will have many systems of learning, and people will use different systems in the course of their lives. For example, there is a growing desire of legislative and professional bodies to require continued recertification. Currently, so many credits are required periodically from

established schools. It would be better to make open learning modules available and permit the professional to choose those that suit his problems and practice. Diversity will become a source of strength, not of problems.

The second response from Max Rowe turns one of Dr. Badran's questions on its head.

If an open university remains an institute on its own, on the margin of education, it will serve some social purpose, but it will be at least a partial failure. However, if the conventional universities start using the same methods, then it will truly be a success. One university in Israel suggested that it was rather foolish for all universities to be offering the same basic courses with indifferent success. They suggested that an open university might take over first- and second-year courses entirely.

We perceive in these debates the beginnings of differing educational philosophies between developed and developing nations. The developed world is struggling with questions of economic access to a scarce commodity for an ever widening sample of its population. The Third World, on the other hand, is seeking to foster the development of an intellectual elite to promote economic growth. It is undoubtedly unfair to both sides to state the distinction so simplistically because there are many nuances of opinion, sources of agreement, and areas of common thinking inherent in the basic dichotomy. But one cannot disguise the fact, implicit in the views of Archer,[9] that the nature of innovation is modified by the goals of innovation and that these goals are not entirely congruent among diverse societies.

6
New Clienteles

In many countries, two forces are operating to cause the university to seek to open its doors to a new kind of student. The first is demographic. Universities have expanded over the last twenty years to accommodate the postwar bulge in the birthrate and the rising educational expectations which have drawn a greater proportion of the relevant age group into college. Recently, though, the birthrate has fallen precipitously. Siegfried Grosse summarized the problem in West Germany, pointing out that the constitution of the Federal Republic guarantees educational opportunity for all. "In spite of our having built twenty new universities," he said, "there will not be enough places for the students demanding entry in 1985. The trend has reversed, however, so that while in 1965 there were 1.2 million births, in 1975 there were only .6 million. When we consider that 60 percent of our students intend to make careers as teachers, we can see that jobs will not be available for them."

The second force promoting awareness of new clienteles is a growing antipathy to the elitist image of the university, and to the concept that education should be essentially completed by one's early twenties. In response to both of these forces, many educators feel the need to "open" the established university rather than to establish an open university, as Sven Caspersen put it. He continued by saying:

> In Denmark we believe our educational purpose is not simply to improve the individual skills and possibilities of the citizen's working life, but also of his family life, his leisure life, and his life as a member of society. We would wish to take seriously the injunction that education should provide something to live for, not just something to live with.

L'Université Ouverte-Vincennes

An example of an attempt to "open up" the conventional university to new types of students is Vincennes University. A literal translation of "L'Université Ouverte" is "Open University," but Vincennes is radically different from the Open University in Great Britain and Everyman's in Israel. Dr. Guy Berger described the goals and methods of Vincennes in this way:

> While we have excellent relationships with our colleagues in the Open University in Britain, our purpose is quite different from theirs. The main purpose of the Open University is to provide a second chance for people to obtain the same diplomas that other students obtain. New students are asked to forget their life experience once they enter the symbolic doors of the university. Our purpose at Vincennes is more social and cultural, as well as educational. We do not wish to extend further opportunities to members of the middle class. We want to extend cultural opportunities to new types of students and, in fact, 40 percent of our students are from developing countries or are migrant workers.

> The final result is a change in the function of the university. We are trying to extend to foreigners and housewives the opportunity to confer and exchange, to discuss and analyze their former experience while also obtaining a formal diploma. Our fundamental pedagogical problems are threefold: (1) How to consider student heterogeniety with regard to cultural background, age, and academic level, not as an obstacle to progress, but as a means towards educational advancement. (2) How to use individual and group research as a process for teaching and learning. (3) How to get away from traditional means of transmitting knowledge and find ways for the students themselves to produce new knowledge, new theories, new modes of transmission. As an example, we have excellent audio-visual equipment, but we do not use this to give conventional lectures and classes--or at least not only for that. We encourage the students to make their own productions covering problems that interest them and to take them back to the community as a means of instruction and analysis for members of the community and for the students themselves.

It is difficult to understand the nature of the changes sought at Vincennes without some understanding of the traditional French educational system and of the alterations precipitated in that system by the extensive student demonstrations of 1968. State control of education is very evident in France. The remark attributed to a Minister of Education of the Second Empire, that at a given hour all the pupils in every school in France will be translating the same page of Virgil, is probably apocryphal. But the implications of that statement are quite real. Professors, like all other teachers, are civil servants appointed by the Ministry. While this may not have restricted academic freedom, it has certainly inhibited change.

The modern university dates from the Imperial University of Napoleon, and as Archer[1] points out, Napoleon was explicitly creating an instrument of government. During the nineteenth century, the French university became a collection of faculties, in which the true power resided. And if the faculties of science, of letters, of law, and of medicine were the kingdoms within the Imperial University, then the professors—the heads of individual disciplines—were the dukes and counts. With little opportunity for educational innovation, the disciplines turned inward upon themselves.

Meanwhile there existed in France an alternative system formed by the Grandes Écoles. While any student who matriculated in France could, by law, attend the university of his/her choice (and most who could chose Paris), entrance to the Grandes Écoles was highly competitive. Their graduates had, and still do have, an inside track to the highest posts in government, industry, and the army. However, the professions, including teaching, have remained the prerogative of university graduates. In addition, between 1963 and 1966 Instituts Universitaires de Technologie (IUTs) were established paralleling university faculties, to provide two-year courses for middle management and supervisory positions. Because these IUTs did not prove as popular as hoped, they failed to relieve pressure on the universities. By 1968 all French universities, but especially Paris, were badly overcrowded. All matriculants had the opportunity to attend, but many were eliminated by the examinations concluding the first cycle of instruction. Together with overcrowding, this high elimination rate was a source of great bitterness among students.

The student demonstrations of 1968 resulted, and they bordered upon insurrection. As a result, the Loi d'Orientation de l'Enseignment Supérieur was passed by Parliament in November of that year, with the goal of drastic university reform though without interference in the Grandes Écoles. The three principles endorsed by this law were multidisciplinarity, participation, and autonomy.

   Multidisciplinarity was to be achieved by replacing the old faculties with Units of Teaching and Research (UERs). These were to be formed by alliances of disciplines, and following the principle of autonomy, each university was free to form its own UERs. A minimum of 800 students and a maximum of 2,500 defined the size of the organizational units. Participation was to be ensured essentially by establishing committees to replace the old professorial fiefdoms. A university would, henceforth, be characterized by collections of UERs, and to take the pressure off Paris, students would be required to attend their local university.

   Overall, success was mixed. At many universities the old faculties survived by merely reorganizing themselves as UERs. In larger universities, sheer size forced faculties to split into several UERs; but a faculty of science, for example, would turn itself into a physics-chemistry-mathematics-natural science UER--hardly multidisciplinary. Similar tactics were employed by faculties of letters. Medicine or law would sometimes form a single UER, based more on political affinity than on a concern for multidisciplinarity.[2]

   Vincennes was created, in short, both as a relief for overcrowding in Paris and as a site for experiment and innovation. It represented a notable departure from traditional higher education in France. Dr. Merlin described it as follows:

   If the university wants to play a role in the development of society, it must give evidence that it is a social force. The university in developed countries must make a choice. Either it delivers professional education to people, in which case their numbers must be dictated by the available market for their services; or it must adopt the cultural model, where it educates citizens with no guarantee that they will receive a highly paid job, but with the goal of enabling them to adapt to the changing values of their society.

   Vincennes was created by the Gaullist government after the 1968 riots. It was focused on four kinds of experimentation: (1) new pedagogical methods; (2) special attention to the arts; (3) teaching addressed towards contemporary problems; and (4) a new population of students to be served, especially those already established in professional life. Its student body has perhaps given the university its greatest challenge and has been the source of most outside opposition. In 1974 a government commission concluded that other universities should be opened to "walk-in" students; its report was rejected. We are permanently at war with the government.

Opening the institution to new students has
repercussions throughout the whole of university
life. Our students are diversified by age from
18 to 60 years old. We have 107 nationalities
represented. And finally, they are diversified by
professional and personal experience. The professor
cannot speak to such students as he did before. For
example, I cannot talk in my course on new towns in
the same way to people who have been involved in
building and living in new towns as I would to 18
year olds. The professor must be both more rigorous
and more concrete.

Our working student will frequently have less
intellectual ability, but generally shows more eagerness to take advantage of his second chance. Both
faculty and students prefer evening classes to accommodate walk-in students. Students want to share
their experience and will interrupt the professor and
discuss questions among themselves. Traditional
students are also eager to take advantage of these
opportunities once they enter the new milieu.
Education takes place by constant dialogue, and the
professor must be ready to rethink his subject.
Students papers will frequently reflect work
experience and not simply the learning experience.

We cannot depend solely upon conventional faculty.
We must invite professionals who bring to the class
their working experience. The students must be
allowed a great deal of freedom to create their own
programs, and there is considerable discussion among
students about the need for new courses and new
programs. For many students, the degree is not the
main thing. They come to obtain professional
improvement or cultural widening. So we cannot
evaluate our programs by the number of degrees
awarded. In fact, because the usual criteria of
admission do not apply, many students will not
receive a degree. It is a future-oriented university
designed to respond to the problems of contemporary
society. It may not sound very revolutionary, and
yet the government is anxious not to extend this
experiment further among working people.

Vincennes tends to describe itself by what it is not.
LES DOSSIERS DE VINCENNES[3] emphasizes the denial of traditional processes and values of the French university--a
refusal to select students, a refusal to adopt traditional course structures, mass-produced examinations,
discrimination by level of study, and other conventions.
Yet, Vincennes claims to be a university like the
others, with the same basic standards and equivalent

achievements, while it maintains a critical stance towards education and towards society.

A major innovation has been to replace the characteristic large blocks of coursework, each leading to a certificate, with a large number of smaller "unités de valeur" (UVs). Conventionally, a French university student will undertake four major courses in three or four years. At Vincennes, a semester system has replaced the previous trimester (or quarter) system. A full-time student is required to complete five UVs per semester, each of which is constituted by three hours of classwork and an estimated six hours of preparation per week; this system, in fact, closely parallels the American system of courses. Furthermore, the three hours of classwork are often given in a single block in the evening because some 50 percent of the students work full time, compared with only 5 percent of the general population of French university students.

The UVs are helpful to part-time students and to those seeking personal development rather than a degree. They are deliberately structured to have few or no prerequisites; they do not form sequences, but each stands on its own. Students can thus construct programs of study suited to their particular needs, rather than being forced in lock step through predetermined programs, a process Vincennes refers to as "Xerox copying." Finally each UV is delivered mostly through discussion and small group projects, rather than by a magisterial series of lectures.

Vincennes is not a small university; it has 28,000 students and 850 teachers. As an example of the university's philosophy and operation, the Department of Urban Studies is representative. About 25 percent of the students in this department are new students, about 25 percent are students who have completed the equivalent of 4 years of higher education, and about half have completed some work in other departments, such as architecture, social science, or economics. The faculty consists of 3 architects, 2 engineers, 2 sociologists, 2 geographers, 1 philosopher, 1 social planner, and 1 urban planner.

The department's instructional program is divided into two cycles, adhering to the usual French practice. In the first cycle, the student must complete eighteen UVs chosen as follows:

1. Three UVs introducing problems and methods of urban studies--an introduction to urban problems, to methods of analysis, and to the role of the city in time and space.

2. Four units of value in social sciences--an introduction to urban sociology, to urban economics,

to public rights, and to the relationships of man and environment.

3. A double UV (one year of study) on instrumentation and spatial and statistical analysis.

4. A double UV studying a specific urban situation.

5. Four UVs composing a coherent theme--examples of such themes would be "The Neighborhood," "The City," "The Urban Region," or "Urban Problems in Underdeveloped Countries."

6. Five elective UVs.

The second cycle, leading to a license (degree) in urban studies, consists of the completion of ten additional UVs, together with participation in a two-semester research seminar and the completion of a two-year research project. The selection of the ten UVs is completely elective for students who have completed the first cycle of instruction in urban studies. For students who have completed their first cycle in other disciplines, requirements are imposed.

Very little needs to be added to make the nature of this program instantly recognizable to anybody familiar with the catalog of an American university, an observation which should not be interpreted to mean that the Vincennes program is a "copy." Division of the curriculum into small, discrete units is inevitable if the possibility of transfer between units and the opportunity for self-paced study are to be developed.

The future of Vincennes is now in doubt. Pierre Merlin and Guy Berger repeatedly stressed that the experiment was unpopular with the educational establishment, and their concern for the future has been justified by events. According to Domenach,[4] the City of Paris never ratified the oral agreement which provided a site for Vincennes. Consequently, it has been obliged to leave its original location and move to a much smaller site in Saint-Denis, a Paris suburb. Domenach asserts that the university is continuing and will continue its former role, and as a consequence, is bursting at the seams because of persistent high enrollment. However, the future is in doubt. While the numbers of non-traditional students in the nontraditional programs is said to be holding up, there were 28,500 students enrolled in 1980, only 3,500 less than the previous year. Whether it can continue to do so in the face of official hostility remains to be seen.

The New Learner in the United States

If the open university is the innovation that has aroused most interest in recent years, surely the response to a growing audience of learners is securely in second place. The two situations are certainly not unrelated because the open university is, indeed, reaching a new clientele of learners. In the United States, however, many (if not most) universities seem to be seeking a broader role primarily in adult education, rather than through adoption of the open university concept. Vice Chancellor Edwin Speir of the University of Wisconsin-Whitewater described the experiences of his own institution as follows:

> The University of Wisconsin-Whitewater realized about five years ago that our service area was the area within 100 miles of the campus. We have now developed the largest enrollment of any State institution in Wisconsin of part-time professional students away from campus. We export our faculty to centers of instruction throughout our service region. The method of instruction is largely didactic and preceptorial, with lectures and discussion formats; but many faculty are treating student groups, and even individual students, as clients and developing courses in consultation with them to meet their needs. The second element of our approach is to develop methods to evaluate learning that took place outside of the university and providing credit for such learning towards a degree. Dr. Kleinjans asked whether people can be taught about the real world from books that are taken up with the rhetoric of conclusions. Now, this should be turned around and the question should be asked, "What have people learned in the real world that is creditable towards a degree?"

In one sense this is no more than a logical extension into a new era of the Wisconsin Idea that the boundaries of the university are the boundaries of the state. But the goals go beyond earlier objectives in agriculture and home economics to encompass students interested in personal development, in completing a degree for which some credits have already been accumulated, or in starting a degree and having other types of learning experience credited toward it.

A noted specialist in the challenges of educating this "new clientele," Patricia Cross,[5] believes that the population of actual or potential adult learners in the United States may presently approach 75 percent of all adults. She suggests that the typical adult learner is young, white, well-educated, employed in a technical or

professional field, and making a good income. All
indications are that learning is addictive and the desire
for it essentially insatiable. And, in fact, Cross
believes that adult and continuing education could
replace college degrees as the socio-economic sorter of
American society. Employers, instead of asking potential
employees about college degrees, may begin to ask what
candidates have done recently to keep abreast of a
rapidly changing world.

The phenomenon of the adult learners' need to keep up
was addressed at Wingspread by Charles Wedemeyer:

> Lifelong learning is not new. It is simply that we
> are only now recognizing it. In the future, we will
> need more systems of learning because people will
> wish to use different systems throughout their lives.
> For example, we may well find that as the learner
> matures, the initiative for establishing a connection
> with the learning institution will come from the
> student and not from the institution.
>
> There is another factor at work; namely, the growing
> desire of legislatures and professional bodies to
> require periodic recertification. Currently, the
> easy way out is being sought by requiring so many
> credits from particular schools. It would be better
> to make open learning modules available and let the
> professional choose those which suit his problems and
> practices.

With regard to adult learners, Wedemeyer called the
attention of the conference to the work of Tough and his
associates, which has been summarized in a recent
paper.[6] Over the past 7 years many basic surveys and
in-depth interviews have revealed that adults spend a
remarkable amount of time each year at major efforts to
learn. To be specific, a typical adult learning effort
occupies 100 hours of time, and the typical adult conducts 5 of these per year. In terms of man-weeks of
effort, this is equivalent to 10 weeks of full-time
study. While some variation occurs among populations,
the overall figures are remarkably consistent for such
diverse groups as doctors, ministers, and unemployed
adults in New Jersey. Similar consistency is observed
over geographic areas--from Tennessee to Jamaica, Ghana,
and New Zealand. Neither does the amount of time spent
vary greatly with the level of educational attainment.

Some studies indicate that job-related learning
accounts for less of this time investment than does
learning for personal development, hobbies and
recreation, home and family, projects, and general
education. Professionals are more likely than nonpro-
fessionals to undertake learning related to their

vocations, but overall these studies parallel other
surveys which indicate that personal interest is as
important as advancement in selecting further education.
Only 20 percent of these adult learning projects are
planned and supervised by professionals in instruction;
most are self-initiated and self-planned. However, Tough
concludes that most adults do desire competent professional help in planning and guiding their projects.
Such help simply is not generally available to them.

There is no reason to think that all of this demand
can or should be satisfied by universities, either
through degree programs or extension services. But it
does show why well-planned efforts such as those of the
Open University, Everyman's, Vincennes, and the
University of Wisconsin-Whitewater are heavily patron-
ized. The demand exists, and most efforts to satisfy it
have simply been inadequate. According to all indicators, efforts similar to those at these universities will
both enjoy success and satisfy real social needs.

7
Innovations in the Land-Grant Tradition

The American land-grant college was the result of three Acts of Congress. The first was the Morrill Act signed into law in 1862, which provided to each state a 30,000-acre allocation of Federal land; one such parcel for each of that state's senators and representatives, for "the endowment, support, and maintenance of at least one college in each state where the leading object shall be, without excluding other scientific and classical studies, and including military tactics, to teach such branches of learning as are related to agriculture and the mechanic arts." This phraseology amounted to a redefinition of the college as it was then known because of the new emphasis on practical education. It was a far-sighted redefinition, however, because it did not exclude liberal education for practical men and women.

As Beale[1] has pointed out, there were immediate problems. There simply was no science of agriculture and the mechanic arts to teach, a problem which drove the early professors to work on local or college farms in order to develop a curriculum. Such pioneering research work led to the Hatch Act of 1887, which established an agricultural experiment station in association with each of the land-grant colleges. The success of the experiment stations led state after state to set up demonstration plots and extension courses to distribute the results of research to the farmer, which in turn led to the Smith-Lever Act of 1914, establishing extension programs in every state. The resulting marriage of instruction for practical pursuits, of research, and of extension has characterized the land-grant institution ever since.

The land-grant colleges rapidly entered the mainstream of American education, characterized by the elective scheme of Eliot at Harvard and the absorption of the influence of the German tradition of research. Nevertheless, a look at the experiences of women students

at Michigan State in the 1870s shows just how practical
the education could also be:

> In lieu of agricultural labor in the afternoons,
> they worked in the horticulture department, cutting
> seed potatoes, setting tomato plants, and helping
> in the greenhouse. In 1896, a woman's course in
> household economy was established. Here, promised
> the catalog, "science would involve a sweeter, saner
> mode of living, simplify and systematize duties and
> labors that at present hold our women in practical
> slavery, bring on premature exhaustion, and take
> away from life all dignity." There was only one
> instructor. In the absence of suitable textbooks she
> prepared a set of printed cards for each day's
> lesson. Following these outlines, students learned
> what they could of nutrition and the principles of
> boiling, stewing, baking, and broiling. They learned
> how to work, how to wash dishes, and how to set a
> table.
>
> Meanwhile, in sewing classes, they learned how to
> embroider samples, apply a patch, and eventually use
> the sewing machine. The social graces were not over-
> looked. The catalog explicitly promised "instruction
> in the accomplishments."[2]

From these beginnings developed such noted ornaments
of American education as Berkeley and Cornell, Michigan
State and Wisconsin. And the land-grant principle
remains a potent force for innovation, both in America
and overseas. "We must take the land-grant tradition,
which has never really been applied to problems other
than agriculture, and apply it to other areas of human
life," said Chancellor Weidner of Wisconsin. "We must
take the university to the people rather than the people
to the university," qualified India's Chitta Mitra. And
James Perkins, director of the International Council for
Educational Development, echoed this land-grant
philosophy in his definition of the university:

> A place where the production of research, of learning
> and instruction, and application up to the point of
> implementation are all integrated. The uniqueness of
> a university is that it combines in a single organi-
> zation a preoccupation with the interrelationships
> between these three primary functions, without being
> the exclusive agent in any one of them....A model of
> such activity might be the Cornell School of
> Agriculture, where in the same building some of the
> most fundamental work in biochemistry is being
> carried out, while adjacent offices are occupied by
> people who are concerned with the application of that

work to agricultural problems. The spectrum extends
from the most fundamental science to the county
extension agent.

The University of the Philippines at Los Baños

A strong plea for the further development of the
land-grant philosophy in the Third World was presented at
Wingspread by Abelardo Samonte:

> We should remember the tradition of the land-grant
> college that teaching, research, and extension are
> mutually reinforcing. It is this philosophy that we
> have adopted at the University of the Philippines.
> But adopting such a philosophy does not automatically
> solve the practical problems of developing an effec-
> tive interdisciplinary approach to specific research
> projects. On entering a university that was strong
> in the biological and agricultural sciences, I found
> that something was lacking; namely, the ability to
> transmit the findings of the natural sciences into
> human skills and programs to meet human needs. Our
> rice production project in the Philippines was suc-
> cessful not because of new scientific data, but
> because we were able to organize an entire tech-
> nological package from production to marketing. We
> achieved a marriage of science and technology with
> management that enabled us to deal effectively with
> farmers, with banks, and with government so that the
> Philippines now produces a rice surplus.
>
> To achieve such an interdisciplinary approach it is
> necessary to have a mechanism to establish task
> forces to attack problems of specific social and
> national significance. The professor must not assume
> that he knows either the problem or the answer but
> must interact with policy makers, farmers, and
> administrators. In the Philippines, we have
> established a Center for Policy and Development
> Studies with a small core staff that is able to
> attract people with the expertise to deal with speci-
> fic problems. One mechanism is the policy confer-
> ence, a meeting of professors with policy makers,
> administrators, businessmen, and farm leaders to
> discuss general topics such as food production,
> nutrition, or agrarian reform. Issues are defined;
> then studies are initiated, preferably in collabora-
> tion with administrators who come to the campus on
> sabbatical. A follow-up conference report results
> and recommends programs of action. The university is
> involved from initiation to implementation of a
> project.

The University of the Philippines at Los Baños (UPLB) grew out of a college of agriculture that had 12 students and 4 teachers when founded in 1909. Today, it has a campus covering 800 hectares, including 500 hectares of experimental farms, demonstration farms, and research facilities. There are 15 colleges, institutes, and centers and a staff of 1,300 serving over 5,000 students, including 1,100 graduate students. It became the first autonomous campus of the University of the Philippines in 1972, when that system was created.

Its College of Agriculture offers curricula in five areas: agriculture, sugar technology, food technology, development communication, and agricultural chemistry. The College of Forestry, which grew out of the College of Agriculture, provides trained manpower for the development of the nation's forest resources and educates the citizenry in the value and importance of forests. It offers degrees in forestry, forest products engineering, and a two-year forest ranger course.

The College of Sciences and Humanities seeks to expand the base for the discovery, dissemination, and proper use of knowledge for the enrichment of human experience. It also provides general education and basic science foundations for the professional programs. Ten undergraduate degrees are offered: applied mathematics, biology, botany, zoology, chemistry, mathematics, statistics, agricultural chemistry (a joint program), communication arts, and sociology.

The Graduate School administers all graduate programs. It offers the Ph.D. and master's degrees in science, agriculture, forestry, and agrarian studies.

In addition, a number of specialized centers and institutes are affiliated with UPLB. The Center for Policy and Development Studies conducts policy conferences and undertakes in-depth studies on problems affecting agriculture and rural development. The Institute of Human Ecology focuses on the study of man and the environment, encompassing such topics as population studies, human nutrition, resource technology, and management and environmental planning. The Institute of Agricultural Development and Administration is concerned with agricultural economics, agricultural business management, and development administration. The Institute of Agricultural Engineering and Technology focuses on agricultural processing, agricultural machinery, land and water resources, and agrometeorology. All these institutes grant degrees.

There is also an Institute of Plant Breeding, a National Crop Protection Center, a Postharvest Horticulture Training and Research Center, a National Training Center for Rural Development, a Regional Network for Agricultural Machinery, a Program on Environmental Science and Management, and a Museum of Natural History.

Several of these programs have a strong problem orientation or interdisciplinary focus. For example, Environmental Science and Management provides a mechanism for interdisciplinary research and teaching and helps formulate local and national policies on the management of the environment. Others have an international component; thus, the Regional Network for Agricultural Machinery, for instance, works with experts throughout Southeast Asia to develop equipment and machinery suited to Asian farms.

Finally, six affiliate institutes are located on campus. These are the International Rice Research Institute, the Southeast Asian Regional Center for Agriculture, the Philippine Council for Agriculture, the Industries Development Commission, the Forest Research Institute, and the Education and Training Center of the Department of Local Government and Community Development.[3]

This is an impressive array of activities and institutes, some of which, such as the International Rice Research Institute, enjoy great fame. And research results are equally impressive. Certainly UPLB represents a major success in adapting the concept of the land-grant university to the problems of development in a milieu not strictly limited to agricultural issues.

Recently, UPLB has shifted from open admissions to a policy of selective admission. At the same time, it has endeavored to provide financial aid and scholarship programs for needy students.[4] In addition, attempts are made to provide remedial support for students from disadvantaged backgrounds whose prior education has been inadequate.

UPLB has also attempted to encourage awareness of alternatives in higher education by the establishment of technical institutes to supply middle-level manpower; these are not, however, affiliated with the university. Another project, the Barrio Development School, is designed to prepare high school students for self-employment as business (as opposed to subsistence) farm operators. Both of these developments are best regarded as demonstration projects in education rather than as university extension.

UPLB is committed in the education of its students to the land-grant concept of "Science with Practice." Thus, it has initiated a social laboratory approach to development; technicians and students have been sent into the field to assist farmers in the barrios of the small town of Pila, Laguna in organizing themselves for the improvement of farming practices. It is expected that this will both encourage a high level of practical technical competence in university graduates and yet discourage the kind of sophisticated specialization that makes students of some programs "ripe for export."[5]

The University of Wisconsin-Green Bay

The idea of applying the land-grant approach to problems other than agriculture is widespread. Beale[6] notes the need for this adaptation:

Beset by overcrowding, jammed transportation, delinquency, crime, decaying neighborhoods, water and air pollution, community health problems, inadequate schools, and a dozen other nightmares, the cities' teeming masses are in urgent need of the kind of attention the land-grant colleges gave to rural Americans a hundred years ago.

And, indeed, the challenge is being met. New campuses have been established which take up the search for solutions to urban and environmental problems, using the same techniques of trial and error which character- ized the early approach to rural problems. Examples are the University of Illinois-Chicago Circle and the St. Louis campus of the University of Missouri. Nor have the old, established land-grant universities neglected such problems. Many are now massive multiversities, often themselves in highly urbanized situations, and they have turned their resources toward the problems closest at hand. Sometimes the approach has been through the establishment of new campuses, sometimes through new schools on existing campuses, and sometimes through problem-focused institutes.[7] The University of Wisconsin-Green Bay (UWGB) is an example of a new campus that has adopted a novel structure in an attempt to orient itself positively toward education to solve emerging problems through interdisciplinarity. Chancellor Weidner has described his institution as follows:[8]

In many ways, the principles of Green Bay's academic plan were similar to the principles that had been part of the best colleges of agriculture in the United States for decades. Nevertheless, there were two major differences: First, the new university proposed to apply these principles to the liberal arts and sciences, and not just to a particular pro- fession such as agriculture; second, the new univer- sity proposed to give students far more freedom of choice and a much greater degree of student-initiated education than had traditionally been true in colleges of agriculture.

At the time of its establishment, higher education was being attacked from many quarters. Faculty members, students, authorities on higher education, parents, and other critics said that contact between professor and student was no longer close and was becoming ever more distant; that the liberal arts colleges were without theme or flavor; that the universities tended to restrict themselves to the basic disciplines, even at a time of major knowledge explosion. Many persons accused colleges and universities of reproducing mainly their own kind--that is to say, professors were primarily interested in their basic disciplines and in students who would help preserve and extend the boundaries of those fields. At the same time, they castigated liberal arts education for being overly general, covering a little bit of everything and not much of anything. Certain humanities programs, American studies, and international studies were especially criticized on these grounds. Students were more restive than ever before, largely because college education had little or no relevance to the world in which they lived. Students wanted to be involved. Furthermore, the teaching, research, and public service activities of universities were carried on in isolation, if not actually in opposition to, each other. Universities seemed to be run on the theory that the undergraduate should not be concerned with research or with what goes on in the community outside the university. Finally, the critics asserted that the course content of a college education remained heavily culture oriented or culture conditioned, and students were not encouraged or required to compare cultures.

As the planners of Green Bay reflected on these and other criticisms, they came to feel that the crux of the difficulty was the nature of the traditional academic department: It was based on a discipline; its professors normally had great authority over programming, personnel, and budget decisions; and they had little incentive to relate their intellectual interests and programs to those of other departments. In some ways they existed in splendid isolation, turned inward on their own concerns and the concerns of their discipline. At most, they paid minimal attention to the world outside the university or to the interface between subject matter and society. Thus, given the mission of innovation, the planners had to reconsider the traditional department.

The University of Wisconsin-Green Bay has tried to retain what was useful from the past, modifying it to fit new goals. Its academic year is organized traditionally into 2 semesters, but sandwiched between is a 4-week interim during which less conventional packaging of course content is encouraged. According to the usual

American practice, 124 semester credits are required for graduation. Many of these credits can be obtained through traditional 3- or 4-credit courses, but single semester or year-long packages are also permitted. Thus, a living/learning commune was organized, carrying 15 credits for a structured immersion in an inter-disciplinary field for an entire semester; and an ACTION program, funded by the Federal Government, at one time permitted students to earn 30 credits for a year-long field placement.

Disciplinary departments have not been abolished, but the basic unit or organization is the interdisciplinary concentration. There are eleven of these. Representative titles of such units are Science and Environmental Change, Population Dynamics, Human Adaptability, Urban Analysis, Regional Analysis, Managerial Systems, and Humanistic Studies. Each focuses on a distinct array of problems. For example, Science and Environmental Change brings biologists, physicists, chemists, mathematicians, and other scientists together to attack problems in the biophysical environment. Population Dynamics brings biologists and anthropologists into alliance with sociologists and demographers to study all facets of population. Humanistic Studies includes members from most branches of the humanities.

In addition to concentrations, the university is organized into disciplinary programs and professional programs. Disciplinary programs are in such traditional disciplines as Mathematics, History, Physics, Sociology, and Anthropology. Most faculty belong both to a disciplinary program and to a concentration; but funding, recruitment, promotion, and academic organization are carried out through the concentration.

The third category of academic unit is the professional program, organized around a potential career goal. Examples are programs in Education, Environmental Administration, and Mass Communications. The University of Wisconsin-Green Bay does not possess faculties speci-fically in such higher professions as medicine and law, but does provide preprofessional programs in preparation for such careers.

A student must major in a concentration, taking thirty credits of upper division courses. If none of the existing concentrations is appealing, students may design their own concentration in association with a faculty advisor. At least twenty-four credits will probably be required at the freshman/sophomore level to obtain pre-requisites for courses in the upper division. In the lower division, the student is required to fulfill dis-tribution requirements, taking nine credits each in the natural sciences, social sciences, and humanities or creative arts. Courses to fulfill these requirements are separately organized, rather than following the custom of the student's selecting introductory courses also required of students planning to major in the field. Many such courses are themselves organized around problem themes, e.g., River Basins in Transition. Tool subjects may also be required--six credits in mathematics or a foreign language, for instance.

It is quite possible for a student to major jointly in a concentration and a disciplinary program, in a concentration and a professional program, or even in a concentration, a disciplinary program, and a professional program. To major in a disciplinary program, twenty-four upper division credits are required, but half of them will usually apply also to the concentration major. To major in a professional program, eighteen credits are required, but again some of these credits may be applicable to the concentration or disciplinary program major. Should a student choose a joint major, then most of that student's credits will be tied to the major.

From this summary, it should be clear that what UWGB is offering is student choice within a well-defined structure. Requirements are not minimal, but they can be met in a wide variety of ways. Conventional grades are given in all courses, but to encourage experimentation, courses may be taken on a pass-fail basis, except in one's major. A degree may be obtained in a discipline or in a career-oriented field but only within the context of an interdisciplinary concentration. Students can certainly prepare themselves to enter the job market as accountants, technicians, planners, and teachers; but the goal of UWGB's educational philosophy is to prepare students for careers within the context of the traditional values of a liberal education. While students in the United States are not sensitive to the distinction between a job and a career, on the average, they will change their field of work three times during their lives. Liberal education, such as that encouraged at UWGB, is preparation for a world in flux.

Two elements are essential for successful problem-focused education. The first is that the identification and solution of problems must form part of the education because a student learns how to solve problems by attempting to solve them. The second is that education must be interdisciplinary. Creative problem solving demands participation by thinkers from a variety of disciplines, and it cannot be achieved by simply breaking up the initial problem into facets appropriate to each separate discipline. Rather, creative problem solving requires experts, each of whom has an intelligent perception of the philosophy and methodology of the other disciplines involved, each contributing individually and yet synergistically interacting with the contributions of others.

UWGB grew out of a great land-grant institution, and its accent on problem solving echoes the concerns which led to the Morrill Act. The basic goal is to seek and apply knowledge for the benefit of the community. Thus, to understand problems of air or water pollution, knowledge is sought through the disciplines of Physics, Chemistry, Biology, Economics, and even Sociology and History. This approach forces study of the etiology of problems. Professors and students linked by a common focus identify and analyze current problems. As projects materialize and mature, they attract other professors and students in a sort of mutually enriching synthesis.

Beyond the campus activity associated with such problem solving, many problems are community problems because community involvement developes naturally. Traditional barriers between town and gown are thus breached. Then, too, research, teaching, and public service are no longer separate entities but dissolve into a common concern for societal needs. The university ceases to be an ivory tower and becomes instead an intellectual resource interacting with the community for mutual social, cultural, and economic enrichment.[9]

8
Comprehensive Higher Education

Educators in most parts of the world agree that postsecondary education should include more than the traditional university program terminating in a bachelor's degree. Needs exist for diploma courses; higher education beyond secondary school, but below bachelor's degree level. During the Wingspread conference, Claudio Gutierrez of Costa Rica addressed these needs as follows:

> The problem of unequal opportunity versus unequal talent forces diversity upon us. Each national system must diversify itself if it is to offer equal opportunity to unequally or differentially talented young people. There are perhaps three aspects to such diversity: (1) diversity as to professional fields--such diversity will, if well designed, also begin to address effectively the needs of social relevance; (2) diversity of geographic location, secured either by decentralizing large existing institutions or integrating several smaller separate institutions; and (3) diversity of levels; opportunities should be presented for early graduation.

In Britain, the Higher National Certificate and teacher training colleges have filled this role, and the French Instituts Universitaires de Technologie have already been discussed in a similar context. In the United States, systems of technical colleges and community colleges exist in almost every state to serve those students seeking higher educational certification short of the baccalaureate degree. Such solutions are suitable where resources permit a multiplicity of institutions, but such sufficient resources are not universally available. Furthermore, the danger of a hierarchy of educational opportunity is that technical education (on the bottom of the hierarchy) tends to enjoy

little prestige, especially in cases where opportunities
to transfer credits between institutions are scarce or
even nonexistent. As a result, the system may create a
self-styled educational elite (graduates from the top of
the hierarchy) for whom employment is not readily
available, while it fails to produce qualified and
employable specialists in technical support services.

An alternative to this dilemma is the blending of
so-called "professional" and "technical" programs in a
new context:

> ...comprehensive programs, or the parallel training
> in the same institution of professionals (doctors or
> engineers, for example) with technicians at senior,
> middle, and elementary levels. Not only are such
> programs economical in terms of training facilities
> and staff but, more important, they also exhibit a
> functional approach, with the formation of develop-
> ment teams that can undertake all the important
> aspects of field activities. The approach so far has
> been used most effectively in the health sciences,
> but it is equally applicable to rural development,
> development engineering, and agricultural training.
> The programs of Tanzania, Cameroon, and Ethiopia
> provide specific illustrations of these several
> cases.[1]

While the above comment refers specifically to
Africa, the idea of comprehensive education is more
widespread. In the United States the land-grant college
frequently made two-year programs available for practicing farmers, quite aside from these institutions'
extension activities. In fact, the University of
Wisconsin-Madison still does offer such programs, making
them available in winter so that young working farmers
can conveniently attend. Many State systems of higher
education in the United States operate a range of
colleges, including two-year institutes as well as four-
year campuses. In some cases, as at Northern Kentucky
University, the two-year college is actually integrated
with the four-year college programs, and technical subjects are offered alongside the more traditionally
academic curriculum. Thus, while the examples below are
taken from developing nations that generally doubt their
abilities to afford extensive and diverse systems of
colleges, other institutions have elected just as
enthusiastically--for nonfiscal reasons--to serve
students' and society's needs more comprehensively by
integrating their various technical and professional
programs of study.

Yarmouk University, Jordan

There are two universities in Jordan, the older University of Jordan in Amman and the newer Yarmouk University. Adnan Badran described the foundation of Yarmouk:

Our university was established in an isolated rural area, lacking even the most rudimentary infrastructure. In a developing country, almost all services tend to be concentrated in the capital, and certainly it is much easier to build a university there. As the first person appointed to the university, I visited the region where it was to be established and promptly asked the Ministry why on earth they would choose such an isolated spot to start a university. Why not start it in the capital? "Oh no," they replied, "we have been wondering how to develop that area, and having tried and failed with everything else, we have decided the thing to do is to put a university there."

We had to do everything from scratch--power lines, sewage lines, roads, bus service, everything. Then we tackled the problem of how to attract faculty. Again, everybody wanted to be in the capital where schools were available for children. Nobody seemed anxious to risk their reputation by coming to what seemed fated to be a second-class institution. So, we launched our program by sending about 100 people abroad and establishing fringe benefits such as furnished housing and excellent research facilities. As a consequence, we were able to compete with the university in the capital and attract excellent faculty. We even had success in overcoming the disadvantage of being so far from the source of funding: With the aid of a very active Board of Trustees we succeeded in lobbying effectively in the capital in competition with the university located there. And getting away from politicians does enable us to concentrate on academic and educational matters.

Initially, we had problems attracting the better students, who preferred to go to the University of Jordan. But we now feel that we are competitive because of the new trends, techniques, and methodologies which we have been able to introduce and which are attractive to students. So while the initial problems of establishing an innovative institution in a rural area are very great, subsequently we have discovered advantages. The very isolation forces all to join in the process of innovation and participate in the running of the

university, and creates its own dynamic and sense
of community. This is equally true for trustees,
administration, faculty, and students. We feel that
we will not only establish a good university, but
that we will also attract development and improve the
socio-economic status of the region at the same time.

The goal at Yarmouk is to establish two kinds of
qualifications. The first would be the equivalent of an
associate degree, from which students would immediately
proceed to employment. The second would be a bachelor's
degree. However, students earning the first qualifica-
tion could also return immediately or later to complete
the baccalaureate. The desirable ratio of the two types
of graduates has been estimated at three to one or even
five to one.

Looking at its development, Jordan anticipates severe
shortages of technicians, assistant engineers, assistant
doctors, medical technicians, nurses, secretaries,
accountants, translators, and hotel and restaurant
managers. A polytechnic college already exists in
Jordan, but it is not expected to produce enough technical personnel of the kind needed.[2] Badran examined
this problem as it affects developing nations in general:

An important question is, what kind of universities
should developing countries attempt to establish?
In England, with many traditional universities,
when the progress of industrialization demanded an
increase in trained manpower, they established some
thirty additional polytechnic universities. In the
nineteenth century, the United States established
the A&M and land-grant colleges to respond to the
needs for agricultural manpower. Now they are
establishing community colleges for similar purposes
in the cities; this is a luxury that developing
nations cannot afford. They cannot establish universities for each and every purpose. Rather,
universities in developing countries must be multipurpose and serve the entire spectrum of higher
educational needs. Furthermore, they must also be
tailored to provide the immediate manpower needs of
the society. The university in a developing
country must provide the services of a community
college and also of an extension service. It must
provide refresher courses to keep the professional
community up-to-date; and the teacher must be
involved in teaching, research, and extension
simultaneously. As an example, let me cite our
School of Business Administration in which there
are nine specializations arranged in a cluster
around the core. Examples of such specializations
are banking, accounting, and personnel management.

The student can design an initial program around the central core incorporating just some of these specializations and can return later to the university to acquire more of them as the needs of his job change. At the same time the university is able to fulfill the functions of the community college, the regular undergraduate college, and graduate work.

The University of Botswana

Another institution innovatively responding to its nation's need for multilevel higher education is the University of Botswana, founded in the early 1970s. It grew out of the breakup of the University of Botswana, Lesotho, and Swaziland (itself founded only in 1964), which originally had its main campus in Lesotho. The disintegration of this supra-national institution was virtually inevitable since the three countries had little in common except their physical proximity to the Republic of South Africa and their erstwhile status as British protectorates.

Botswana itself is a large, arid country with livestock raising as the principal industry. It may have considerable mineral resources, but they are yet largely underdeveloped. The country is sparsely populated and has one of the lowest per capita incomes of Africa. Consequently, it is likely that the nation would not be able to support a proliferation of institutions of higher education; it must opt instead for a blending of development programs within one institution. Rector Setidisho described the function of the development university as follows:

> The single rational principle which guides most of our government policy is to ensure that development does take place. A measure of development is an increase in per capita income. However, even where per capita income is rising, it is frequently the case that only a few benefit. The well-qualified and highly placed receive high incomes while the majority continue to live near starvation. We need to consider providing programs for the majority of students who cannot attend the university, rather than focusing on new curriculum developments for the minority who can. We should consider the design of new universities to take the university to the people, ensuring that all, whether they live in urban or rural areas, are able to benefit from the existence of the university.
>
> Such universities would seek to identify and solve problems not because they are uniquely qualified to do so, but in order to participate more fully in the

life of the society. For example, almost everybody in Botswana is a livestock farmer. If a way could be found to improve the livestock of the country and to give people a greater awareness of the markets available for livestock, then their lives would be improved immeasurably. The university will not be relevant to the problems of the developing countries as long as it concentrates on those few people who have completed primary and secondary education and now seek out the highest academic and professional qualifications.

But, of course, the first task must be to identify the true needs of the people. We must not assume that people within the university understand these at present, for they do not. We need a new type of university that will not simply provide formal education, but will also provide informal education to the mass of the people and integrate it with the formal education which is imparted only to the minority. Such programs might assist in primary and secondary education or in meeting the needs for functional literacy on the part of the agriculturist. Or we might establish programs that would assist the small businessman in the countryside, who often has difficulty knowing whether or not he is making a profit because he does not know how to keep proper records. Such people need knowledge, not certification.

All conventional students should receive some instruction in informal means of communicating their knowledge to the people. For example, we have a program in Botswana that gives ministers of the church some instruction in community development and adult education so that they can act as leaders of the community and not simply attend to its spiritual needs.

Setidisho[3] has written at length about the future development of the University of Botswana and the role it should play in national development, with special emphasis on multilevel tertiary education. He envisions a two-level training strategy that can be summarized as follows: The first education level should consist of (1) technical occupational training for the production of middle-level manpower; (2) the first part of a university academic education; (3) adult education through formal and nonformal programs; and (4) provision of services directed to national and community needs. The second level should consist of (1) the concluding two or three years of academic education; and (2) the next two to three years of further technical or professional training.

This two-level training must be structured so as to allow students to move to different levels on the basis of their personal aptitudes, abilities, and talents. However, one of the purposes of a two-level curriculum is to produce relatively large numbers of trained middle-level personnel. To meet this goal successfully, the university, and society in general, must promote a more prestigious image for these middle-level positions. Such employment must not become regarded as the reward of failure. On the other hand, selection for the second educational level must be based to a considerable degree on strong academic performance at the first level. Some difficulties with reconciling these rather contradictory requirements might be eased if the curriculum were so structured that students graduating from the first level could have realistic opportunities of returning later to complete full professional training.

Setidisho maintains that to be educationally effective, the traditional structure of tertiary education--in which instruction in the first years is typically of an abstract, difficult, and theoretical nature--must be modified. Part of the abstract content should be shifted to the later years, and part of the concrete, applied training should be given in the early years. It is essential that the two-year graduate understand the "why" of what is learned, not simply the "how." On the other hand, four-year graduates may well benefit from being introduced at an early stage to prac-tical concepts. Setidisho refers to this concept as a spiral curriculum, with an alternation of theory and practice, each reinforcing the other.

The Alexander Report,[4] which was instrumental in establishing the University of Botswana, recognized the advantages of such an arrangement of course work:

There is immense value, especially in developing countries, in having a great deal of postsecondary education concentrated in a single institution. The economic advantages have been referred to, but there are perhaps even greater academic advantages in having teachers, nurses, agricultural and social extension workers, technicians, and potential gradu-ates taught together--so that a schoolteacher can become aware, for example, not only of what he or she has to do for the children, but also what the exten-sion worker can offer the parents--and the future graduate be aware of both. Also, there is a great tendency to overlook the flow of ideas which can come from students themselves in joint seminars and dis-cussion groups, especially important when a substan-tial part of the teaching will be done--initially at least--by expatriates, most of them new to the country. These arguments hold whether this consolidation is under the wing of the university or not, but its value is greatly enhanced by the academic and research backing the university can provide.

The University of Botswana has continued its association, although in a more limited form than before, with the University of Swaziland. Some courses are offered at both locations, others in only one. Botswana offers level one studies in humanities, economic and social studies, science, agriculture, and education. Students are admitted there after only five years of secondary education, a departure from the British tradition commonly bequeathed to former colonies, which required seven or more years' preparation. Other African nations are also giving up the more extensive admission requirement, which, in the terminology common to Britain and its former possessions, amounts to accepting entrants with School Certificate (or O levels) rather than requiring Higher School Certificate (or A levels). Setidisho sees this modification of admissions as an adaptation of the Botswana degree program toward a more American structure.

Training at level one for middle-stratum manpower needs (i.e., terminal nondegree training) has so far been restricted to certificate and diploma courses in accounting, business studies, statistics, and teacher education. Agriculture training at this level has been provided at the Botswana College of Agriculture, where such training is expected to continue, but the University of Botswana also intends to establish a faculty of agriculture at the university. Both Botswana's college and its university will jointly conduct the diploma course and establish a degree program. Currently, degree programs in agriculture exist only in Swaziland.

Level two teaching in the humanities, science, and economic and social studies already exists at the University of Botswana, and will be strengthened. Majors are still to be established in education, with options in teacher education, planning and administration, adult education, and curriculum development. Plans are also still on the drawing board for bachelor's degrees in soil science, plant pathology, analytical chemistry, geological studies, and other applied sciences; nor has provision yet been made for training environmental specialists in such fields as hydrology, social science, land surveying, urban and regional planning, and land utilization.

Finally, Botswana's demand for training in commerce, accounting, business administration, and law is increasing. Graduates are needed to satisfy the personnel requirements of government, as well as of parastatal and private sectors of the economy; current diploma courses may have to be augmented by full degree programs.

The University of Botswana represents a development similar to Yarmouk University, but in an economically poorer nation, striving to overcome rather different problems. For example, agricultural development seems of much more immediate concern in Botswana than it does in Jordan. Interestingly enough, management training, which is stressed at Yarmouk, also seems to be important at Botswana. Both universities are attempting to combine in a single curriculum all levels of postsecondary training. Each recognizes the need to combine such training with extension work, both for its intrinsic merit and for strengthening the problem focus of the curriculum.

Both nations regard this comprehensive educational approach as necessary to prevent the production of baccalaureate graduates beyond the economy's capacity to absorb them, and simultaneously to ensure an adequate supply of middle-level manpower to support the effectiveness of professional-level graduates' effectiveness in national development. Each university is conscious of the dangers of promoting a caste system within the university and seeks to avoid this by teaching both groups of students in the same classes and by offering opportunities for technical level graduates to upgrade their qualifications later. At the same time, they both believe that the association of students at the two training levels can be mutually beneficial by promoting fruitful interchange during the educational process as well as effective cooperation in later employment situations. However, educating both groups simultaneously requires a restructuring of the curriculum, principally a reordering of the sequence in which theoretical and practical education is offered. As both Yarmouk University and the University of Botswana are new, only time can prove the sucess of their plans.

9
Interdisciplinarity and Problem Focus

As knowledge has become more compartmentalized, much innovation in higher education has centered on the effort to relate the various disciplines and to focus learning on problems that draw their potential solutions from a number of disciplines. Skills must be integrated and transferable, rather than narrowly defined, if they are to provide an adequate foundation for careers that often change during a lifetime. At Wingspread, educators expressed concern that one's education should not be made obsolete by social change. Siegfried Grosse, for example, pointed out that changing demographic patterns might foreclose a teaching career, traditionally pursued by a great many German graduates. How can their education then be made useful for other fields? Pierre Merlin observed that in France, and perhaps elsewhere, the demand for professionals has not kept pace with the extension of university education to an ever greater proportion of the population. The university, he said, must also prepare people for a more fulfilling personal life rather than merely opening doors to prestigious jobs that, paradoxically, may not always exist. Rector Caspersen of Denmark shared this concern, and Wisconsin's Chancellor Weidner further pointed out that skills easily become outdated in a rapidly changing world. What a university should promote instead is the ability to acquire skills continually throughout a working lifetime and an understanding of the way in which such skills can be applied to solving problems.

Such worries about educational obsolescence are widespread, especially in light of the generally accepted truism that, at least in America, people are likely to change fields at least three times in their professional lifetime. To complicate the matter further, engineers, for example, find that little they learned at school is applicable to their professional tasks even ten years after graduation. Max Rowe of Everyman's also observed that in England scientists have almost never occupied a

103

leadership role in society, perhaps because the
over-specialization at the university almost excludes the
graduate scientist from general service to the community.

One answer to stemming such premature obsolescence,
then, may be for higher education to move toward greater
interdisciplinarity. While interdisciplinarity can exist
without problem focus, problem focus cannot exist without
interdisciplinarity. Piaget[1] has pointed out, with
regard to scientific research in general, that we are
compelled to look for common mechanisms and interactions
in investigation; interdisciplinarity thus becomes a
prerequisite for progress. As a consequence, he suggests
that purely disciplinary teaching is likely to be a poor
preparation for research because it divides knowledge
into presumably watertight compartments.

Of course, not all training is for research; much is
vocational. But in the latter case as well, Heckhausen[2]
of the University of Bochum has called attention to what
he calls the chronic mismatch between the current state
of a discipline as a science and that same discipline as
a vocational field of practice. Vocational practice per-
sistently lags behind theory in disciplines with strong
vocational obligations (such as engineering or medicine),
he says. Vice Chancellor Willett of Australia's Griffith
University referred to the reverse problem: the curious
academic purism which can arise in university teaching in
fields such as engineering. When he was a student of
engineering at Cambridge, he said, a common boast of the
"pure theorists" there was that only in the third year
did a student come to realize that a steam engine can be
driven by steam.

Most participants at Wingspread, though not all,
approached interdisciplinarity through problem focus;
that is, by pragmatically relating education, research,
and the problems experienced by the community at large.
As Zeferino Vaz said with respect to his own institution
in Brazil:

> The functions of the university are both to improve
> knowledge and extend it to the community. The
> activities of the university in providing direct
> services do not jeopardize research and teaching
> activities. On the contrary, through contact with
> the community our faculty members improve in maturity
> and in moral and didactic authority. Furthermore,
> students who participate in the problems and activi-
> ties of the community acquire a new attitude. The
> benefits are observed not simply in the region
> immediately surrounding the university, but through-
> out the whole state of São Paulo.

The problem-focus approach need not be confined, of
course, to vocational education. Education without an

explicit vocational goal, such as education in literature or chemistry, needs also to be linked to problem solving. Vocational education, medicine, engineering, or business administration require similar linkages, but not necessarily in the same way.

Not all educators who were at Wingspread saw interdisciplinarity and problem focus as the answer to higher education's problems. Max Rowe, for example, entered this plea for more traditional educational methodologies:

> We are often asked why, in our new university, we do not revolutionize by being more relevant, or by being more community-minded. But we ask ourselves how can we be a university and still become relevant? One cannot even answer the question as to what is relevant because relevance changes with life and changes with time, and above all it changes with a man's philosophy. For one man, the most relevant thing is to close the trade gap while for another it may be research on solar energy....

> Now, of course, this does not mean that the university should not become involved in closing the trade gap or solving the problems of solar energy. And certainly universities should encourage their students to carry out community health work or assist disadvantaged youth. Good things are always good. But these things are marginal to the problem of innovation. Universities should concentrate on doing a little better what they ought to be doing anyway; namely, educating the individual.

Rowe spoke further of the need to train leaders:

> The overspecialization of the university, especially in the sciences, almost excludes the graduate scientist from service to the community. The proposal now being made in England is that if a person studies physics, he should be directed to also study technology so as to understand how to use science, and perhaps also history and philosophy, in order that he appreciate his place in society and his obligations to the community. Such a curriculum might produce a man who is less of a scientist, but perhaps more of a citizen. My main point is that universities become irrelevant if they simply engage in any kind of thing that is good for the community. Such activity is marginal to the heart of the university, which should aim to improve the curriculum and research plans in order to make individuals more useful citizens.

Hamdan Tahir, however, offered a different viewpoint:

In Malaysia, we have 5 universities for a population of 11.5 million, and we think it is enough. We plan no new universities. The 20,000 students at our present universities are augmented by 30,000 students who are studying overseas. The government has determined that each of these 5 universities shall have the fundamentals of science and the humanities in their curriculum, but over and above this each university is required to define a unique mission for itself that will fit its graduates for subsequent employment. Consequently, one specializes in agriculture, another in technology and engineering, another in medicine and science....

In 1969 the founders of my own institution, the University of Science, felt that they had to declare an intention, a special focus or mission. As there was already a university dealing with heavy engineering, they settled on light engineering. In fact, we do not use the term engineering, preferring applied science. We specialize in such studies as electronics, polymer rubber, chemical science, and applied technology. I would emphasize that we do not do this simply in response to government directives but for the sake of the student. Our graduates have had no difficulty in finding employment, except possibly in the social sciences. Many people in Malaysia query the need for social science, so we encourage students in the comparative social sciences to take subjects such as computer science or computer mathematics. And in fact the mathematics we do is concentrated in computer mathematics or service mathematics rather than in conventional pure and applied mathematics. Such are the fundamentals of multidisciplinarity as we practice it.

Let me go into the specifics of one problem-focused field among many; namely, housing, building, and planning. We expect graduates of this program to go into business as developers, but as developers knowledgeable in the fields of architecture, engineering, and related fields. They are practical people who fit the market and the needs of the country rather than professional architects or professional engineers.

I feel that we, as educators, should look again at the spectrum of qualifications which the university grants. Holders of the bachelor's degree should be generalists and should be fitted to serve the needs of society at large. Some specialization may be

desirable at the master's level, but only during
doctoral study should the student attempt to become a
master of one field. If the bachelor's degree is not
a general degree, there is a chance that its holders
will not be relevant to the needs of society and will
end up unemployed and unemployable.

The immediate impression from the observation is of a
contrast between two perceptions of the university. Max
Rowe is speaking of the traditional function of training
minds; Hamdan Tahir is talking of vocational education.
In part, this is due to the differing contexts of Israel
and Malaysia. However, vocational education does form
part of the curriculum at Everyman's University, for
example, in electronics and electrical engineering; and
vocational education does not form the entire curriculum
at the University of Science, although it might motivate
much of it. The differences are certainly real and do
reflect differing views of the role of the university,
but they are by no means absolute.
In fact, the conflict between vocational and
nonvocational education in the university has to some
extent been resolved. Even in such long-established professional schools as medicine, law, and engineering, the
teaching of both pure and applied subjects may have
retreated so far from the real world, become so confined
within disciplinary boundaries, as to fail now in the
production of adaptable minds. Can a problem-oriented,
interdisciplinary approach reverse such failure?
Chancellor Weidner of the University of Wisconsin-Green
Bay is convinced that, under the right conditions, it
can:

There are many points of view as to what
problem-oriented education might be, and to what its
purposes might be, and what its necessary organizational framework might be. I think there is a major
difference between institutions that are trying to
train people to solve specific problems and those
that are trying to expose students to problems and
use this as a vehicle for liberal education. In the
second instance there is a liberal learning
objective, and in the first instance there is a
skills objective. These are quite different from a
pedagogical point of view and in their educational
objectives. There are real problems with training
people in particular skills because they may not be
transferable to new situations. Consequently, we
have a continuing problem of reeducation in new or
emerging skills. On the other hand, if we approach
problem focus as a means of teaching people to work
together in seeking solutions to problems in general,
then this may have a more lasting effect.

Many difficulties can be avoided if we take a liberal
learning approach. I think most people would agree
that problem-oriented education should not prescribe
action for society but should leave that to the
policy-determining branches. It should concentrate
more on the identification of problems, working with
people from many different backgrounds and many different points of view, and should work to develop
alternatives before letting the policy-determining
branches of society take over. The university is in
this way distinguished from a political party or from
a government agency, which is an important distinction to maintain. The nonprescriptive approach will
avoid many of the pitfalls that have been identified
in problem-oriented education.

The type of approach I am recommending has long been
part of the American educational scene in the land-
grant college. Unfortunately, this philosophy, which
is truly interdisciplinary and truly problem focused,
has never been applied to problems other than
agriculture. What we are trying to do is to take the
College of Agriculture tradition and apply it to
other areas of American life.

Lest it be thought that once again we have only an
isolated view from a developed country which can afford
the luxury of the impractical, consider the words of
Lewis Mughogho of the University of Malawi:

A graduate in agriculture is expected to be
immediately useful; however, nobody is immediately
useful in that way. All that the university can do
is expose the student to the type of problem that
might occur in agriculture and provide the tools to
attack such problems. Only when the student has
acquired a sufficient amount of experience is he
going to be useful in the field. Furthermore, if a
problem is identified as being urgent and it takes
three years to train somebody to attack that
problem, then the nature of that problem will have
changed by the time the person is trained.

The essential problem then is to train minds, and
that is not a new thought. Harold MacMillan tells of his
professor at Oxford half a century ago who said,
"Nothing you learn here will ever be of the slightest use
to you except this--you will learn to detect when a man
is talking nonsense." But the problem with emphasizing
thought processes more than tangible skills is that the
consumer of mass higher education may be skeptical. Most
people are unlikely to be willing to spend three years
learning something which they find difficult (and perhaps

even boring) if they are aware that it is, by definition,
useless. As Confucius is reputed to have said, "It is
hard to find a man who has studied for even two years
without hope of profit." Is it not possible, however, to
learn to perform useful skills and also learn to discern
when someone is talking nonsense? If not, the public may
begin to question rather closely the qualifications of
those teachers and administrators whom they are being
taxed so heavily to support. The university, for good or
ill, can never again be merely a marginal good in
society.

The answer that both interdisciplinarity and problem
focus bring to such questions is not only that it is
possible to impart useful knowledge, but that it is the
duty of the university to do so. Knowledge does not
naturally integrate itself. But the university is
devoted to studying nature in the broadest sense, and
nature does comprise a cycle of interrelationships. For
example, physics and sociology may be viewed as
distinctive fields with little in common, but physics is
important in understanding chemistry, especially at the
molecular level, and chemistry pervades biology in its
more reductionist aspect. Many behavorial biologists,
furthermore, are convinced that their subject has
insights to offer sociologists, and some would maintain
that these relationships will become increasingly clear
as biology begins to probe more deeply into the molecular
roots of the nervous system and evolution. While
sociologists disagree, few have been able to ignore the
hypothesis. This oversimplified but hardly fanciful
illustration demonstrates the sometimes subtle ways in
which disciplines are linked. It also characterizes one
of the more vigorous intellectual debates of recent
years, the socio-biology dialectic which has been
obscured by the various sides' relative ignorance and
disrespect for the achievements and traditions of the
others' disciplines. The rather closed-minded quality of
this debate itself points to the need for greater
interdisciplinarity in higher education.

Of course, not all knowledge is directly applicable
to concrete problems, but all is potentially applicable.
Where connections exist, they should be examined. Where
possible applications exist, they must be explored. And
this pursuit of connection should occur not in isolation
(not discipline by discipline), but among disciplines,
spiraling back and forth between the concrete and the
abstract. Abelardo Samonte affirmed this view in
relation to the University of the Philippines:

Innovation must be related both to the cultures and
values and also to the socio-economic realities of
the country. Consequently, I believe that the most

important task for the university in a developing
country is to marry the two needs of relevance and
the maintenance of standards. But we must take care
not to impart misplaced values to our students. For
example, in Southeast Asia there is a great aversion
to manual labor and a belief that education is the
road to avoiding such labor. This is a misconception
that can only be overcome by an integration of education in the national development process through
greater cooperation between universities and other
institutions, such as extension agencies, training
centers, and agencies for nonformal education.
Liberal education must be balanced with practical
training, and students made to realize that classroom
and field experience are both important. We have
established a social laboratory in a small town about
thirty miles from our campus, which we use to enable
professors and students not simply to observe, but
become active participants in, the development
process. We are not only taking the students to
learn from the people, but enabling the people, the
professors, and the students to learn from each
other. Research perspectives also emerge from this
interaction. Unfortunately, we have found that these
field projects tend to duplicate each other. We have
another project in which medical and health science
students are exposed to rural areas. I now believe
that we should not fragment our developmental
approach according to disciplines, with one village
exposed to medical scientists, another to agricultural specialists, and so forth. We have initiated a
new project in which we will integrate the medical,
economic, and developmental processes, enabling us to
obtain a more holistic insight into the problems of
rural development.

To illustrate the existing disparity of opinion and
approach, Guy Berger[3] has produced Table 1.1 which
contrasts representative characteristics of the
innovative, interdisciplinary university with those of
the traditional university. While it is not very fair to
the traditional university, his contrast deliberately
highlights the viewpoint of those educators who esteem
interdisciplinarity and see themselves as consciously
innovating--that is, reacting against the old. Certainly
the table summarizes the attitudes of many, if not most,
of the educators who convened at Wingspread.
The goal of interdisciplinarity, then, is to make the
barriers which compartmentalize knowledge a good deal
more permeable than they usually appear to be. There are
two reasons for doing this. The first is that novel
insights often appear on the borderlines between
disciplines. The second is that the solution of

Table 1.1

	Traditional University	Interdisciplinary University
Teaching..........	school-boyish abstract	lively concrete
with the aim of...	knowledge	know-how
transmitting......	old knowledge	rejuvenated knowledge
applying the teaching method..........	of repetition	of discovery
emphasizing.......	contents	structures
teaching based on.	passive acceptance of a final academic sub-dividing of knowledge	continual critical and epistemological reflection
the university....	is stuck in "splendid isola-tion" and setting up a kind of know-ledge which kills life	overcomes the gulfs between university and society, know-ledge and reality
It requires.......	a purely hierarchical system and rigidifying syllabus	restructuring based on how the institution works on the whole
It favors........	isolation and competition	collective activity and research

problems, both in pure and in applied fields, often demands intelligent interdisciplinary interaction. But problem focus is not simply an objective of interdisciplinarity; it is simultaneously a useful instructional tool for effective blending of the disciplines for the value of interdisciplinarity can often be best apprehended by illustrating its usefulness in real life situations.

The following examples illustrate these twin principles of interdisciplinarity and problem focus as they assume dramatic but different forms at four progressive universities.

Griffith University, Australia

Griffith University is a newly established (1970) Australian university, which admitted its first students only in 1975. It is an example of an innovative university, problem focused and interdisciplinary. Located fairly near the older and larger University of Brisbane, Griffith is permitted a considerable degree of experimentation through the flexible funding policies of the Australian government. F.J. Willett, its first vice chancellor, described Griffith as follows:

> We were fortunate in being called upon to establish a new university in a moderately large city where a university already existed. Planning began in 1970, and the process of planning responded to the ideas current in the late 60s and 70s. We reacted to this process with essentially four thrusts. They were (1) to avoid conflict with the large existing university. The existence of conventional programs made it possible for us to assume that students who wanted such programs would be able to find them elsewhere. We would concentrate on broadening the range of educational experiences available to the people of Queensland. (2) We believed very much that a great deal could be done to improve undergraduate teaching in the British mode, which is the conventional mode in Australia. (3) We believed that opportunities existed for students to explore the transitions from the university to the outside world. Basically, this produced the idea of problem solving in groups or teams by students. (4) We believed that it was necessary for a university founded in the 1970s to develop a service relationship with its social and community environments.

> Putting these four things together, we defined a university that takes as its basic approach problem orientation, which has now become our own orthodoxy. However, a problem that we have not yet examined, but

will ultimately have to, is how to make the
university accountable for its interventions. The
problem does not exist for the classic university,
which has been doing what is expected of it. While
it does intervene in society, it does not do so as a
conscious change agent. Griffith is consciously and
explicitly intervening in society as a change agent,
which is an orientation which it shares with universities in more clearly developing nations.

The university, in its planning stages, took as its
focal definition the statement that we were concerned
with human adjustments to changing physical, social,
and intellectual environments. This is not a process
statement because it implies nothing about ends. It
does not define itself in terms of improvement or
betterment, but simply in terms of examining those
questions. We developed four specific schools, each
looking at a particular set of problems. The School
of Environmental Studies has a fairly readily
definable set of problems upon which to focus. They
could choose, for example, from the constellation of
problems surrounding the management of natural
resources or the delivery of health care in rural
areas. We could define the School of Modernization
Studies, which would examine the relationships of
some Asian countries within themselves, with each
other, and in relationship to Australia. A bigger
problem was presented by the humanities, which
perhaps tend to resist the imposition of problem
focus. They themselves came up with communication
and change of human values as a definition which
would enable them to develop their own approach.
Below the schools, there remains the problem of
defining sets of courses for particular problem
fields.

The significance of Griffith is perhaps that it
imposes interdisciplinary innovation within a tradition,
the British tradition, which is often presumed resistant
to change. It is important then to note what has not
been done at Griffith. Neither a "foundation year" of
distribution courses nor the American cafeteria system of
course offerings has been adopted. Interdisciplinarity
and problem focus have been achieved instead by the
establishment of the departments and schools that characterize the conventional British model. (A comparable
endeavor in Britain is the University of Sussex.)
Consequently, we see that, at least for new schools,
determined innovators can overcome limitations within
their given system of higher education. Vincennes, too,
is an example similar to Griffith but developing in a
different context. The next example will perhaps

114

demonstrate the limitations that a system can impose upon
creative innovations.

University of Bochum, Germany

Interdisciplinarity was not a primary motivating
force in the foundation of Bochum in 1964-65. Rather, as
Siegfried Grosse pointed out, it was demographics:

> One of the biggest problems in German education is
> the democratization of education. We have experi-
> enced an enormous increase in the number of students
> attending universities. For example, in 1950 only 5
> percent of the appropriate age class attended
> universities, whereas in 1985 27 percent will
> attend....However, the German Constitution guarantees
> educational opportunity to all who wish it.

Bochum was founded in the Ruhr district between
Cologne and Münster to relieve pressure on those two
universities. It was also intended to provide an opportunity for university education in a densely populated
area, especially for social groups for whom the possibility of convenient commuting might be an incentive
toward their decision to attend. The university was also
designed to provide a needed cultural center in a heavily
industrialized area.

In Germany, as in France, universities are very much
a service of government. Unlike France, it is the Land
or State government rather than the National government
that is responsible. Nevertheless, professors are civil
servants; and all details of university governance,
including curriculum, fall under the purview of the
"Land" (State) Minister of Education. This does not
preclude academic freedom, which is firmly established.
It does, however, inhibit innovation. Rolf Dahrendorf
has said, "It is but a very slight exaggeration to say
that the only person who can reform a German university
is a Minister." As Siegfried Grosse pointed out, since
all "Gymnasium" graduates with an "Abitur" are legally
entitled to be admitted to a university and since most
courses of study at the university culminate in an examination conducted by the State, universities find themselves in the difficult position of preparing students in
whose selection for admission they had no part and for
examinations which they themselves do not administer.
This leads to definite constraints on the curriculum.

An additional feature of the German university is the
traditional pre-eminence of the individual professor.
This attribute has both good and bad implications for
innovation. Professors can use their prestige to inhibit
change and even the exploration of new research pathways

initiated at the middle faculty levels. On the other hand, the status of the professor under which the student studies is more important than the status of the university itself, no small advantage for a new and innovative school able to attract noted faculty. Thus, the cachet awarded to a "Harvard" or an "Oxford" degree does not really exist in Germany.

Possession of the Abitur or High School Graduation Certificate is traditionally believed to represent the culmination of general education in Germany, and this is true as well virtually throughout Europe. With the "Gymnasium" behind him, the student is then faced with the departmentalism and disciplinary emphasis which characterize the traditional German university. As in France, but not in Britain, Germany's universities have also tended to be organized into distinct faculties under the influence of a powerful professoriate. Thus, the organization of Bochum into departments on a single integrated campus (except for the medical program) represents at least a step towards multidisciplinarity. All main academic disciplines, incidentally, were included in the new university--including theology, for which there was inadequate student demand.

The principal academic work at Bochum, including research, takes place in institutes. These may be departmental or interdepartmental institutes, but a primary goal is to encourage and facilitate cross-disciplinary exchanges. The institutes also incorporate the famous seminars to which American education owes so much. A publication describing Bochum explains its cautious movement toward blending the academic disciplines.

It has rightly been regretted that the disciplines and faculties of our universities have moved further and further apart into positions of isolation, so that the principle of "university" itself is dissolved, and cooperation of research endangered. Furthermore, scientific development calls for close cooperation between hitherto separated disciplines. The task then is to counteract the thrust of disintegration and, even more important, to create the best possible facilities for cooperation in research, thus enabling science to demonstrate its unity and close integration convincingly and effectively to every student, both in research and in academic teaching. The structure intends to achieve these aims by deviating from the traditional "faculty" pattern and organizing science in "departments" instead. This principle is based on the conviction that it will be easier and more natural to establish the necessary and flexible ties between such departments

116

that correspond to the true units of science and are not just accidental accumulations of subjects.

The main purpose of the departments then is to establish, or rather reestablish, the meaningful units of related disciplines that the faculties once were. Still, there remains the danger that wherever the dividing line between subjects is drawn, new barriers to interdisciplinary cooperation will arise. Wherever /the Bochum founders/ foresaw it, they have institutionalized such links through double or triple department memberships of an individual professor, the assignment of disciplines in various departments to cooperate in one institute, and the establishment of certain institutes (e.g., East Asian Studies) which have special "supra-departmental" positions.[4]

In German terminology, a department is not a discipline. The discipline tends to be delineated by the "chair" or the professor occupying that chair. Thus, departments characteristically have many professors and many corresponding disciplines. In 1970 there were twelve chairs in history at Bochum, with such specific designations as social history, history of economics, art history, and other subject areas; these designations, then, are the actual disciplines.

Consequently, in a sense Bochum offers a counterpoint to the more radical changes at the University of Vincennes. Within similar (though by no means identical) traditions of higher education, Bochum has pursued inter-disciplinarity by modest reform within the mainstream, attempting to locate pressure points at which innovation will result in genuine and substantial change. Vincennes, on the other hand, has consciously and vigorously moved out of the mainstream of French education, accepting not willingly--but inevitably--all the tribulations inherent in such iconoclasm.

Linköping University, Sweden

Traditionally, the Swedish system of higher education, to which Linköping is the sixth and most recent addition, has much in common with the German system on which it was in fact modeled. Both professors and administrators in Sweden are civil servants, but the path to university administration is through, not the professoriate, but the Ministry of Education. Power, say Premfors and Östergren,[5] lies at the top (the Ministry) and at the bottom (the professors) of the structural hierarchy. But to become a professor in Sweden, as in most of Europe, is the culmination of an academic career, while below the professorial rank are many assistants; professors-in-waiting, so to speak.

Until recently in the Swedish system, the professor was autonomous, loosely bound to a faculty and surrounded by a collection of students and assistants. Within this group of students and assistants there tended also to be a division between teachers and researchers.[6] The professor was a research leader, and research provided the path to advancement. Most undergraduate teaching was carried out by the lecturers and assistants, who were not necessarily researchers.

The Swedish system, however, is currently undergoing profound change. Without minimizing the noticeable innovation in Germany, it occurs there primarily within the traditional system. Sweden, on the other hand, seems intent on "breaking out"--an easier task, perhaps, in a smaller country. In the 1950s, without affecting the traditional position of the professor, departments became the customary units of Swedish academic organization and the primary vehicle for undergraduate education, while the older faculties persisted as organizations for research. The division between teaching and research was thereby deepened.

Standing educational committees came into being within the faculties in 1953, each consisting of the dean, three teachers, and one assistant. There has been subsequent expansion of these committees, including equal representation by students. The committees have also expanded their influence on curriculum, in alliance with departmental committees, on which students are also represented. This pattern of educational management represents a distinct and effective break with the old system of an all-powerful professoriate.

Premfors and Östergren[7] diagram the structure of a modern Swedish university in Table 1.2.

The program committees are responsible for study programs, which are varied and conducive to a good deal of student choice. First, there are general study programs intended to reflect national educational needs. These are grouped in five sectors correlating with the labor market: technical professions; administrative, economic, and social professions; medical and nursing professions; teaching professions; and cultural and informative professions. Second, there are local study programs, which may reflect local need but may also be experiments directed towards the establishment of a new general study program. Finally, there are individual study programs, designed by students for themselves. Provision is also made for offering individual courses exclusive of the needs of particular programs.

Two facts here are worthy of note. First, a great deal of interdisciplinarity has been added to the entire Swedish higher educational system in the last two decades, the structure of which has been dominated by the

perceived needs of the labor market. Higher education in
Sweden is perhaps unique in being consciously directed
towards career goals. Secondly, the study programs
differ radically in length, ranging from 40 to 220 points
or credits, with 40 points being approximately equivalent
to 1 year's full-time study. The Swedish universities,
too, are comprehensive institutions of the kind represented in the preceding chapter by Yarmouk University.
Linköping, described here by its rector, must then be
viewed as an innovation within an innovation:

> Our university is only 12 years old and now has 7,000
> students. We have a medical school and a school of
> technology, together with undergraduate programs in
> the natural sciences, social sciences, liberal arts,
> and teacher training. The programs in the medical
> school and the school of technology were quite
> conventional. To a greater extent than in the United
> States, we in Sweden--and indeed in Europe in
> general--are sticking to the concept of the professor
> as being a king within his discipline. But we did
> ask whether specialization within disciplines was
> going too far. For example, while a few years ago
> there were 3 sub-disciplines in my own field of
> physics, it is now broken up into 10.
>
> There is a real question as to whether a university
> can serve society when people specialize in this way.
> Young people cannot use what they have learned in
> these narrowly defined fields, but require some over-
> view of what is happening in the different branches
> of science. Consequently, we have built up a program
> around four themes within which integrated research
> is planned:
>
> (1) Technology and Social Change
> (2) Water in Nature and Society
> (3) Public Health and Medical Care in the Community
> (4) Communication--The Transfer of Information
>
> We believe that this will permit the process of
> undergraduate education to have that contact with
> research that it needs, while at the same time
> promoting interdisciplinarity.

As with the research institutes established at
Bochum, the goal at Linköping is to establish interdisciplinary programs within a pre-existing system of
departments. But the themes at Linköping are deliberately designed for social relevance, or problem
orientation, rather than merely for a structural merging
of disciplines.

Governance of the themes is in the hands of Linköping's Theme Council, composed equally of researchers from the theme departments, other scholars and researchers, and interested individuals from outside the scientific community. Provision is made for the inclusion of associates and assistants, as well as professors, and also of guest researchers from industry or other research organizations.

Within each theme, sub-themes are projected. For example, possible sub-themes within Public Health are "The Public Health Organization in Society," "Problems of Information and Contact," and "The Individual's Health and Social Background." In Communication, possible sub-themes are "Language and the Individual," "Communication at the Molecular Level--The Membrane as a Structure of Interaction," and "Models for Communication." The interdisciplinary nature of the themes is nicely illustrated by the preceding sub-themes--linguistics, for example, in the same unit as molecular biology.

While Linköping's themes are primarily oriented towards research and graduate studies, the university anticipates effects on its undergraduate programs as well. Sub-projects initiated by the themes will overlap with some degree courses, the themes will initiate additional courses to be available as part of the established degree structure, and teachers involved in undergraduate education will participate in research projects within particular themes. Consequently, the new theme structure is expected to nullify the old research monopoly of the faculties and to reintegrate graduate and undergraduate education to some extent. Finally, the themes will complete the reorientation towards interdisciplinarity and problem focus which has characterized change in Swedish higher education for some time.[8]

Autonomous University of Guadalajara, Mexico

The study of medicine is inherently interdisciplinary and problem focused. Medical education, however, seldom reflects this. Multidisciplinarity, the simultaneous or sequential study of disciplines without exploration of the connections between them, is common in medical education. And the tendency to neglect experience in public health in favor of a purely clinical approach (delaying even this clinical experience until the end of the training) is standard procedure. The University of Guadalajara, however, represents a pace-setting attempt to break with such tradition. Luis Garibay described his university's innovations as follows:

There are no simple problems which are important and no important problems which are simple. In considering the university curriculum we must regard it

as a dynamic, changing thing. We should regard
innovation, not stability, as the normal and orthodox
thing. I would like to describe a situation from my
own experience where a program which began as an
attempt, through extension, to give health services
in the community became altered as the focus sharp-
ened through interdisciplinary interactions among
those tackling the problem.

While the initial goal of the program was to provide
service, we soon found that we were changing the
attitudes, values, and beliefs of the students.
They came to realize that doctors were unwilling to
leave the cities, in spite of the shocking health
needs of the countryside, and that medical attention
was becoming dehumanized and failing to serve the
individual. In fact, a dichotomy had arisen between
the training itself and the purpose of the training.

In traditional medical training, the clinical base is
separated from the scientific base, and the theoretical base is separated from the practical base. The
study of medicine often separates the student from
himself and from other human beings. The student
spends his first year with animals, skeletons, and
cadavers; and then during the clinical experience, he
comes across patients who are themselves isolated
from their own physical environment. To overcome
this, we place the student in contact with the community from the beginning of his study. We began
doing this as a service to the community, but ultimately realized that it led to an improved teaching
process and restructured our curriculum accordingly.
We began to emphasize interdisciplinarity and problem
focus. Not only did we change the nature of the
curriculum, we also changed its distribution. The
conventional ordering of the medical curriculum is
not adequate if the student is quickly faced with
patients in need. Theory will not necessarily pre-
cede practice but alternate with it, each reinforcing
the other. The student is also forced to better
organize his time, protecting the time necessary for
theoretical study while also finding time to work in
the community.

The advent of this program has had repercussions
throughout the university. A medical student working
in the community cannot simply be a doctor, but must
also be a change agent. Ill health is a consequence
of the condition of life in the village, not an
unforeseeable catastrophe. Therefore, the student
becomes involved with other subjects in the university in a multidisciplinary fashion. Every student

spends twenty hours per week in the field, and
current evaluation shows profound changes in the
attitudes and values of students--enhancing the
transmission of knowledge, linking theory and
practice, and placing a helping role at the center of
the student's training.

Interdisciplinarity in Medical Education

Modification of medical training towards problem
focus and interdisciplinarity, as described by Garibay,
is occurring in several other countries as well. The
goal is to train doctors who are more responsive to the
true health needs of the community, who are as concerned
with public health and health maintenance as with the
cure of those already sick. Two universities that have
done pioneer work in this regard are the University of
Valle, Colombia and Hacettepe University in Ankara,
Turkey. While neither institution was represented at
Wingspread, their experiments are certainly pertinent to
this discussion of innovative education.

The University of Valle is a new university by Latin
American standards, having been founded in 1945.
Although from its inception the new university served its
region, it was not until the 1960s that it accepted a
truly major responsibility for development when its rector at that time enacted his belief that the university,
through a dynamic and pragmatic reciprocity, should
become immersed in the life of its nation. The university has since evolved a full range of scientific and
technical programs to serve national needs, but of primary interest here is its program of medical education
and extension, which has attracted much acclaim and
emulation.

Originally, each second-year medical student at Valle
was assigned to a family for whose health he was
responsible, with a requirement to write a paper on the
socio-economic, environmental, and health condition of
each member of the family. This attempt at interdisciplinarity ultimately had to be discontinued because of
the tendency for both student and family to become too
emotionally involved with each other. Therefore, the
Division of Health established a health center in the
town of Candelaria which offered facilities for teaching
and research in rural medicine. Teams composed of
doctors, nurses, paramedical personnel, students, and
volunteers compiled, through this center, an impressive
record in health maintenance and health care delivery,
collaborating meanwhile in medical, sociological,
demographic, and economic studies.

The success of this program ultimately led to a
program known as PRIMOPS, which stands for the Spanish
translation of Research Program for Systems of Health

Care Delivery. The objectives of PRIMOPS are (a) to design, implement, operate, and evaluate an efficient model of health care delivery; (b) to deliver maternal and child health care, reducing perinatal mortality and improving prenatal health and nutrition; and (c) to modify teaching and curriculum to prepare better qualified health care professionals and para-professionals.

Under PRIMOPS, there are 5 levels of community health care. The first level is the home, which is the responsibility of health employees resident in the community. The health promoter serves and reports on about 420 families. She usually has only an elementary education, plus 6 weeks of special training. She visits each family once every 3 months and reports the results of her visits to a nurse's auxiliary. The nurse's auxiliary, in turn, trains and supervises health promoters and supervises midwives. She typically has 2 years of post-high school education and is responsible for primary health care of about 7,000 people, referring cases she cannot handle to a health center physician. Midwives, too, are traditional participants in such health services, but they nevertheless receive 6 weeks of special training under PRIMOPS. They are paid by the women they attend rather than by the municipality.

At the second level of community health care, each political district (with a population of 10,000 to 20,000) has a health post managed by a nurse's auxiliary, under the supervision of a supervisory nurse. The post processes statistical data, gives first aid, treats numerous diseases, provides prenatal care, and delivers other basic health services. At the third level of care is the health center, responsible for all of the 90,000 people in the PRIMOPS district. Its staff consists of several physicians and dentists, nurses, and various auxiliaries. Seriously ill patients are referred to the health center, which has laboratory and diagnostic tools. The head doctor of the center also supervises through his staff the 2 preceding lower levels.

The upper two levels in PRIMOPS are the urban hospital and the university hospital. These have the most resources and are able to deliver the most complete care when needed. This entire system was designed by university personnel who continue to advise it. The university, for example, has prepared general training manuals for promoters and auxiliaries, and such materials as programmed manuals for first aid instruction.[9]

This is an example of a program that had its origins in a need for training programs more closely related to the true needs of the population, but which has grown more towards delivery than training. Direct participation by university students has lessened, not increased. However, very significant and positive effects on

training have resulted from the participation of
university personnel in the health care delivery program.
    An interesting comparison with the University of
Valle medical program is provided by Hacettepe University
in Turkey.[10] Here the emphasis is on community medicine
as part of the early training of the prospective doctor
has been retained. In Turkey, medicine is not a postgraduate program; hence, the first year at Hacettepe is
devoted to teaching basic science in an integrated
fashion. In the second and third years, however, the
student is assigned to a family in which there is either
a pregnant woman or a child of less than one year. The
student assists in periodic medical checks under the
supervision of the doctor assigned to the family,
gradually assuming increasing responsibility. Meanwhile,
the student engages in a series of second-year courses,
in cell and tissue biology and in such traditional topics
as metabolism, mechanisms of cell and tissue injury, and
the cardiovascular system.
    The fourth, fifth, and sixth years are primarily
occupied with medical clerkships in the university
hospital, again according to the sequence and fashion
typical of European medical education. But during the
fifth year, the student is assigned to live in a village,
where he serves as a research health intern. The university maintains seven health centers staffed by faculty
for this purpose. The instructors live in the village
also and serve as rural health officers. Not the least
of the advantages to the student is this opportunity to
work with a health service team consisting of nurses,
para-professionals, and public health officers.
    Hacettepe is a full-spectrum university, not simply a
medical college. Organization is interdisciplinary
throughout, and there is again an absence of authori-
tarian chairs or professorships. A series of institutes
(biology, biochemistry, physiology, anatomy, and
pharmacology, among others) interact with the respective
faculties of such programs as dentistry, medicine,
pharmacy, and health sciences. Other institutes interact
with the faculties of science and engineering. In
addition, permanent Interdisciplinary Committees of Cell
Biology, Cellular and Tissue Injury, and Community
Medicine exist.[11] Many departments exist within each
institute and are represented on each committee. Thus,
the Cell Biology Committee represents microbiology,
biochemistry, histology, embryology, genetics, and
physiology, but biochemistry and histology are also
represented on the Cellular and Tissue Injury Committee.
Consequently, neither institutes nor committees are
allowed to become watertight compartments without
exchange between them.
    These examples of innovative, interdisciplinary
medical education programs at Valle and Haceteppe, then,

complement the four previous case studies to bolster the
assertion that constructive and pragmatic change is not
only possible but profitable--for universities, for their
students, and for the public they serve. Less compart-
mentalization of knowledge and more interaction among
ideas and personnel from traditionally separate disciplines is a trend the Wingspread participants generally
applauded. Not only does such interdisciplinarity re-
vitalize higher education, but it also seems to offer
more effective mechanisms for solving the day-to-day
problems of both developing and developed societies.

10
Extension
and National Development

      Taking the university to the people, rather than
bringing the people to the university, is the goal of
extension. The concept of extension has roots not only
in American history--notably, in the Chautauqua movement
and in the early belief that the university had responsibilities beyond the campus--but also in European institutions and practices. For example, early extension
educators in the United States were conscious of the successes achieved by the Workers' Education Association in
Britain, of the external degree programs of the
University of London, and of the Workingmen's College
that ultimately became Birkbeck College within London
University. In fact, as late as 1926, William Lighty (in
Wisconsin) could reflect that the English general strike
of that year had not led to revolution because of the
mental discipline that such British adult education
programs had provided labor leaders.[1]
      In common with many early leaders of extension,
Lighty saw education as a means of protecting the political status quo from violent change. This attitude viewed
from the present gives some poignance to the following
statement made at Wingspread by Dr. Turner of Cornell:

> There is a mystique in America that education
> transcends political variables, whereas in fact
> American education has traditionally been very def-
> erential towards government and the private sector.
> Your point (the political neutrality of education)
> might hold more strongly if American institutions
> were open marketplaces for ideas. But we find, in
> fact, that this is not the case.

Particularly when considering other governments' ties to
their nations' universities one should bear in mind that
U.S. universities have never been as separate from
political currents as they have sometimes claimed. The
American universities' early extension movement, in fact,

shares many similarities with more recently established
government-sponsored outreach services by modern development universities.

Another of Wisconsin's pioneers of extension, Charles
McCarthy, was imbued with an intense respect for German
political and industrial efficiency, which he attributed
in large part to the interrelationship of the
universities, government, and industries in that
nation.[2] Although the role of the German university in
the formation of the American university has often been
documented, the effect of German models on the concept of
extension has generally been overlooked. But if extension is considered to include, as it must, the service of
intellectuals as experts in the solution of societal or
technological problems, then one must admit certainly
that such a tradition had its origins in nineteenth
century Germany.

The techniques of extension (both historically and
presently) have been consultation, demonstration, short
courses, and correspondence or distance education. All
of these activities and their development are extensively
documented in the history of Wisconsin extension.[3]   As
early as 1907, for example, an engineering professor at
Madison undertook a series of firing tests with the goal
of smoke abatement from industrial furnaces. The tests
resulted in a series of lectures and demonstrations to
heating engineers and janitors in several Wisconsin
cities. Another instance occurred in 1908, when at the
request of a group of bakers, a Bakers Institute was
organized to demonstrate the importance of food value, as
well as control of adulteration and vermin; the session
was sufficiently successful to be repeated. Even
earlier, in 1890-91 Henry Jackson Turner, one of the
greatest American historians, delivered a lecture series
on North American colonization to audiences in cities
near Madison; he also carried on considerable correspondence with students for many years as a result of his
extension courses. In addition, prior to the First World
War, Dean Louis E. Reber initiated correspondence courses
for mechanics throughout the state, and correspondence
study at the University of Wisconsin was sufficiently
well established by 1917 for the state to offer free
tuition for such study to Wisconsin soldiers serving in
the war.

The purpose of this brief historical review is to
demonstrate that much that is currently presented as
novel in "outreach" is not new at all. "The work of the
extension division has remained the extension of the campus to the farthest boundaries of the state, or the
greatest possible enlargement of the student body;...the
lengthening of the period of education for the
individual; and...the expansion of the services of the
university to include opportunities other than those

offered in the academic curricula." That very
contemporary-sounding statement was made by Wisconsin's
Dean Reber in 1922.

The Open University and Everyman's University are
examples of innovative institutions that in large part
are assuming and expanding many traditional extension
functions. While they may currently emphasize, as they
should, their degree-granting functions, it is clear that
they have developed a technology for the transmission of
training that will increasingly be applied as well to
nondegree functions. The British Open University is
already accepting this challenge with its nondegree
courses for associate students on such topics as
"Consumer Decisions" and "Energy in the Home." It has
also been invited by the British Department of Trade and
Industry to prepare two learning packages on micro-
processors as resource material for in-house company
training programs.[4]

Equally clear is that Vincennes University was
accepting responsibility for further education, though
not correspondence education, within the Paris region.
The majority of its students were nondegree students, and
within its own national tradition, much of its activity
fell into categories that other institutions designate as
extension.

On the other hand, some countries are still eager to
develop extension programs. When Chitta Mitra spoke at
Wingspread of successful businessmen in India not being
reached by the university, or of scientists being
regarded as parasites, he was seeking a type of involvement such as that historically pursued by the University
of Wisconsin in its extension services. So also was
Rector Setidisho in his quest to reach cattle farmers,
businessmen, and clergymen in Botswana. Their goal is to
make the boundaries of their universities the boundaries
of their states. In fact, nearly all the universities
represented at Wingspread were attempting to establish or
significantly develop traditional extension functions.
Three noteworthy programs to be discussed at length
follow.

The State University of Campinas, São Paulo, Brazil

An outstanding example of a university attempting to
develop in modern form a mission parallel to those just
briefly considered is the University of Campinas
(UNICAMP). Zeferino Vaz described the role of his
university:

> Brazil imports one million barrels of oil a day--80
> percent of its needs. We are looking at sources of
> alternate energy, such as hydro-electric power and
> power by dissociating water into hydrogen and oxygen.

This involves physicists, chemists, engineers, biologists, agronomists, architects--all working together on a common problem, and it is producing practical results. Another problem is the need for research on the production, drying, storage, and exporting of soybeans, which is an expanding export crop in Brazil.

Research, extension, and teaching are not separable; the best professor is dedicated to all three. Furthermore, the distinction between basic and applied research, which is often made, I find to be entirely artificial. There is only good science and bad science. Eighty-five percent of our 2,000 faculty members are devoted to teaching and applied research to develop technology and service to the community.

What kind of problems do we face? We have millions of people suffering from Chagas disease and schistosomiasis--diseases that lower the work capacity of man. Such people are poor and cannot pay taxes to support services, including the university. We must break this vicious cycle of poverty, where no money means no research, which in turn means further poverty.

Now it may be that in providing formal education, the university is elitist. It is not really the university; nature itself is elitist. We can enroll only ninety people each year in the faculty of medicine. In order to adequately prepare professionals and scientists we must seek out those people with the necessary intellectual capacity.

But the university can do more to provide informal education in the community. For example, in the Campinas region we have 1,200 industries, only 50 of which would be considered large--that is, employing over 500 workers. The proprietors of these small industries are former workers themselves. They are intelligent, ambitious, but know nothing of modern principles of management. We provide free short courses for 20 such people at a time, and so far we have served 650 proprietary industries with impressive results on production and profitability.

Uterine and mammarian cancer are very prevalent among our women, and we have had a program for many years to detect precancerous lesions. We had first to overcome feelings that the necessary examinations were an offense against chastity and morality. But we have examined 40,000 women and saved many lives.

Finally, always remember that scientific research is more important to developing than to developed nations. Brazil pays two billion dollars a year for imported technology. One responsibility of the university is to help the nation escape from this dependence.

Vaz describes the classic extension university, one in which extension permeates all activities and where agricultural extension plays a role, but not a dominant role. Furthermore, he provides a justification for outreach that was heard from others at Wingspread. In developing countries, universal education lies a long way in the future. The university in these nations is inevitably an elitist institution that can educate--at least for the present--only a minority. While attempts can be made to draw that minority from a wider population, the economically privileged are likely to be overrepresented for the indefinite future, as they indeed are in every nation of the world. Consequently, the university has a duty to extension, a responsibility to distribute its resources as widely as possible. The nonextension university is, according to Vaz,[5] a luxury that only rich nations can afford.

He also points out another key to effective extension: the need to promote and publicize the specific services being offered. In developing nations, the community often fears the university, regarding it as inaccessible and unintelligible. And poor communities often cannot see the solutions that may be readily available for their problems. No one responded to the University of Campinas' first newspaper advertisements of its courses for leaders of small industries. University representatives finally assembled the first class of twenty by talking individually to the proprietors of small businesses in their own plants, convincing them that they would be able both to understand the material presented and to profit from it. After the first course, fifty applicants applied for the second. Success breeds success. Currently, this scheme is spreading to other states, and UNICAMP has prepared a six-month course to train professors and other professionals from elsewhere in Brazil to deliver such courses.

Similarly, university health workers had to overcome initial objections to uterine and mammary screening for cancer. But success in reaching large numbers of people has enabled UNICAMP to enlarge its health role; it has encouraged breast feeding, both to reduce the incidence of mammary cancer and to improve the health of children. (In the absence of rigorous hygiene, bottle feeding spreads deadly disease among nursing children in the tropics.)

Surely one factor in UNICAMP's success is its healthy respect for the culture in which it exists, coupled with disdain for narrow nationalism, which Vaz calls a false nationalism.[6] He points out that progress in the United States in recent decades has been in no small measure due to the importation of scientists. Following that example, UNICAMP has 230 foreign professors on its faculty, while at the same time attracting back to its campus some 160 former faculty members who had emigrated. On the other hand, in developing its extension education program the university gave considerable thought to the characteristics of the region. It selected for a pilot program a segment of the city of São Paulo designated as AR2, which included the richest quarter, two middle-class quarters, a State housing project, and some very impoverished slums. The region chosen thus provided an economic cross-section of the population.

After considering its clientele, the extension program identified such serious societal problems as malnutrition, maladjustment, and drug abuse; then it sponsored meetings with elementary school teachers, neighborhood clubs, and leaders of Catholic, Protestant, Spiritualist, and Syncretic churches--groups that could not be identified with the establishment, as well as those that could. These meetings were designed to inspire confidence and cooperation among diverse elements of the population, and to parcel out responsibilities among community leaders.

The program that emerged has two components: (a) services related to formal education, such as refresher courses for teachers, adult literacy classes, school meal service for children three to twelve years of age, vacation schools for both education and recreation, and school medical services; and (b) services related to informal education, including short courses in hygiene and nutrition for women and couples, as well as semi-professional courses to train manicurists, hospital auxiliaries, office assistants and secretaries, and chiropodists.

In addition, contract projects have been completed in conjunction with the Brazilian Company of Telecommunications (TELEBRAS), with the Subway Company of São Paulo, and with branches of the food processing industry, among many others. Much of this research could be characterized as "applied," if one accepts the distinction between pure and applied research which Vaz rejects. However, the Enzymology Department of the biochemistry faculty worked both on texturized soya protein (research many would categorize as "applied") and also on the synthesis of 6-amino-penicilamic acid, indispensable in the production of broad-spectrum antibiotics (research more likely to be labeled as "basic" or "pure"). Simplistic labels aside, the important principle at UNICAMP is that actual societal need, rather than arbitrary scientific categories and competition, evokes the appropriate research.

Clearly the developments Vaz describes could not have taken place without relatively abundant funds. Nevertheless, the aggressive and successful alliance of teaching, research, and public service can be documented for other countries (e.g., Ahmadu Bello University in Nigeria) and other universities, especially those in developing nations, can profitably imitate this model of interdependent, integrated functions in their own drive toward self-sufficiency.

The Cooperative Extension Service of the U.S. Department of Agriculture

A recent report[7] has pointed out that in the 1930s American farmers were no more productive than their Third World counterparts. Since then, however, grain yields in the Third World have remained below 1.5 tons per hectare, American yields are now around 3.5 tons per hectare. The report goes on to suggest that economists have dwelt more on the failures of the Third World than the triumphs of the United States; consequently, the importance of the cooperation existing among universities and farmers in the United States has been neglected.

Many comments at Wingspread indicated that Third World educators do not underestimate the importance of this cooperation between American academia and agriculture. The Cooperative Extension Service of the U.S. Department of Agriculture, in fact, has been described as the largest single organized adult education program in the world.[8] Its story is worth telling here, both as an account of what can be achieved from modest beginnings and as an illustration of an effective system towards which much of the Third World is striving.

Most nations have agriculture extension or advisory services. They traditionally formed part of the governmental network in former colonies as well as in developed nations, but usually they had no formal links with universities; where such links did exist in the developmental stage (as in Britain), they were soon severed. It proved difficult outside of the United States to integrate the muddy boots of the extension specialist with the more philosophic attitudes of the professoriate. And, indeed, such conflicts were not unknown in the early days of agricultural extension in America. Scott[9] characterizes this schism:

> The overwhelming majority of the professors of traditional subjects made no effort to hide their contempt for agriculture and for those who sought to teach it. When Isaac P. Roberts arrived at Cornell

in 1874, he found a cool reception. "Because agriculture was then regarded by most of the classically educated members of the Cornell faculty as quite unworthy of a place in education beside the traditional subjects," he recalled later, "we suffered a sort of social neglect and felt ourselves in an alien atmosphere." As late as 1891, according to Alfred T. Akeson, the president of West Virginia University, "we looked upon agriculture as an undesirable invasion of the holy precincts of classical knowledge."

Scott also notes that the epithet "Cow College" was hardly used to express affection and esteem, persisting even into recent times long after many of the universities so described had attained international stature.

It would be pleasing, of course, to record that early extension efforts at least had the support of farmers, but Scott provides evidence to the contrary:

Particularly distressing was the dislike or contempt for the colleges that most farmers displayed....A convention of farmers in Illinois...denounced the curriculum at the Illinois Industrial University as being totally irrelevant to the needs of agriculturalists. According to the malcontents, the college would not "allow a boy to go there and study such agricultural or mechanical branch as he may choose without taking everything else in the curriculum. If a man has peculiar faculties for blacksmithing, in God's name, let him be a blacksmith. Metaphysics, what is it? Ten pages will contain the substance of all the metaphysical fools from Aristotle down."

In the early extension days, it was sometimes said that nothing emptied a hall of farmers as fast as the announcement of a speaker from the university. Most probably it was only the increasing value of land itself that led the farmer to welcome a scientific agriculture and to accept the worth of farming as a career for which training was required. In much of the world, even today, agricultural land still has little value, and the attendant skepticism and even contempt toward academic involvement in farming continue.

In U.S. universities a unique cooperative organization has evolved. The extension workers themselves are federal employees and, consequently, make few demands on the resources of the university itself. They report, however, to the extension director, who either is himself--or ultimately reports to--the dean of the College of Agriculture. Frequently, extension workers hold faculty rank within the university structure. The foot soldiers of the service are the county agents, and

each U.S. agricultural county now averages three such
agents.[10]   They are backed up by campus extension
specialists in all branches of agriculture, who themselves interact with the university and U.S.D.A.
researchers on campus.   This close relationship among
field and campus personnel has been a vital element in
the success of the system.
    The other vital element has been the dedication of
the individual extension workers and their ability to
relate directly to their clients. Watts and Weick[11] tell
a typical story of such devotion:

> The sun was just touching the gable of a sparse cow
> town train depot as the home demonstration agent
> stood beside her assorted packages and satchels.
> Tied to one of the heavy canvas bags was a monstrous
> pressure canning kettle. That was the reason she was
> here--to teach pressure-cooking canning to homemakers
> scattered throughout that large southwestern county.
> It was going to be a long week. It had already been
> a long day since three a.m. when she boarded that
> train back at the college where her home base was.

> Before the week was over, that home demonstration
> agent had put on over 20 canning demonstrations.
> She'd taught the wives of mayors, Mexican house-
> keepers, bachelor cowboys; she'd been to mining com-
> munities and remote ranch homes. She'd worked over
> kerosene stoves and oil drums for stoves and she'd
> logged over 100 miles on horseback as she moved
> through the country borrowing horses and saddles as
> she went from place to place. Tying her canvas
> satchels and her pressure cooker to the saddle, she'd
> ask directions and set out equipped with the latest
> techniques of food preservation....

    Women's liberation came early to the southwestern
United States, if by liberation we mean sharing perils
and privations. And the key to extension's effectiveness
has always been to reach out to the people on their own
terms.   Rosentretter[12] tells of early debates between
Beach and Adams on the virtues of long-season versus
short-season corn. Beach would refer to Adams as being
like his own corn: early maturing, but small. Adams
would counter that Beach was like the corn he favored:
large, but never matured. While such banter may have
seemed too vaudevillian for the ivory tower, it was
calculated to hold its audience--and it did so!
    The three pillars of U.S. agricultural extension have
been agriculture itself, home economics, and the 4-H
movement.   The instructional techniques in all three
areas have been demonstration, institutes, and

correspondence (the latter including pamphlets and other publications). The 4-H youth movement, in particular, with its focus on "Head, Heart, Hand, and Health" exemplifies a simple but effective merging of instruction and practice. Farm children throughout the world are familiar with daily chores, and the 4-H Clubs simply harnessed those chores to education. Farm children were encouraged to grow a plot of corn, raise a heifer, can vegetables, bake, indeed undertake any farm or household activity with the incentive of competition at county, state, or even national levels. While purely social activities formed an important part of the club's program, advice on the farm project was always available through the club leader, usually a local resident who was backed up, at least in theory, by the entire resources of the extension service. Because 4-H reached the youngsters and got them to adopt improved practices, the children themselves not only learned to be better managers but, equally important, also sometimes influenced their parents toward more progressive farm and household management. And it should be recalled that, at least in these early days, farm parents were often immigrants with limited literacy in English and with considerable problems in adjusting to the New World. The influence of 4-H thus often transcended strictly agricultural improvements by helping such families settle more successfully into the changing American culture they were helping to create. The 4-H movement, by the way, has since been extended to other developing nations, such as Kenya with its 4-K Clubs.

Home economics and agriculture, the other components of extension, have always gone hand in hand. In the United States, the canner-on-horseback of yesteryear is now likely to be a nutritionist instructing both rural and urban welfare mothers in dietary principles; but the idea remains the same, and the methods are still home visits, home demonstrations, and "how-to" pamphlets. Institutes and workshops (voluntarily attended meetings for one or a few days) are the other formats commonly used by extension for instruction in home economics and agriculture. At one time these meetings would have concerned themselves purely with "farming" topics--good fertilizer or pest control practices, the choice of crop varieties, and other field-oriented studies. Now, however, they are as likely to consider agricultural finance, the utility of small computers, or estate planning.[13]

A successful workshop, of course, will rapidly lead to related publications, and indeed a continuous stream of written material emerges from the cooperative extension service. In general, these publications tend to be of two types--the pamphlet (sometimes termed "bulletin"), which contains essential information on a given topic in easily understood terms; and the technical publication, which examines a topic in considerable detail and requires serious study for mastery of the material. For today's extension programs, these two types tend to reflect extremes, although less distinct extremes than in the past, both in the spectrum of technical information distributed by extension and in the range of sophistication characteristic of its audience. The public communications media have also become important in disseminating extension information; local newspapers, as well as television and radio stations, readily provide space and time for agricultural extension programs and reports.

The origination of the demonstration farm technique, another important instructional format used in United States extension services, is usually ascribed to Seaman Knapp. In the early 1900s the cotton boll weevil invaded Texas from Mexico, threatening the state's entire cotton-growing industry. The insecticides of that day were quite ineffective; indeed, even with today's insecticides, control of the boll weevil is difficult. The most sophisticated agricultural theories of the time suggested that control could be achieved through a combination of revised procedures, changes not only in field practices but also in traditional cultural attitudes toward cotton farming. Shorter season varieties would, for example, perhaps permit harvest before the major weevil attack in late season. Careful sanitation (burning of crop residues, prevention of recurrent "volunteer" plants by thorough weeding) would reduce the carryover of the pest from season to season. Fertilizer and careful husbandry would strengthen the crop, enabling it to withstand a mild attack with little loss. The essence of the suggested control plan, then, was a package of interrelated improvements in cultural practice, any separate element of which would fail while the entire package would succeed. The proverbial "catch," of course, was that this integrated plan could succeed only at the expense of appreciable additional effort on the part of the farmer, who nevertheless faced ruin unless he overcame the pest. Such a fundamental but complicated problem is, to be sure, not merely a quaint glimpse into Texas agricultural history; it exemplifies a critical and all too familiar challenge facing under-developed agriculture throughout much of the world today.

To control the boll weevil challenge, in 1903 Knapp suggested to a group of local businessmen and farmers in Terrell, Texas that a suitable farm be selected for a demonstration site. A seventy-acre plot was chosen on the Porter farm, and Mr. Porter agreed to carry out all the required operations under Knapp's instruction. Although no help other than advice would be given, any loss the farmer might suffer would be compensated.

138

In fact, at the end of the season Porter himself
estimated he had cleared an extra ten dollars per acre
from the demonstration plot. From this modest but successful beginning, through further demonstrations, the
improved methods spread throughout the threatened region
of Texas.[14] The essence of this achievement was that
farmers had been shown that a neighbor, using only those
resources available to themselves, could substantially
improve his yield in spite of the pest; or more
generally, they learned that improved techniques could
help them use present resources to overcome threatening
agricultural problems.

The demonstration method has continued with
adaptation to this day. The principle has been variously
named, but might be called the "master farmer technique"
because the most able farmer in a region is persuaded to
adopt a practice and demonstrate it to his neighbors.
Results of this approach have been criticized on the
grounds of equity. By concentrating first on the most
able farmers, the rich tend to become richer. The poorer
farmers, however, ultimately do become richer as well,
and many believe that the abundance of the American harvest is a testimony to the overall success of agricultural extension. Nowadays, the extension service is also
becoming interested in the organic farming movement,
which has been successfully adopted by some farmers even
in the teeth of opposition from the best technical
opinion. Again, some of these farms are being used as
demonstration sites, and if the price of fuel and such
fuel-intensive inputs such as fertilizer continues to
grow, then more will be heard of these organic
demonstration farms.

The cooperative extension service currently is an
enormous enterprise with widespread effects. It is
represented in all but a handful of U.S. counties. Its
technique, described as informal education for action,
spreads far beyond the boundaries of the farm into the
towns and cities in which most Americans now live. While
the connection of the local agent with the university may
sometimes be distant, the association is very real.
Because information flows readily in both directions, the
extension service seems certain to remain a permanent
element both in American life and in the American land-
grant university.

The University of the Philippines at Los Baños

Other nations, too, have developed their own
variations of extension services. The University of the
Philippines at Los Baños (UPLB), for example, is striving
towards leadership in cooperative extension in the
Philippines, so far with limited results. Some of these
efforts have already been described in Chapter 7 in

relation to the land-grant tradition and will here be
expanded upon. At Wingspread Chancellor Samonte was
emphatic, in his discussions of extension, about the need
to develop a set of related innovations, echoing an
opinion he has explained elsewhere:

> Oftentimes a combination of technologies is more
> useful than relying on only one. Moreover, serious
> effort should be made to link the technological
> innovation with other educational or developmental
> measures. For instance, innovations to educate stu-
> dents and farmers to use modern technology of agri-
> cultural production must be related to new measures
> aimed at promoting agrarian reform, strengthening
> cooperatives, and improving the system of financial
> credit. Innovations to democratize the schools must
> be related, among others, to the improvement of
> community nutrition....
>
> Before the...technology thus chosen is adopted on a
> large scale, it is necessary to test it on a pilot-
> study basis. Thus, there should be a better evalua-
> tion of its functionality in terms of the specific
> culture and environment. Intended as well as unin-
> tended consequences of the technological innovation
> should also be determined, and its impact on the
> community assessed. Furthermore, weaknesses or gaps
> in the new...system, such as inadequate staff
> training, poor logistics, and lack of interagency
> coordination and public understanding should be
> identified and remedied.[15]

The emphasis upon a related set of innovations is
reminiscent of the earlier example of Knapp's efforts
against the boll weevil. The comparison is even more apt
if we parallel the Knapp example with one cited by
Samonte; namely, the introduction of improved varieties
of rice, the so-called Green Revolution. The introduction of new varieties alone would not produce conditions
sufficient for positive change. More specifically,
because the new varieties' value is in their ability to
profit from intensive fertilization, the new varieties
and new fertilizer practices must go hand in hand. In
many regions, the improved strains are more susceptible
to pests and diseases than the locally adapted strains.
Consequently, the introduction of the new varieties must
also involve improved methods of cultivation and pest
control. The entire package is necessary to obtain a
good return, but the return will more than compensate for
the cost of pest control. In fact, the return on the
package is spectacular, as much or more than 100 percent
yield improvement. Certain sociological consequences,

however, were less anticipated. The better farmers
adopted the new techniques first, profiting themselves
but driving down the value of the poorer farms' smaller
yields. This repercussion, as Samonte emphasizes,
illustrates the need for an effective extension
attempting to foresee and ameliorate such potentially
destructive consequences. Many technologically plausible
innovations have been severely criticized in the past,
and rightly so, for their failure to anticipate social as
well as agricultural effects.

Another example of an integrated approach at UPLB is
a project to assist farmers in the barrios of the small
town of Pila. In cooperation with the Southeast Asian
Regional Center for Graduate Study and Research in
Agriculture, researchers, students, and technicians were
sent into the field to help organize the farmers to
improve their agricultural practices. This pilot project
in extension was intended to train extension workers as
well as to develop effective farming methodologies.
Meanwhile, in the nearby town of Bay, several UPLB
colleges were starting a similar project--The
Comprehensive Community Health Program. Both were
integrated attempts at extension, but as Samonte points
out,[16] unfortunately they were not integrated with each
other. Health, nutrition, and agricultural production
are all facets of a single process: the life of the
peasant. They are experienced in an interrelated fashion
by the peasant, so they should be approached in an
interrelated fashion by the extension worker. As a consequence of observing the operations of these two
programs, community health has been adopted as an additional dimension of the social laboratory at Pila.

UPLB does not supervise extension for a region in the
sense that a U.S. land-grant college does, but then the
extent of supervision by the university in the United
States should not be exaggerated. Cooperative extension
workers are employees of the U.S. Department of
Agriculture, not of the university, but the chain of
activity does extend from the university to the field.
Similarly, in the Philippines extension workers are
employed by appropriate government departments. While
often they do not cooperate with the university very
effectively, the university participates in training
extension workers and exploring new paths to more effective extension. Thus, UPLB has attempted, in partnership
with the government of Quezon Province, the Integrated
Rural and Agricultural Development Program. The goal of
this program is to mobilize leadership at the village
level--an objective again reminiscent of the U.S.D.A.'s
achievements through its 4-H programs and its master
farmer technique, among other methods.

UPLB has also established short-term training courses
for government and private sector employees in

postproduction technology for rice. (Storage losses are very large in the tropics.) This service has involved the development of equipment to harvest, dry, mill, and store grain. It has also investigated extension practices to promote multiple cropping by upland farmers. And, like the U.S. farm institute program, it provides a continuing education program for farmer leaders, production technicians, supervised credit technicians, extension workers, business executives, radio broadcasters, and indeed for all personnel involved in agriculture and rural development.[17]

In its own way, in a manner responsive to its own time and place, UPLB is developing and maintaining what has been called the two-way street of extension. Knowledge is carried from campus to field; questions are carried back. Results will, quite likely, amply pay for the investment, just as they have in the United States. No doubt there will be, as Samonte suggests, some unforeseen and perhaps unfortunate consequences of innovation similar to those that have occurred in other nations, including the United States. But if the traffic of experimentation and information continues to move freely in both directions, failures will provide lessons for the future, and the university will grow in knowledge and stature as it contributes to societal development.

11
Research

As much as any function, research defines the
university, distinguishing it from other institutions of
learning. In the European tradition, freedom of inquiry
has always been regarded as essential to the university's
role, and teaching loads have characteristically been
comparatively light to provide time for such
investigation. Consequently, when the British government
decided that an expansion of higher education could not
be achieved economically within the existing university
philosophy, it established polytechnics which awarded
degrees but had a diminished research role.[1] These
institutions were deliberately not called universities.
Similarly, the California Plan (which distinguished the
University of California from California State universities and colleges) provided a substantially lighter
teaching load for faculty in the University of California
System to promote research as a primary activity there,
as opposed to its secondary role at the State colleges.
Nevertheless, significant research continues to arise
from both the British polytechnics and California State
universities and colleges, largely because scholars themselves hold their own research role in such high esteem.
    As Schauer[2] has pointed out, the value of a research
component in the undergraduate program is being
increasingly recognized even in liberal arts colleges.
He suggests that not only in the sciences, but also in
other disciplines, infusion of the spirit of research
into the educational process may well be an inspiration
for active and creative scholarship. But it would hardly
be fair to suggest that the principal reason for the
existence of research within the university has been its
contribution to teaching. Wolfle[3] has pointed out that,
at least in the United States, the university has been
the principal site of scientific achievement since the
nineteenth century; and what is true for science is
doubly so for the humanities. Without the university,

the explosion of knowledge in the last fifty years would probably have been little more than a muffled thud.

Among innovating institutions, the role of research in developed countries tends to differ from its role in less developed countries; and in both types of nations, newer institutions seek a research role different from that of the large established universities. In the United States researchers must contend with teaching loads several times heavier than their European counterparts, with the consequent need either to compete for external funding or to relegate their research into their "leisure." As in other developed countries, however, the intense research activity in the nation as a whole provides a certain security of status for U.S. faculty involved in research. University researchers are certainly attached to the research establishment even if they are not at the center of it.

In the Third World, on the other hand, intellectual resources are sparse, national needs are urgent, and every university is a rare center of excellence striving to survive in relative isolation. As a result, research must be conducted with very limited funds and, at the same time, be relevant to the pressing needs of development. Nevertheless, faculty in developing countries must also strive to keep a foot in the door of the international research community; otherwise they will lose status as scholars, a serious loss for their nations, as well as for themselves. Perhaps worse, Third World institutions must worry about losing their best investigative scholars to emigration. As Luis Garibay of Guadalajara pointed out, even the most rudimentary research infrastructure may be absent in such development universities:

> In colonial times, universities in Mexico were oriented towards research, but in the last century, because of conditions inside the country and the emphasis on training professionals, research ceased to be a major activity. However, in the 1930s conditions changed, and the National Institute of Mexico started several institutes for research in which at least some of the professors are full-time researchers. But we have often been handicapped by a lack of research policy, by a lack of funds, and by a lack of people trained to do research. In 1957, there were very few graduate students in Mexico.

> In 1962 there were only five national research councils on the American continent--those of Argentina, Brazil, Canada, Mexico, and the United States. More are in existence now and are developing research policies, but research is supported almost entirely by the government. Private industry gives

very little support. We are trying, by cooperation among the national research councils, to develop collaboration among Latin American universities on research projects. This will enable them to do more of the work the research councils want done and make better use of national resources.

One urgent need is for more research on education itself. Furthermore, if we are to establish better institutions, then we need more institutional research. Finally, Latin America lacks centers of information. While we are short of funds for research, much research is being duplicated. Venezuela is trying to establish such a center in Caracas in cooperation with UNESCO. We are trying to establish another in Costa Rica and perhaps soon will be able to establish yet a third at Guadalajara to deal with research and information in education. But these projects are at a very early stage.

Despite these differences between developed and developing countries' attitudes, two research ideals inspire most of the institutions represented at Wingspread: relevance and interdisciplinarity. Throughout the conference these two principles were continually stressed, and most participants could agree with Chancellor Farhad Riahi's observation:

It is not necessary that one always be working at the frontiers of knowledge in a specific discipline. Practical problems exist that are simple to define but nevertheless lead to intricate questions within scientific disciplines, questions for which solutions are lacking. Consequently, if we define research within the university as problem oriented, then we can avoid the fear of being provincial and absorbed in applied research.

Furthermore, by cooperation it should be possible to develop and generalize approaches and ways of dealing with problems that are applicable across national boundaries. Within the so-called developing countries there are down-to-earth problems such as health improvement and the increase of literacy, which are common to all. Cooperative efforts may provide means of attacking such problems, which can subsequently be adjusted to local cultural contexts. The search for such general methodologies is one way in which the developing university can participate in the international research community.

Both Garibay and Riahi introduced research-related issues that arose again and again at Wingspread: The rejection of the assertion that "basic" research is necessarily more worthy or more intellectually signifi- cant than the research for immediate application to problems; the significance of solving problems to con- tribute to immediate gains in living standards; the importance of an interdisciplinary, problem-oriented investigational approach; the belief that this approach can lead to basic (or "pure") knowledge as readily as can defining basic research problems in isolation from prac- tical considerations; the lack of funds, nongovernmental funds, and the absence of planning agencies to promote research efforts; the importance of cooperation among researchers and their institutions; and finally, the need to establish a tradition of intellectual excellence where one may have never existed before.

Interdisciplinary Research in Developed Countries

Multidisciplinary research programs have not generally been developed within regular university faculties, possibly because, as Wolfle suggests, univer- sities have not yet been very successful in such investigations. Interdisciplinary research, Wolfle further points out, is impeded by the problems of allo- cating costs and credits to departmental budgets as well as by the departmental and disciplinary rivalries among the faculty. The beginning scientist knows that advance- ment depends on gaining the respect of senior scholars in his own discipline, and while the approval of colleagues in other fields may not be a hindrance to advancement, neither is it much help.

Green Bay's Chancellor Weidner has suggested that these problems are not insuperable and that one alter- native is to create new institutions, or segments of institutions, that focus their entire attention on interdisciplinarity. The University of Wisconsin-Green Bay (UWGB) has been organized to this end.

As described in an earlier chapter, members of the faculty at Green Bay are grouped into interdisciplinary departments called concentrations. It is only within these concentrations that faculty members can receive professorships, get promoted, earn merit increases, and conduct the normal voting and collegial functions of a faculty. One concentration at UWGB focuses on urban analysis, another on social change and development, and yet a third on science and environmental change. The disciplines are subordinate to these concentrations though they do exist, but without conventional budget and personnel functions. Rather, they are formal groupings of people with similar academic interests. A faculty member belongs to a discipline and a concentration. A UWGB student must major in a concentration, but can co- major in a discipline if he or she chooses.

    While only a few examples of the research engendered
by UWGB's innovative plan are noted below, Prange[5]
provides a more extensive summary for the interested
reader. To understand the research role of UWGB,
however, one must first be somewhat familiar with the
northeastern Wisconsin natural and social ecology of
which this university is a part.
    The city of Green Bay lies at the mouth of the Fox
River which flows northward into the bay, itself a long
arm of Lake Michigan. Sixty-four kilometers below the
city, the river flows out of another lake, Lake
Winnebago, and the stretch of river between Lake
Winnebago and Green Bay is occupied by one of the
greatest concentrations of paper-processing plants in the
world, all using water and discharging effluents. In
addition, the city has a considerable food processing
industry, involving cheese manufacture, butchering, meat
packing, and food canning. These industries contribute
substantial loads of pollutants to both air and water.
The metropolitan sewage system is also a significant
contributor to area water pollution.
    But this is hardly the whole story. The surrounding
catchment area for the Fox River is a rich region of
dairy farming. During the severe Wisconsin winters, considerable difficulties surround the disposal of animal
waste from these farms, much of which is washed into the
river system by spring's rapid snow melt and run-off.
UWGB students and faculty have, for several years, been
studying this contaminated river water; they have
concluded that the nutrient load originates mostly from
Lake Winnebago and various municipal treatment plants.
Urban run-off and industrial discharge, surprising
enough, are of minor importance with regard to their
nutrient effect. Most of the half million kilograms of
phosphate and the one and a half million kilograms of
nitrogen running into the bay each year, in fact, can be
attributed to run-off from rural sources while the ground
is still frozen. While 75 percent of the 3,000 kilograms
of nutrients per day during summer can be attributed to
the municipal sewage treatment plant, the fourfold
increase each spring can be attributed largely to agricultural run-off.
    On the other hand, 90 percent of the biological
oxygen demand (BOD) loadings are of industrial origin.
The paper industry, especially, deposits masses of
organic matter, and this excessive loading causes anoxic
conditions in portions of the river, leading to ammonia
release. The river itself would benefit from an increase
in algal release of oxygen, but on the bay algal blooms
fueled by excess nitrogen and phosphate are a menace to
fish and to recreation. UWGB personnel have also done
considerable research on the physical pattern of water
flow into the bay, especially regarding cooling water

from a major power plant located at the river's mouth.
Because this cooling water is chlorinated, there is a
potential problem involving chlorination of organic
compounds, which are now suspected carcinogens.
    This is but a brief review of what is, in fact, a
major research venture. Faculty researchers in association with their undergraduate and graduate students,
continue to monitor, sample, and analyze the bay and
river conditions; and the story is by no means complete.
For instance, a major municipal waste treatment plant has
been constructed at the mouth of the river; the operation
of the plant will modify the nutrient and BOD loadings in
both the river and the bay, and these effects must be
monitored.   Furthermore, a question arises concerning a
suitable disposal mechanism for municipal sewage sludge,
now that regulations prohibit its deposition in the
river.   Present plans call for it to be incinerated,
which would possibly exacerbate an already prevalent air
pollution problem. But another group of UWGB faculty and
students are investigating the possibility of on-land
disposal, perhaps as land fill, fertilizer, or feedstock
to generate methane gas. Problems that must be resolved
in this case are the possibility of ground water con-
tamination by nitrites, heavy metals, or other noxious
chemicals, such as PCBs, and the potential nuisance
effect of disposal as fertilizers.
    Not all research projects at UWGB are on such a large
scale. Neshota Park, for example, is a 200-acre tract
established several years ago in Brown County but, as
yet, little developed as a park. A group of students,
under a faculty advisor, set out to produce a master plan
for the park that would preserve and develop the natural
features, while simultaneously using these features to
meet recreational needs. The completed plan calls for
doubling the size of the park and provides for swimming,
fishing, camping, picnicking, nature trails, along with a
playground, a horse ring, and even 5 acres for seasonal
berry picking. The students recommended that a careful
study of the natural history of the area would be an
essential prerequisite to the park's development, as
would a study of the needs of potential park users. It
was suggested that existing camping sites and a horse
ring be relocated to better drained ground. The students
recommended substituting 5 small lakes for the proposed
large lake, which the students felt could not be kept
clean. The success of this small but pragmatic research
project is attested by the fact that similar university
help was requested for planning a neighborhood park in
the nearby town of Howard.
    These examples represent the extremes of UWGB's scale
of research activity--at one end, projects with a
sophisticated research component and extensive faculty
participation backed by strong student support; and at

the other end, projects applying existing scientific knowledge and principles to community problems, involving faculty only as advisors to the students who actually conduct the work. A project that falls somewhere in the middle has been initiated on the Kewaunee River watershed, which is an area of about 140 square miles set in the midst of dairy farms. This project, as a matter of fact, has formed the focus of an extensive student-directed investigation for undergraduate degree credit. The physical problems identified in the area include agricultural run-off, causing siltation and chemical and bacterial pollution, allied with poor sewage treatment facilities in the small communities along the river. The main socio-economic problems are a decrease in farming, high unemployment, and disproportionate out-migration. The students divided into two topic area study groups: socio-economic and biophysical. After attending classes on all aspects of the watershed, sessions often conducted by community leaders and planners as well as by university faculty, the groups then identified specific topics they wished to tackle. Studies investigated such factors as soil, vegetation, animal populations, and land use. Extensive monitoring generated reliable information on water quality. Meanwhile, the group studying social problems gathered data on such factors as the nutritional status of the aged, demographic characteristics, livestock density, occupation types, and the economy of the watershed region. Obviously, then, besides providing useful experience for the participating students, such intensive study of a restricted area can uncover inter-relationships and reveal new insights of genuine scientific and community interest.

In summary, three general conclusions may be inferred from this brief account of UWGB research activities. First, faculty and undergraduate students are working together to produce significant scientific discoveries in the field of ecology. Second, through these efforts by its faculty and students, the university is making a measurable contribution to the understanding of the region in which it exists and will thus have a real impact on the area's future development. Third, the experience students are obtaining by working on these projects is turning out better graduates with greater potential for occupying leadership positions in society.

Linköping University in Sweden has developed interdisciplinary research projects similar to UWGB's in four areas: technology and social change; water, nature, and society; public health; and human communication. The funding successes of Linköping's Rector Hans Meijer, however, would arouse envy at Green Bay. Having asked for 2 million kroner, the university was pleased to have its request raised by the Minister of Education to 2.5 million kroner while the parliamentary opposition proposed an increase to 3 million kroner. With additional strong support from trade unions and industry, Linköping's research and other programs operate from a stable fiscal base that few institutions enjoy.

The Aalborg University Center in Denmark is perhaps too young to have a research record; yet a lengthy account of the economic, demographic, and social impact of the university on North Jutland has already been published.[6] Again, at this institution, the evidence of multidisciplinary research, together with a close involvement with the local community, is clear.

At Griffith University in Brisbane the titles of funded research in the School of Australian Environmental Studies[7] indicate interests similar to those examined in earlier examples: "Investigation of Ground Water Hydrology of the Cooloola Sand Mass and Noosa River Catchment;" "Human Health and Ecology;" "Evaluating the Environmental Bases and Human Consequences of Land-Use Legislation: A Case Study in the Erosion Districts of the Darling Downs;" "Health Servicing of Urban Children;" and "The Park Ecosystems of Brisbane."

Each of these innovative institutions would undoubtedly detect in all the others a common philosophical thread, a similar approach to problems conditioned by shared concerns. Indeed, while the University of Paris-Vincennes[8] suggests that its research is no different from that of other, more traditional French universities, some of the research projects cited sound the familiar chorus of interdisciplinarity and problem focus that seems more typical of innovating universities.

While the foregoing contains a note of cautious optimism about the vitality of university research programs, other Europeans at the conference were less sanguine about future prospects. Siegfried Grosse described a recognizable plight when he characterized his own University of Bochum in Germany:

> The University of Bochum is 14 years old. It was planned for 12,000 students and now has 26,000. It was hoped that the new university would stop the growth of Münster and Bonn, but they just went on growing alongside us. As a consequence, the social context of education has changed in Germany, producing difficulties and changes for research. For example, one of the oldest principles of the European university is the connection between teaching and research. The presence of such large classes of students /now/ undermines both the condition of research and its relation with teaching. Democratization of the university brings its own problems and its own tasks. The government wants as many students as possible taught, and consequently the time available for research declines.

Administrative tasks also increase, which further curtails research activity. And the shortage of money in recent years has had its own impact.

Some fields of research have simply deserted the university by founding independent research institutions. Some disciplines have become schools where teaching is virtually the sole activity. In these circumstances, how long will it take for the latest research results to be incorporated into teaching? The government is anxious to reduce both the cost of the first degree and the time taken. Consequently, we have been faced with the following proposal: All students will have the opportunity to study for three years, fulfilling the constitutional requirement to provide higher education for all who qualify; following that, a small minority (say 5 percent) will have a chance to continue their education and engage in research; only those universities accommodating these students will be research universities.

My response is to say that this is to reinvent the nineteenth century university. We have no adequate criterion to select the privileged 5 percent. Furthermore, after 1985 the potential population of students will begin to fall quite sharply, and the sixty to seventy universities of the Federal Republic will have grave difficulty in maintaining enrollment. I have no answers to these problems, but we must recognize that they exist.

Political leaders often expect research results to emerge too quickly. Relevance is a magic word, one which we can all support, but who defines relevance? We cannot find those fields which are applicable to societal needs without exploring widely, and universities must often begin projects which do not initially appear relevant. We should also remember that there are fashions in research as in everything else, and many fashionable lines of inquiry will not yield the promised results. Finally, an increasing problem for research is growing academic unemployment. It is hard to persuade fresh doctoral graduates to undertake three to five years of research when they doubt if employment will be available at the end of it.

Certainly, many academics would recognize Grosse's predicament as closer to their own circumstances than, for example, Meijer's enviable experience with research funding at Linköping University. Rector Ikola of the University of Turku, in fact, expressed his surprise at how close the German situation was to that in Finland.

The Finnish government, he said, considers the most important function of the university to be teaching; opportunities in research have thus declined. We have already noted that nonresearch universities have been established in Britain, where they are called polytechnics; and similar institutions have long been part of the American scene, as well. However, British polytechnics do not neglect research any more than do American colleges, some of which tend to regard themselves as major research universities "in-the-making." The University of Wisconsin-Green Bay, though, has enjoyed considerable success not by aiming for international distinction in research, but rather by seeking and serving the local spectrum of investigative needs.

In considering the university's research role as well as its pedagogical function, Ikola expressed doubts about the wisdom of organizing to promote interdisciplinarity. He said that in Finland, as elsewhere in Europe, professors are the "kings" of their disciplines. Because the Ministry of Education wished to promote interdisciplinarity and problem orientation, the University of Turku organized around several large interdisciplinary departments such as foreign languages or biological science. The consequence has been that where there was once a king, there is now a council of professors, assistants, and students--resulting in more bureaucracy and less flexibility. Perhaps, Ikola suggested, it would be better if apparently unrelated disciplines just joined naturally together to tackle problems as they emerge. Disciplines could be maintained as organizational units, with cooperation between them promoted to enhance both instructional and research programs.

Interdisciplinary Research in Developing Countries

THE BIRLA INSTITUTE OF TECHNOLOGY AND SCIENCE

Perhaps one of the conference's most eloquent exponents of a new role for research was Chitta Mitra. Listed here is his summary of the concept of research at the Birla Institute since its formation from three rural colleges.

1. An alternative model and a new pedagogy can be discovered through innovations and experiments in intimate contact with the real world.

2. Educational structure must integrate all disciplines because real life does not recognize the codifications of knowledge made by men.

3. The foundation years must include components of
   mathematics, natural sciences, social sciences,
   languages, humanities, and professional and
   analytic skills.

4. Narrow, bookish specializations are to be avoided,
   and extreme alienation of academic research
   discouraged by continuous encounter with the real
   world.

5. The search for relevance can be institutionalized
   through critical involvement of the
   teacher/student teams outside the classroom where
   teachers and students educate one another through
   the mediation of the real world.

6. Voluntary involvement of a student in social
   service should earn academic credit irrespective
   of the degree for which he or she is enrolled.[9]

At the conference, Mitra described progress that had
been made at the Birla Institute towards achieving the
above goals:

Over the past decade, we have attempted to transform
the role of the university. We have done this in
part by defining a new role for research. Our university was formed by breaking away from a larger
university and began by being very traditional, very
discipline oriented. Our professors were kings
within their disciplines, and the characteristic
research mode was what Eric Ashby has described as
moving along the frontiers of knowledge with a hand
lens. We came to realize that we needed to define a
role for ourselves which we could fulfill within our
limited resources, which was suited to the region in
which we exist, and which was not already being
filled by others. Some of the areas we fixed upon
were (1) water resources in a sunny, arid zone;
(2) unconventional energy, especially solar energy
and biogas; (3) reuse of agricultural and industrial
waste; and (4) science, technology and development,
with special reference to our immediate surroundings.

Let me share with you some of the issues we
encountered. The government wanted solar energy
research. However, because this was research with
a clear social purpose, there were those who considered it too pedestrian, too lacking in intellectual content, for our university to become involved.
When we did become involved, we found that problems
in high physics were integral to the questions which
arose. I have to believe that it is frequently the

academic politicians who decry applied research.
Our experience has been that those people who had
been productive in narrowly defined conventional
disciplinary fields were unable to cope with applied
problems because they did not know enough. Those who
succeeded had a broad knowledge of their field and
were willing to accept unconventional challenges. It
is the latter quality, not the former, which universally distinguishes excellence among scientists.

Now there is a conventional viewpoint that the
dictation of research directions, thought to be inherent in much applied work, is inimical to academic
freedom. I suggest that this is a false distinction.
My doctoral work was supported by the United States
Atomic Energy Commission and was directed towards
liquid metal reactors. The purpose was training as
much as the production of new knowledge--training
with the goal of providing me with a passport into
research. And the usual thing would be for me to
continue my research on the same lines, producing a
few papers and several research studies each year.
Such is the common pattern. What, in fact, it
reduces to is that I took up the loose ends of somebody else's research where it had been left off. I
can see no reason why this cannot be done, equally
meaningfully, with regard to problems which emerge as
being of practical importance.

Let me further point out that there have always been
two aspects to research within the university. The
first has been the search for new knowledge, but the
second has been the codification of existing knowledge and has been geared to application. I would
suggest that in the United States in recent years
these two aspects have become unbalanced, with the
search for new knowledge given unwarranted
predominance. People should occasionally remember
that MIT was originally a strongly "applied" research
institute, and only in the last thirty years has it
emerged as a major instigator of "pure" research.

We have spoken often of the extension functions, of
taking science to the village. Now this can be
perceived as taking a particular piece of apparatus
into village schools and performing certain
illustrative experiments. That I would characterize
as the reactionary, unimaginative approach. The same
scientific principles can be expounded by developing
a curriculum and a pedagogy which is related to the
surrounding conditions of life. The village lives in
a situation where science is manifest. This fact is

not used when the university takes science to the
village. It always seems that the role of the outside world in our pluralistic society reduces to the
most sophisticated university work at one end and the
village at the other, with nothing in between. But
you can teach science in the village without import-
ing apparatus if you are sufficiently imaginative.
You can tackle such problems as how to devise a solar
device that can pump water without moving parts, made
as much as possible from local materials. And when
you do so, you face problems which are challenging in
terms of high science, not simply in terms of
relevance.

What is at issue here is not inadequate funding
levels; it is not even the essential infrastructure
of science itself. What is at issue is an attitude
of mind, a sense of social purpose. Consider two of
the scientific giants of our century--Fermi and Von
Neumann. Not only were they great physicists, but
great engineers, great managers, great improvisers.
The first nuclear pile was constructed in a disused
squash court! Von Neumann contributed game theory to
mathematics, which has achieved great significance in
management. What would such minds have made of the
problems of development, had these been the problems
which came to their attention? These are the ideals
which we should hold up to young scientists: not
simply the research results of these great men, but
their dedication and the sense of practical problems
to be solved which motivated their research.

In spite of all the money spent in the United States,
a new Einstein does not emerge every day, nor does a
new theory of evolution. Research goes on, but most
of it simply discovers that in this area, too, the
fundamental laws of nature apply. It does not
discover new hypotheses or establish new laws. In
those circumstances, we need not blindly follow the
developed nations. It seems to me almost criminal
that a nation which has sent a national abroad to
obtain an advanced degree should be expected to provide him with the cultural milieu he found abroad.
Rather, he himself must combine the ingenuity of the
German tradition, the innovation of the American
tradition, and the intellectual perseverance of the
British--instead of which so many return to the
developing countries and simply want the outward
paraphernalia and manifestations of these cultures
rather than their true strength.

Illustrating Dr. Mitra's concern for a practical,
creative synthesis of theory and action is the Practice

School Program at the Birla Institute. Its students of
engineering, technology, natural sciences, social
sciences, pharmacy, and languages--together with their
teachers--spend eight to ten months in practice school
stations in industries, research laboratories, teaching
establishments, and design organizations. Part of the
educational process is thus transferred from the classroom to the practical world, the time for this practice
made available by discarding certain conventional
courses. The resultant interflow of people and ideas has
had an impact on traditional courses and also, says
Mitra, on the attitudes of the students. They
demonstrate greater self-reliance, initiative, ability to
make decisions from insufficient data, and willingness to
adopt a global perspective.

The institute has also implemented master's programs
in science and technology development in India, as well
as in museum studies. The former program trains students
to analyze the development of science, to assess technology and the interactions of science and society, and
to disseminate relevant science information through the
popular media. Museum studies, on the other hand, represents an attempt by the institute's science and
technology museum to take the message of science directly
to the villages, to help people understand scientific
principles more readily and inexpensively through the
phenomena of everyday life.

THE AFRICAN UNIVERSITY

Ex Africa semper aliquid novi, said Pliny--out of
Africa, always something new. Certainly, that observation seems true of the emerging African university.
Treating "the African university" as a generality no
doubt leads to some distortion of the individual nature
of each institution. Nevertheless, there is a common
array of problems besetting Africa between the Sahara and
the Limpopo, problems instrumental in defining the
character of Africa's new universities. In the midst of
cultural plurality, nearly all Africans share in three
overwhelming problems--the need for rural development
within a framework of traditional societies, a colonial
heritage which has suppressed cultural autonomy to a
great extent, and the effects on colonial universities
that evolved from the insensitive and even obtuse trans-
plantation of European models to an alien environment.

In light of these problems, Vice Chancellor Mwanza
explained the present goals of the University of Zambia:

Because our initial thrust was to develop trained
manpower, our first emphasis was on teaching.
However, we have tried to develop research programs
which would address the need for applying scientific

knowledge to our country's problems. Now, in a developing country there are more priorities than we can possibly handle, and the problem is to find those that are most pressing and which provide the most promise of rapid solution. To compete for government funds against other priorities we must emphasize the contribution that we can make. The basic areas we have chosen are (1) curriculum development and educational research, not just for the university, but for the school system and for informal means of communication and mass education. Our goal here is to develop an educational system that is more compatible with our needs than that left to us by the colonial power, seeking methods that are cheap and which produce effective results; and (2) we have to collect and codify base-line data on things like demographics and material resources--to some, this might not seem appropriate for university research, but a primary need in Zambia is the assessment of national resources and devising the means for their exploitation. The main thrust of the nation's development must at present be in rural development and mining. But, of course, we cannot neglect human relationships and the manner in which human resources can be mobilized for the tasks of development.

We have to organize our research projects around interdisciplinary teams, both for expedience--the shortage of funds precludes much disciplinary research--and because of the nature of the problems being tackled. One fundamental task is to establish the relationship between an imported technology and the characteristics of the society in which it will be used. People do not realize what a large stock of knowledge exists that is currently not being applied for development purposes. A university in a developing country must apply itself to finding out how to use this stock of knowledge in specific situations. The development of Japan, Taiwan, and Korea has been largely funded by the application of scientific discoveries made elsewhere to the solution of technological problems. We must train people who are flexible enough to seek out and apply this knowledge. Do not misunderstand me, we do have fundamental research problems, but they are seldom the most important ones. The question is often not how to develop a plow suitable for Zambia, but how suitable can a plow already available in Japan be made for Zambian conditions.

In summary, lacking funds for basic research, we must devote the bulk of our time and our energy to teaching and applied research. In doing so, we must

maintain credibility with the government, which is
our primary funding agency, and that means obtaining
results. Finally, we must devise a curriculum which
produces graduates who will not only work in the
community, but who will live in the community
applying broadly-based skills which will have a
multiplier effect.

The University of Zambia has already made substantial
changes during its relatively short history.[10] It no
longer requires a Cambridge Higher School Certificate
(A-levels) for entry; this elimination of what, in
British parlance, is called the "Sixth Form" has
broadened the base for student recruitment. In addition,
the single-subject degree has been abolished; a degree
program consists of sixteen degree courses, which can be
broadly selected from a range of fields, thus enabling
students to defer as long as possible irrevocable commitment to a single program. University of Zambia students
have also been involved in community building:
constructing a medical center, cooperating in preventive
medicine programs, digging wells, and contributing to
public service through voluntary organizations.
    Despite these changes, however, Tembo[11] suggests that
the utilization of Zambia's university facilities by both
government and private industry has as yet been limited,
at the expense of the nation's development. There is a
need throughout Africa to integrate existing research
centers with appropriate university departments and
faculties, to achieve greater economy and a better mix of
pure and applied research. Furthermore, African universities need to assume the lead in research on the relationship between education and national development.[12]
    These, then, are the ends towards which African
universities are striving, and one notable example of
progress has been Ahmadu Bello University in Northern
Nigeria. Although the vice chancellor of Ahmadu Bello
was unable to accept his invitation to Wingspread, his
institution well exemplifies an African university in
which the healthy integration of research, instruction,
and development has been achieved.
    Even though Northern Nigeria has an area of 250,000
square miles and a current population of 50 million,
the region enjoyed relative neglect in colonial times.
Fairly remote, with a well-developed Islamic tradition,
it was a prime candidate for the British policy of
indirect rule. It is not a poor region, however, and at
independence and immediately after, it acquired great
political significance. More recently this area, along
with the rest of the nation, has experienced considerable
continued development greatly facilitated by its oil
wealth.

Zaria, in Northern Nigeria, was a political center of some significance when Ahmadu Bello University was founded there in 1962 by the amalgamation of four existing institutions.[13] The headquarters branch of the Nigerian College of Arts, Science, and Technology became the main campus, providing Faculties of Arts (including fine arts which represent a strong local tradition), a Faculty of Science, and a Faculty of Architecture (subsequently reorganized as Environmental Design to accommodate urban and regional planning, and building technology as well). Faculties of Education and Engineering also existed, and Social Sciences, Medicine, and Veterinary Medicine were soon added.

Also in Zaria ws the Institute of Administration, founded in the 1950s by the then government of Northern Nigeria to provide government and administrative personnel. This institute became the nucleus of the Faculties of Administration and of Law, providing programs in public administration, business administration, accounting, and international relations. The third institution in the merger was the Research Division of the Northern Nigerian Ministry of Agriculture, together with the Extension Liaison Service, both only 13 kilometers from Zaria in Samaru. Since colonial times, Samaru had been one of the best agricultural research stations in Africa, and it was undoubtedly a great advantage to the relationship between government research and the university that the 2 communities were so close. Fourth and finally, the Higher Muslim Studies Section at the School for Arabic Studies in Kano, 110 miles to the north of Zambia, became the Faculty of Arts and Islamic Studies, thus rooting the emergent university in the culture of the region. As a consequence of this merger, a vital and responsive new institution evolved, whose current enrollment of some 10,000 students makes it a major university by any nation's standard.

Two of the antecedent organizations were incorporated into Ahmadu Bello University with a substantial degree of autonomy; namely, the Institute of Administration and the Institute of Agricultural Research. They maintained their own governing bodies, with equal representation by government and the university. While teething troubles had to be expected, the arrangement with the Institute of Administration did provide essential links between education and government. Ultimately, the success of this arrangement led to a similarly constituent Institute of Agricultural Research.

It is possible in the space available here to recount only a few of Ahmadu Bello University's successes. In addition to professional and continuing education services to teachers, for example, the Institute of Education conducts and promotes research in all matters pertaining to education in the northern states. It is involved in the development of primary education curricula, both in English and in the vernacular; in the production of primary teaching materials, particularly on local topics and issues; in the testing of new curricula; and in assisting the states with the collection and evaluation of educational statistics.

As another example, The Institute of Agricultural Research, with its six field substations, has carried out formidable work on the development of irrigated and dry crops, for both cash and food. In this regard, it has been a center of truly international repute with studies on cattle, sheep, goats, and poultry currently underway. The institute, for instance, has shown that while indigenous cattle will not support a dairy industry, they are with proper care an adequate beef breed. The parameters of such care are now being determined, and the health and feeding requirements of exotic dairy breeds have also been delineated by institute researchers. Furthermore, this research division monitors pests and diseases for the extension service and technological assistance and information for Green Revolution-style accelerated crop production.

The Rural Economic Research Unit, another component of Ahmadu Bello's research activity, is making progress towards understanding area farmers' resistance to extension advice and has concluded that too often such advice, which is often based on the experience of the Temperate Zone's expatriate experts, neglects the good sense and traditional experience of the native farmer. For example, African farmers dislike monocropping, a practice generally advised for large-scale farming in developed nations; in their precarious climate, Africans prefer intercropping as insurance against the failure of any single crop. The research unit has found that mixing crops actually increases total yield per acre: While each individual crop yields less than it would if the same area were planted exclusively in that one crop, the total yield of the mixed crop is greater. Problems of sowing and weeding mixed crops, of course, are not as great in a hand-hoe agriculture as they would be in a mechanically-based system.[14]

This amalgamation of folk tradition with scientific data represents a rare instance of demonstrable economic achievement by the integration of social science with technical research. Through such open-minded research, Ahmadu Bello is thus producing a body of information and techniques to promote guided change in its nation, offering realistic hope for a breakthrough in the productivity of tropical agriculture and for other aspects of Nigeria's development as well.

UNIVERSITI SAINS MALAYSIA

Southeast Asia shares some of Africa's educational
problems, but differs significantly in several respects.
It shares a colonial past, urgent development needs, and
the necessity for cooperation between government and
national research institutes. It differs, though, in its
generally greater wealth of developed resources and in
its relative insouciance about the overproduction of educated manpower. Since other countries' experts can still
command premium salaries in Southeast Asia, a common
attitude holds that unfulfilled manpower needs exist and
that society can best be served if an abundance of
trained manpower drives down high salaries and reduces
employment differentials.

The University of Science of Malaysia (USM), founded
in 1969 as the second university in Malaysia, was man-
dated to provide, promote, and develop higher education
in the fields of natural science, applied science, phar-
maceutical science, building science and technology,
social science, humanities, and education. Its primary
research mission, however, is in applied science, which
is broadly defined to include such fields as building
technology, applied natural science, and pharmacy.
Hamdan Tahir, its vice chancellor, described the manner
in which research collaboration with the government and
the private sector is managed at USM:

Because we are a public university, we are expected
to assist the government. Our strategy is to concentrate on short-term research which promises
results in two years or less. We allocate small sums
of money to our lecturers and younger professors as
seed money. For example, one such project on the
chemistry of oil products began virtually as a hobby
of one of our professors, but ultimately developed to
such a degree that the government established a
research institute.

We have established a Center for Policy Research,
headed by a political scientist and assisted by two
other professors and a senior research officer.
This center stands outside the regular structure of
the university, and serves as a funnel whereby
requests for government help can be channeled to
schools within the university. As an example, they
were asked to look into the problems of drug abuse,
which involved cooperation with the police, customs,
and health authorities, among others. Much of the
information accumulated and examined was highly
confidential, but with the research falling under the
aegis of the center, we found the government had as
much faith in the university to maintain discretion

as it did in civil servants. Because of the
resources we have, such as the computer center, we
were able to monitor on a countrywide basis.

So, our approach to the organization of research has
essentially two facets: First, we provide seed
grants from State money for faculty; and second, we
use the center to channel funds for large-scale
projects with immediate practical implications.

Ong[15] describes the principles guiding research in
Malaysia as follows: (a) it should be applied in nature
and of direct relevance to national and social needs,
(b) teamwork should be encouraged to tap all relevant
expertise; and (c) an interdisciplinary approach should
usually be followed, best utilizing the system of schools
and maintaining a real-life attitude towards research.
Wherever possible, the choice of problems should be such
that the results can be directly used for the benefit of
society while at the same time increasing the supply of
trained manpower through the production of experienced
graduates.

So far, many of the research programs at the
University of Science of Malaysia relate to the exploitation of the natural resources of the country, such as
studies in the science and technology of rubber, of palm
oil extraction, in the utilization of solar energy, and
in the uses of tin. Much effort has been devoted to
close collaboration with agencies outside the university.
For instance, projects have involved the Economic
Planning Unit of the Prime Minister's Office, the
Ministry of Information, and the Penang local government,
as well as agencies in the private sector. It is
possible, too, for workers in research stations such as
the Rubber Research Institute of Malaysia and the
Malaysian Agriculture Research and Development Institute
to register for higher degrees; and if they do, super-
visors will be appointed both from the university and
from industry.

Graduate assistants at USM may receive limited
financial support from the university, but they rely too
on emoluments from contract research with the institutes.
The facilities of the university are also made available
to government and private research workers, and mutual
benefits result. During the long vacation, for example,
some undergraduates are given research employment and
paid from short-term research grants, grants meant for
projects likely to produce a positive return on effort
within a reasonably short period.

Such interaction among the university, government,
and industry has encouraged applied research in Malaysia.
As a consequence, in its short history of ten years the
University of Science of Malaysia has already been able

to help solve social problems, while at the same time
gaining credibility among outsiders and among the
university's own personnel. Its successful experience
may well provide an encouraging model for other new
universities.

The Role of the Humanities and Social Sciences

The discussion of research at Wingspread focused
primarily upon scientific research for two reasons. The
first is that developing nations stress research for
development; and rightly or wrongly, development is perceived as a largely scientific and technological process.
In relation to Africa, especially, attention to scientific research has taken precedence for a second reason:
lack of a unified cultural tradition. In Asia and Latin
America--just as in Europe--a fully-developed culture
exists, is studied, and provides a source of pride
requiring no justification. The situation is different
in Africa, however, not because an indigenous culture
does not exist, but because it has been less literary.
For this reason, and because African consciousness was
suppressed in the colonial period, the culture is studied
less, and the resulting absence of a cultural context is
felt acutely, as Zambia's Jacob Mwanza[16] has affirmed:

For the African university to fulfill its expected
role in our society, it must not concentrate only on
the techniques of training individuals for specific
jobs, but must concern itself with the development of
a student as a total person who, after graduation,
not only works but also lives and functions meaningfully in society. Hence, the active participation of
our university in Africa's struggle for cultural
revival and promotion becomes of crucial importance.
The concept of culture is not easy to define
precisely; but for our purpose, this will be
understood to mean "all those ways of thinking,
feeling, and behaving that are socially transmitted
from one generation to the next" in any society.
Agents of cultural transmission include all social
institutions such as the family, church, school, and
indeed the university. The African university must
overcome historical obstacles for it to contribute
meaningfully to cultural development. The majority
of these obstacles stem from the origins of most of
the African universities.

Most African universities were established during the
colonial period by either colonial masters or
colonial advisors whose conception of civilization
did not include the values of African societies. In
many cases, these pioneers of universities in Africa

did not accept the fact that Africans could have a civilization or that their values could be civilizing. The consequences of this situation for the university are well known. The cultural curriculum in the African universities was largely Western: Latin and Greek. And when it came to cultural performances, Shakespeare and Molière were invariably staged for their universal artistic merits as theatre.

I am not saying that foreign values should not be taught in our universities. What I am saying is that these values should not be taught on the claim that they, by virtue of being foreign to Africa, embody all that is worthy of being called civilization. They should be studied to complement the basic program of African culture. This is the greatest challenge to African universities today--to provide research and teaching programs that will produce deep knowledge and understanding of African culture. Such a stock of knowledge will provide a firm foundation for the revival and promotion of African culture and insulate it from total domination by foreign influences. I would now like to propose a number of ways in which I think the African universities can help in the preservation and promotion of African culture. They are:

1. Ensuring that the curriculum in the cultural fields is designed in such a way that it reflects the values of African society rather than those alien to it.

2. Helping to develop and improve knowledge of African people through research. (In this area, a start has already been made in many African universities. Our own Institute for African Studies is, for example, engaged in research on Zambian arts, languages, and music.)

3. Promoting the development of performing arts that reflect the values of, and are based in, African societies. (Here again, the University of Zambia has made a good start through its production of African-based plays normally staged at the Chikwakwa Theatre.)

4. Developing close social and cultural links with groups within the society.

Ki-Zerbo[17/18] gives many examples of the imposition of non-African cultural traditions upon African universities. He tells of students in an open-air class

in Ethiopia, for example, studying the digestive system
of the Bourgogne snail. He also cites cookery students
in West Africa required to prepare Sole Meunière as their
final examination; since the sole could not be found in
local lakes, it was flown in by jet from France. As
Ajayi[19] has pointed out, the need to make use of indigenous values and materials in African universities tran-
scends the question of the relevance of curricula. It
involves the whole issue of identity and continuity with
African traditions. A major task of future research must
be to record these traditions and examine them in a world
cultural perspective.

In another Wingspread discussion over research
priorities Iran's Chancellor Riahi maintained that
natural science must be emphasized over social science
because the social and behaviorial sciences have not yet
attained a level of predictive accuracy comparable to
that in the so-called "exact sciences:"

> I do not wish to be too hard on my colleagues in the
> social sciences, nor do I want to press the role of
> the natural sciences to the exclusion of the social
> sciences and humanities. But I must say that the
> methods of the social sciences do not give working
> answers. They view life retrospectively, describing
> what has occurred in the past, when we require causal
> definitions that will enable us to predict what will
> occur in the future.

> Clearly, nobody can disagree that in problem-oriented
> research the social sciences and the natural sciences
> must cooperate. However, we must have tools if we
> are to tackle problems effectively. The current
> tools of the social sciences have been primarily
> developed in the United States, and they simply do
> not seem to work well in Iran. A crucial need is to
> develop methodologies that will enable social scien-
> tists to examine effectively the context within which
> our problems are embedded.

However, Dr. Luykx of the Agency for International
Development suggested that the social sciences are not in
such bad shape as Chancellor Riahi suggests. Nicolaas
Luykx offered this cautiously optimistic view of social
science research in developing nations:

> The social sciences may be stumbling, but if you look
> closely, the natural sciences are stumbling also.
> Much work is going on in relating environmental con-
> cepts in the developing countries, but while one can
> go into a laboratory and experiment with chemicals,
> it is a little more difficult to experiment with an
> entire society. One has to develop simulations and

models, and test them adequately before too many
people get hurt.

There is a real problem of obtaining untainted data,
data that are not drawn from stereotypes. Remote
sensing holds promise for the development of
agriculture, and rank order methods may enable
sociologists to achieve the necessary measure of
quantitative certainty on the basis of early qualita-
tive data. Furthermore, certain kinds of cautious
social experimentations are going on. We have models
in Bangladesh. In Taiwan, Yugoslavia, Tanzania, Sri
Lanka, Israel, and elsewhere there have also been
attempts to organize societies in different ways for
social development. This kind of research in action
also produces data that can be used to influence
policy. Universities thus far have not effectively
linked themselves to these village experiments, nor
are they yet exploiting the network of remote sensing
stations for the purpose of generating data.

The programs of the universities discussed in the
preceding sections mirror Luykx's view of the vital role
which social science must play, especially in rural
development. The University of Wisconsin-Green Bay chose
as its focus Man and the Environment, in part because
this university sensed the need to complement America's
characteristically blithe technological optimism with an
element of social awareness. UWGB undertook as one of
its initial research studies, in fact, an investigation
of the social and economic impact of the university on
its own environment. Aalborg University Center in
Denmark also engaged in such a study, and other young
universities have conducted similar research in their
attempts both to serve and to be assimilated by their
social environments. At Nigeria's Ahmadu Bello
University researchers are convinced they have achieved a
breakthrough in extension service by beginning to understand the peasant's motivation in his reluctance to act
upon well-meant advice. Abelardo Samonte of the
Philippines pointed out that in his nation, for example,
simple adjustments in a traditional system of production
will almost always fail; success can be achieved only
when such adjustments are incorporated in a total system
which will replace the traditional system with little
social friction as possible. Clearly, social science
research must play a crucial role in this process in
whatever nation it occurs.

Rector Phasook of Thailand's Prince of Songkla
University expanded further on the university's need for
understanding and interaction--not only with the peasant

or urban worker, but with local government organizations
and industrial managers:

> Both in developed and developing countries, most
> research results stay in the journals and never get
> into practice. In the case of mission-oriented
> research, we must boldly consider the question of how
> long it will take for results to trickle down to the
> villages. And if the problem is difficult in the
> natural sciences, it is a great deal more difficult
> in the social sciences. A few years ago a consortium
> of universities in Thailand undertook a program of
> research on integrated rural development. This had
> much less effect than had been hoped because there
> was no connection between the researchers and local
> government. Without suggesting that the university
> can solve everything, I do think that ways should be
> sought to integrate the work of the university with
> local government and industry. Other people must be
> involved from the beginning. It is easy to see how
> local government might view a program of local
> development in which they are not involved as pri-
> marily disruptive of order rather than conducive to
> development.

Some Common Problems

Educators and others sometimes forget how recently
research has grown to the proportions of a national
enterprise. Eurich[20] points out that knowledge, once an
ornament of man and society, is now a meal ticket for one
and a charm against disaster for the other. He quotes
Peter Drucker as saying that, prior to the twentieth
century, to be educated meant to be unproductive, so no
society could afford too many educated men. Suddenly, we
find that the rate of growth of our societies hinges on
the number of highly-trained scientists, engineers, and
technicians we can produce. The upper class of the
future, said Drucker, might well be called the
"doctocracy."

At Wingspread, as elsewhere, the common perception
was that the economic hegemony of the United States
resulted from its research activities and from the active
solicitation and utilization of research by industry.
The extent to which the university, and especially university research, has contributed to this process can be
overstated. Nevertheless, the growth of management as a
science, for example, or the recent development of high-
technology companies to exploit advances in electronics
and genetic engineering are but two examples of the very
real role the universities have played. It is probable
that the people educated in universities are more
important to technical innovation than is the actual

168

research conducted at universities. It is also true that
major advances in research have been made by people who
have had minimal contact with the academic world.
Nevertheless, the research university remains the single
institution assuring a continuous supply of competent
scientists and engineers, and acting to absorb technical
advances--wherever made--into the educational process.

Research conducted at the university is important to
the institution itself for three reasons. First, it is
necessary to inform and enhance the instructional
process. University teachers are no exception to the
rule that people do not understand well, or retain long,
knowledge that they do not use. Second, research
activity maintains a problem orientation and retains
education's connections with the world of work. No doubt
there are other ways in which this could be done: shared
appointments with industry or government is one; sabbaticals in industry or government is another. Nevertheless,
research (including the consultancies usually associated
with research) remains overwhelmingly the principal
mechanism whereby university personnel keep intellectually abreast of developments in their chosen fields.
Third, the reputation of a university depends in large
degree on the research production of its faculty. While
many educators deplore this traditional yardstick,
suggesting forcibly that devotion to research detracts
from an institution's teaching role, it remains true that
this criterion is universally applied.

A major problem for many of the universities
represented at Wingspread is the appropriate definition
of their research role. The problem was frequently
described as a conflict between so-called "basic" and
"applied" research, but just as frequently speakers
denied the existence of such a distinction. The real
dichotomy seems between "big, expensive science" and
"small, cheap science." Few, if any, universities in the
Third World, for example, can afford to get involved in
nuclear physics. Even if the money were available, such
research would be too far removed from the immediate
needs of their societies. Similarly, many innovating
universities in the developed world are precluded from
involvement in "big science;" that is, in such sophisticated research fields as nuclear physics and much of
molecular biology. Although they are in positions to
provide the necessary research infrastructure that has
evolved in older centers of excellence, they would be
false to their founding if they did so, and there is
little demand for more university expansion into these
research fields anyway.

Consequently, the innovating universities are seeking
research roles suited to their situations and to their
missions. If they succeed, real scientific advances may
result, for originality is not the exclusive preserve of

the big battalions. Meanwhile, such institutions are
struggling with a professoriate primarily educated in
major Western universities who have problems accepting a
role in which "pure" research is not pre-eminent. From
the perspective of a developing nation, Adnan Badran of
Jordan explained:

> Frequently, in developing countries, the universities
> have failed to address themselves to the social and
> economic development of the country and have failed
> to carry out mission-oriented research. They are
> left without funds by the government because the
> government is not interested in the type of academic
> research the university wishes to undertake. To
> remedy this, the university must become more policy
> oriented.

> I find it difficult to make the distinction between
> basic and applied research because so many basic
> problems arise in applied research, and so much basic
> research ultimately becomes applied. But a balance
> must be struck between basic and problem-oriented
> research which enables them to be carried out
> together and directed towards the development needs
> of the country. One problem is that many univer-
> sities are employing their professors as full-time
> teachers. Greater flexibility is needed in the
> assignment of professors so that some can be assigned
> to a quarter, a half, or even full time to research.
> But the situation where promotions depend on the
> publication of basic research in established journals
> is not appropriate to developing countries. We must
> cease to look down on publications in local journals.

> Another problem is that when people are sent abroad
> for training, they work on basic research problems.
> When they return, they request facilities and funding
> to continue this type of work, and if they do not get
> it, they threaten to leave. In developing countries
> we are just not able to afford it. In basic research
> the best we can do is develop one or, at most, a few
> lines of research. For example, concentrate on solid
> state physics and put all our funding into that.
> Researchers would then have to conform to the line of
> research for which funding was available. However,
> the priorities of the university must be dictated by
> their economic resources, and mission-oriented
> research must have first claim.

> Interdisciplinary or group research is very important
> for mission-oriented research. We also need to
> establish relationships with universities in the
> developed countries. For example, we have

established a relationship with Georgia Tech, a
university which we feel has passed through the same
stages of development that we must pass through. We
can send our professors there to carry out research
for which we cannot provide facilities.

Several problems are evident here. There is the
difficulty of funding--of providing young professors with
time away from teaching. There is also the problem of
defining and fulfilling a role--of satisfying the professor with his own work at his own institution. Most
countries want the best training for their people; and
while they may be able to afford to send them to the very
best institutions overseas to get such training, they
cannot later support these returning faculty members in
the manner to which they have become accustomed.
Consequent dissatisfaction can lead either to unproductive research or to the emigration of talented personnel.
Malaysia's Hamdan Tahir elaborated on this unfortunate
paradox:

Many faculty returning from abroad want to teach at
the level they learned abroad. In their training,
they simply do not learn how to make what they teach
effective. Now, they are going overseas with
taxpayers' money and they have a responsibility to
return and make that expense worthwhile.

We may be obliged to teach our teachers how to teach
in addition to mastery of their subjects, and we must
make people more responsive to the needs of
administration. As they move from lecturer to
assistant professor and so on up the ladder, they
must realize that each promotion entails certain
additional responsibilities for originality and
leadership. In particular, they should become more
aware of the theme in the country itself. They must
be conscious of the political and socio-economic
situation within which they work and must be prepared
to adapt to that situation.

Chitta Mitra of the Birla Institute acknowledged similar
problems:

There are two projects in engineering in India that
involve MIT. One is with a consortium of nine universities in Kanpur; the other is with my institution alone. Our greatest disappointment with these
projects was that while we could find people willing
to go to MIT to be trained in solid state physics,
on their return they were not willing to undertake
the task of properly organizing a laboratory or
creating an infrastructure in which solid state

physics could be pursued. They became the most
resistant to change of all faculty. An embarrassing
fact was pointed out to me by the president of MIT:
It was easier for me to get together with my
colleagues from Kanpur in Boston than it was in
India.

We must learn to respect plurality. I am certain
that there are important innovations at MIT, but we
must also recognize that there are innovations of a
different kind for a different purpose in other parts
of the world. We must foster more interinstitutional
respect.

Mitra went on to address the problem of acceptance
standards, disagreements about which frequently impede
academic innovations. He suggested that we will not be
able to devise satisfactory instruments for judging the
products of research. It is very difficult to decide
immediately whether a particular project has been successful and worthwhile because the overwhelming majority
of research does not lead to wholesale breakthroughs
either in knowledge or technology. Perhaps it is better
to develop indicators which judge the process, assessing
not only the problem but also the way it has been
tackled. Mitra has in mind here overcoming the poor
image some scientists harbor of strictly practical
pursuits--"science in the village," so to speak. No
innovative institution can be successful, he said, unless
we create instruments to judge the inner logic of the
pursuit of excellence and the pursuit of scholarship, no
matter what the particular circumstances of their
external manifestation.
The need for interinstitutional respect for diverse
research roles is as great in the developed world as
elsewhere. Plurality of institutions is ultimately a
source of strength, not weakness; and plurality is
perhaps easier to achieve if there are multiple sources
of research support. Dependence on government funding is
to be expected in developing nations; but the research
enterprise can be greatly strengthened, as has been noted
in the case of Malaysia's Universiti Sains, by culti-
vating other sources. In the developed world as well,
except for the few major research universities, future
government support will be limited; furthermore, local
problems can often be approached best through local
financial support. A fine example is provided by the
University of the Andes in Colombia, as described by
Rector Muñoz:

The University of the Andes was established primarily
as a research university, and we do 78 percent of all

the research being done by private institutions in
Colombia. We do many kinds of research--much of it
problem oriented. We have done fundamental work in
the areas of health, of administration, of politics,
and on the organization and administration of justice
in our country. We also do other kinds of research
which is proposed to us by members of the faculty,
proposals which we send to the Ministry of Education
for funding if we find them appropriate. We do have
a small amount of our own funds available as seed
money, but much of our research is financed by private enterprise, to whom we propose research projects
which might be of interest. In fact, some of our
faculties, such as economics and administration, are
almost research institutes in their own right. In
these cases, faculty and students work together on
research projects. We find intense involvement in
research by students, and great benefit to them from
such involvement. We are now trying to form a committee that will bring together industry and government to provide large sums so that all universities
can benefit from research activity.

On the other hand, the Latin American Development
Bank, both a producer and consumer of research, had difficulty in eliciting fundable projects from academics,
according to the Inter-American Development Bank's
Francisco Thoumi. The bank requires that research have a
direct policy or project content, and Thoumi said he has
seen no such project that would not be funded. So the
apparent shortage of research funds for some institutions
may simply reflect a lack of research projects directed
towards fundable goals.
Research projects of this kind will frequently be
strengthened if they are integrated with extension, and
many speakers at the conference insisted upon this as a
desirable goal. Abelardo Samonte of the Philippines continually stressed the need for applied research projects
to incorporate into their planning stages those who were
responsible for implementing the results. H.R. Arakeri
of India also insisted that the alliance among research,
extension, and instruction is essential. Without
extension, he said, research is likely to cease to be
problem oriented and become instead highly theoretical;
constant feedback from the field is essential.
Rector Phasook made a similar point with respect to
research in Thailand. In fact, he suggested that
problem-oriented education and mission-oriented research,
blended with extension services, are two faces of the
same coin. And, as Arakeri also pointed out, the benefits to the undergraduate teaching program are manifold.
In the presence of an active research program, undergraduates will have specialists as teachers who are

likely to kindle in the students an interest in inquiry; and by being better informed, the teachers will be likely to bring more knowledge to the attention of their classes.

There are two additional problems with mission-oriented research, though. Chancellor Riahi pointed out that while we can all agree that the university has a bona fide research role in seeking solutions to problems of immediate practical importance, there is also a real need for serious research to define what is, in fact, important. Even in the health fields, he suggested, it is not at all clear which problems should be confronted immediately; discussions on such matters are important, not simply in determining research directions but also in developing the curriculum.

A second problem is that, although the results of research on practical problems are not readily publishable, publications are a widely acknowledge criterion of faculty merit. In part, Mitra was addressing this problem when he spoke of judging the process, not merely the result. In some developing nations, too, journals in which to publish results are scarce. Thompson and Fogel,[21] as well as Yesufu,[22] have discussed these problems in detail. Simply put, there is a need for suitable local publications and other mechanisms to complement the role of revered international journals in disseminating research results of greater than local interest. Otherwise, too many human and fiscal resources may be depleted in the continual reinvention of the wheel under the guise of innovative, problem-focused research.

12
The Management of Innovation

Several themes recurred throughout the debate at the conference. Perhaps the most significant was the need for the university to demonstrate fidelity to the national purpose and to the indigenous culture. Such fidelity may, of course, lead to unique institutions, quite unlike Western models. In the Third World, for example, where national purpose is readily identified as development, the university is expected to impel that activity; it becomes, therefore, the development university. On the other hand, although in Western Europe and North America higher education may be more firmly established as part of the socio-cultural scene, it is still expected to serve the nation by educating the young and conducting research appropriate to the national purpose.

A second theme reiterated at Wingspread was the need for educational diversity, both among nations and within any single nation. Clearly, service to effect development presupposes that systems of education will differ radically among nations. But even within a nation, higher education must serve a variety of constituencies and fulfill a range of responsibilities. Equality of access inherently imposes variety on the form of institutions. Furthermore, it is likely that within a nation, each university will strike its own balance among the competing--yet complementary--roles of instruction, research, and service. James Perkins of the International Council for Educational Development underscored this second theme:

It is vital to undertake planning with a view to maintaining diversity. Otherwise, there is a very real tendency for universities simply to copy established models. For example, in Britain a major problem is to ensure that the new universities do not simply become pale imitations of Oxford and Cambridge. Diversity must be planned with care, and

new innovations require new styles of management.
What is important is that each country develop a
management system which will protect the autonomy of
the university while ensuring diversity and service
to the national purpose.

There are two fundamental reasons why the world's
educators must expect and foster a diversity of
institutions. The first stems from the need to provide
educational services for an increasingly larger cross-
section of society as we strive for equality of
opportunity. The second reason is simply that particular
educational needs differ, both among individual societies
and among the various social settings within a given
society. The first reason, in particular, was addressed
by Claudio Gutierrez, rector of the University of Costa
Rica:

> The problem of unequal opportunity versus unequal
> talent forces diversity upon us. Each national
> system must diversify itself if it is to offer equal
> opportunity to unequally or differentially talented
> young people. There are perhaps three aspects of
> such diversity: (1) diversity as to professional
> fields. Such diversity will, if well designed, also
> begin to address effectively the needs of social
> relevance. (2) diversity of geographical location,
> secured either by decentralizing large existing
> institutions or integrating several smaller separate
> institutions; and (3) diversity of levels.
> Opportunities should be presented for early
> graduation.

This belief in diversity as a means of broadening
opportunity is widespread; it has, for instance, long
been an informal feature of American education. Major
private universities, prestigious liberal arts colleges,
State "flagship" institutions, State colleges, two-year
colleges, and technical colleges all co-exist in an
unspoken, but nevertheless real, hierarchy of
opportunity. It is, of course, a hierarchy with considerable opportunity for both student and faculty
mobility. The able two-year college student, for
example, proceeds to complete a distinguished degree at
the State university and then secures admission to the
Harvard Business School. Diversity is also becoming a
characteristic of British education with the advent of
polytechnics and the Open University. Certainly the
principle has motivated recent changes in Swedish
education, too, and it permeates the philosophies of
Vincennes and Aalborg.
A particular technique for encouraging diversity of
purpose within an institution is the adoption of some

variant of the American credit system. We have seen
earlier, for example, that this enables Vincennes to
serve both its regular students and its many clients not
seeking degrees. Similarly, both the Open University and
Everyman's have adopted a system of courses or credits.
By dividing the curriculum into bite-sized chunks, these
institutions free themselves and their students to
assemble those pieces in a variety of ways--a system
which itself contributes to diversity. Furthermore, the
credit approach permits qualified people to study single
courses, to acquire elements of knowledge needed for
individual advancement or professional development--an
option contributing to continuing education and community
service, as well as to interinstitutional mobility.
Finally, the credit system leads to greater equality of
opportunity, for it makes no sense to apply restrictive
admission standards to people taking only one or two
courses. Nor does it make sense to deny those who successfully complete one or two courses the chance to
complete a full degree. Self-selection, then, inevitably
substitutes for imposed standards.

Equality of opportunity is not a universally prime
concern, though, as Zambia's Jacob Mwanza pointed out:

> While we acknowledge the demand for equal opportunity
> in the developing nations, we cannot achieve it
> because of limited resources. Consequently, the
> problem of relevance to societal needs becomes even
> more important. Since we can only produce a few
> graduates, to what extent can we ensure that these
> few will be effective in meeting the needs of our
> society?

This attitude seems to suggest a gulf between
developing and developed nations' goals; as the former
grapple with the tandem problems of development and scar-
city of trained manpower, the latter are bedeviled by an
overproduction of graduates for which professional opportunities are unavailable. Certainly this interpretation
was inherent in the advice of Pierre Merlin from
Vincennes:

> In considering the function of the university in
> training manpower for social needs, we must distin-
> guish between the developed and developing countries.
> In the developing countries there may, indeed, be a
> shortage of trained manpower which the university
> needs to rectify. However, in the developed
> countries we have difficulty in finding jobs for the
> people who are already trained. In developed
> countries, should our response be to restrict entry
> to those people for whom jobs will be available, or
> do we have a wider responsibility? Should we

concentrate on developing the modern citizen? The
needs of developing countries are economic, and consequently the university can receive priority in the
allocation of funds. In the developed countries,
however, the needs are social; and the university
cannot receive the same priority. If the university
wants to play a role in the development of society,
it must give evidence that it is a social force. It
must make a choice. Either it delivers professional
education to the numbers of people dictated by the
market available for their services, or it uses the
cultural model, where it educates citizens with no
guarantee that they will receive a highly paid job,
but who are nonetheless capable of adapting to the
changing system of values in their society.

Despite the fact that per capita degree production in
the United States is much greater than in Europe, even
the most pessimistic forecasts suggest only about a
5 percent excess production of U.S. graduates. On the
other hand, both India and Latin America suffer from
large numbers of graduates for whom the promise of
employment using their skills is only a dream. One
possible inference from these situations is that the
problem is more likely one of failing to fit education to
needs rather than of simply overproducing graduates.
Nothing worthwhile can be achieved without careful
planning, and the need for such planning in higher education represents a third theme that emerged at Wingspread.
Claudio Gutierrez affirmed this attitude:

Whether it be funds or other aspects, a lot of
planning is required. And governments and foundations prefer to provide funds in response to
well-integrated five-year plans, rather than to
uncoordinated annual budgets of individual
institutions. In Costa Rica we have found that
planning is more effective if institutional planning
offices are dismantled and planning becomes a function of a single national office. We have found that
it is easier to get consensus on a single five-year
plan, rather than to coordinate separate plans which
have been prepared by individual institutions.

This view was enthusiastically supported, with
important qualifications, by Eduardo Gonzalez-Reyes of
the Organization of American States:

The first requirement for innovation is to conduct
research and discover where the needs for innovation
exist and what kinds of innovation need to be
undertaken. This is always very difficult. For
example, when I came to a planning post in Venezuela,

I found that there was little or no tradition of
planning. Even in the United States the ability to
plan is quite limited. It is necessary for each
country to specify precisely what it hopes to achieve
and then to plan innovation to meet those objectives,
even though the objectives might be quite limited in
scope.

At one extreme we have the type of planning that I
observed in Czechoslovakia, which is very precise.
On asking what would happen if the plan needed to be
changed because of some erroneous assumptions or the
like, the response was that we do not make mistakes.
Truly that is superhuman planning. On the other
hand, we have the situation where we proceed with
innovation without any kind of planning whatsoever,
and the results are catastrophic. The Organization
of American States has requested all Latin American
states to produce educational plans, and the majority
have now done so. But, of course, it is not enough
simply to have a plan. You must also have people who
understand the plan, and people with the will and
ability to carry it out.

Finding the right people to carry out a plan,
especially a five-year plan, can be difficult. Faculty
members tend to be conditioned to a concept of
individual, rather than collective, innovation. It goes
against the grain of many to commit themselves to an
extended enterprise in which opportunities for self-
directed innovations may be limited. Paradoxically,
though, this same stubborn individuality and independence
of the faculty is a vital safeguard of the academic
diversity so highly prized. Therefore, while it should
be possible to seek interdisciplinarity without abandon-
ing discipline, responsibility without losing
spontaneity, respectability without conformity, depend-
ability without dependence--it will never be easy.
Perhaps a combination of patience and the ability to
seize fleeting opportunities for change is one of the
hallmarks of successful innovation. Chitta Mitra drama-
tizes this delicate balance through his experience at the
Birla Institute of Technology:

Ten years ago when we started on curriculum reform,
we rapidly developed expressions of resentment which
blamed the bureaucracy and the pigheadedness of the
departments for all the difficulties experienced. A
vocal minority wanted to abolish departments while
the majority favored a less cataclysmic approach.
However, as the core curriculum became strengthened
the departmental hegemony weakened, and it was
further weakened by the development of

180

interdisciplinary research projects. Departments
began to merge. Then after about five years the
government came up with a new salary structure for
universities. Now, of course, this did not automati-
cally apply to us because we are a private
institution. Nevertheless, the Board of Trustees
decided to implement it, and I was told to recast the
budget and come up with the necessary money. I
appointed a committee of faculty and staff, which
debated for three months and finally reached the
conclusion that we should restructure the university,
abolish departments, freeze positions freed up
thereby, and hence come up with the necessary money.
End of battle.

Now we were able, with substantial support, to
abolish departments while retaining necessary elements of collegiality. We established a Division of
Teaching, a Division of Research, a Division of
Registration and Counseling (ten divisions in all) to
replace the former organizational structure. Faculty
and students were given the choice to stay in their
old faculties or join the new divisions. Most opted
for the new structure.

Change requires consent, and we must face the fact
that no organization is ever fully ready for change,
any more than a nation can be fully ready for
independence. We must develop a strategy for change.
Personally, I have noticed that too often change is
initiated rapidly in response to a categorical
imperative or an ideological impulse. Too often this
results in taking ten steps forward but eleven steps
back. More useful is change that is the result of an
empirical process consisting of a sequence of
increments, each small in itself. The optimum
process is to exploit these incremental changes,
advancing simultaneously on all fronts in an integrated way by tiny but irreversible steps. We must
examine our paths for the future in the light of our
ambitions, but always bearing in mind the capabilities of the present.

In striving for change, we cannot ignore man, his
heritage, and his environment. This is especially
true for us of the Third World, who are sometimes
tempted to import new models wholesale. Our disappointment when they do not work is akin to that of
a man who imports a beautiful foreign car and then
castigates the government for failing to provide an
adequate road system for him to drive on. Just
because there is teacher evaluation in the United
States does not mean that we must adopt it. Nor can

we innovate simply by buying equipment. We must ask
of any innovative process whether it makes our people
the object or the subject of change. Is their self-
confidence and self-sufficiency improved? Can these
things be improved if they do not participate in the
process? And remember, participatory democracy is
not simply voting and then going to sleep for another
five years. It is a participation in which dialogue
occurs, and it can even take place in an undemocratic
society.

We make a serious mistake if we think that knowledge
is absolute and immutable. It is culture-bound and
may not be the same in one culture as in another.
The essential thing is that knowledge be associated
with both theory and practice, with practice testing
theory and theory validating practice. Advance in
such a situation occurs in measurable quantum steps.
Above all, let us not be trapped into simply adopting
models from abroad, or even from other universities
in our own culture. We are enablers, not purveyors.
A purveyor simply accumulates knowledge and doles it
out as a consultant. An enabler transmits knowledge,
until the recipient is able to act for himself.

This is an experienced academic administrator's
eloquent statement of faith in the process of change
itself. Mitra is saying, in effect, that we must keep a
clear vision of the future without allowing it to become
a sterile, static vision. Nevertheless, we must not be
impractical; we must take into account the circumstances
within which we function, the needs of those we must
lead. We must seize opportunities more often than we are
able to make them, while continuing to do both. Above
all, we must not expect to achieve our vision overnight.
If it materializes at all, it will do so only as a consequence of a series of carefully managed steps--often
painful, sometimes imperceptible, and essentially
irreversible.

Bu-Ali Sina University, Iran and Aalborg University Center, Denmark

Two noteworthy examples of universities that
deliberately set out to solve challenging management
problems are Bu-Ali Sina University in Iran and Aalborg
University Center in Denmark. They provide instructive
comparisons for several reasons. Both are new
institutions--the former in a developing country, the
latter in a developed nation; and while Aalborg incorporated a number of existing institutions, Bu-Ali Sina
did not.

According to Chancellor Riahi,[1] Bu-Ali Sina University encountered five main organizational problems: (1) recruiting staff; (2) attracting students; (3) establishing clear-cut relationships among instructional, research, and community outreach; (4) gaining recognition from other universities; and (5) designing a suitable promotion and evaluation system for personnel.

The problems of personnel recruitment were central. "We did not have time within the deadlines set by government," said Chancellor Riahi, "to recruit a staff wholly sympathetic to the goals of the institution. Instead, we had to choose among those Iranians educated abroad who were willing to participate in the experiment, and many of them were partly or totally lacking in feeling for the rural area and were consequently reluctant to spend time with students in the villages, as called for by our curriculum. Considerable time and effort were necessary to reorient and reeducate staff." To recruit teachers and researchers interested in its program, Bu-Ali Sina arranged exchanges with other national and foreign universities.

In response to its second challenge, the university hoped to appeal to students from rural backgrounds and from relatively low socio-economic groups, both by giving them priority in selection and by allowing alternation of work and training cycles. It also offered the hope of jobs, first by securing from the government guarantees of appropriate employment in the public sector for graduates, and also by cooperating with the government to establish regional service networks to provide jobs for graduates.

Like most other innovative universities represented at Wingspread, Bu-Ali Sina experienced its greatest difficulty in formalizing the relationships among its instructional, research, and community outreach roles. "We have not been able to develop a clear-cut idea of the interrelationship," said Riahi. "We have organized the university not into disciplines, but into clusters among which we have attempted to distribute the disciplines. But we lack a skilled administrative backbone that will make such a structure successful and truly interdisciplinary."

"Another problem," he continued, "has been our failure to obtain proper recognition by the existing Iranian universities, which are quite conventional in nature. I have no idea how to overcome this resistance and establish fair and friendly contacts based on mutual respect."

Establishing a system of faculty rewards was the final element in Bu-Ali Sina's management challenge. "We have not been able to work out a suitable staff promotion and evaluation system," said Chancellor Riahi. "The traditional arrangement of the assistant professor serving a probationary period prior to receiving tenure as an associate professor, and ultimately becoming a full professor, is not suitable to our situation; but what alternatives exist? At present in our university everybody is either a lecturer or a professor, existing in an uncertain and ill-defined relationship, one with another." Thus while Bu-Ali Sina's management problems were considerable, careful planning helped the university confront its circumstances realistically from the start.

The Aalborg University Center faced somewhat different management challenges in its North Jutland setting, a relatively underdeveloped area of Denmark. In spite of the fact that North Jutland is one of the most populous regions of the country, it has long been characterized by an above-average level of unemployment and a net out-migration of population. It has also exhibited a lower recruitment level of students into higher education than have other areas of Denmark. Consequently, there was appreciable local enthusiasm in North Jutland for the establishment of a new university.

Christensen and Sverdrup-Jensen[2] have described the steps leading to Aalborg's establishment, its structure, and its effects on the region's economy. The law founding the university was passed in 1970, with the provision that it should open in 1974-75. It was termed a University Center, rather than a university, to distinguish its broader than usual mission. Aalborg was intended to incorporate all levels of study from bachelor's to doctoral work and also to include such courses as business administration, engineering, and social work, traditionally taught in Denmark's nonuniversity institutions. It was also expected to accommodate increased enrollments resulting from a generally expanding population and particularly from an increase in the proportion of young people electing a college education.

In addition, plans dictated that Aalborg incorporate a number of other centers of higher education already existing in North Jutland. These were two technical colleges, a school of economics and business, a school of social work, a teacher-training college, a library school, and an academy of music. Consequently, most of the faculty for the new institution would come from these existing sources, and new recruitment would thus be limited. The faculty, as a result, were not uniformly committed to educational experimentation, were familiar with disparate salary structures, and held differing commitments to research and teaching. In actual practice, the teacher-training college was not incorporated into the new center, a condition that severely limited development in the humanities. Nevertheless, temporary faculty exchanges with other institutions have been effected, both to bring in interested scholars and to facilitate the absorption of faculty members inherited from other institutions.

Another of Aalborg's challenges was effective planning of its curriculum to fulfill its academic mission. Aalborg's curriculum was designed to incorporate the concept of a one-year, problem-oriented basic training course prior to subsequent specialization. Four such courses were initiated in languages, art and aesthetics, social studies, and technology, respectively. Figure 1.1 depicts the underlying structure of Aalborg's degree program.

Figure 1.2 encapsulates the broad array of studies possible at Aalborg, requiring various commitments of time and leading to different professional qualifications. The overview also characterizes an approach to interdisciplinarity and problem focus through common foundation courses, an unusual variation within the continental European tradition. Interdisciplinarity is also demonstrated in the nine research institutes which have been established at Aalborg; again, the institutes' relationships with the traditional faculties are neatly conveyed in Figure 1.2.

Yet for all the technical glitter of the Aalborg program, its intention is not solely to train people for employment. As Rector Caspersen said at Wingspread:

> In Denmark we believe that our educational purpose is not simply to improve the individual skills and possibilities of the citizen's working life, but also of his family life, his leisure life, and his life as a member of society. We should take more seriously Dr. Kleinjans' injunction that we should seek in education to find something to live for and not just something to live with.

There have, of course, been problems at this new institution. While prior to the university's establishment there was intense local involvement, once formal planning began local people were not included in the process. However, Christensen and Sverdrup-Jensen clearly document the Aalborg Center's beneficial effects on the local economy, on population and emigration, and on the proportion of North Jutland youth attending college. Although some failures commonly associated with locally-oriented research projects have been experienced, the knowledge thus gained will certainly inform and strengthen future projects. In general, the picture at Aalborg is one of an institution rising to greater visibility as its initial difficulties are overcome and assimilated.

In conclusion, striking similarities characterize the thinking behind Aalborg and Bu-Ali Sina, despite the

185

Figure 1.1
Aalborg University Center, Training Program 1978
(after Christensen and Sverdrup-Jensen)

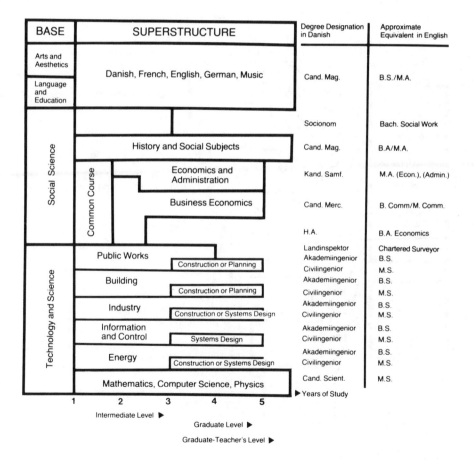

186

Figure 1.2
Research Institutes at Aalborg (after Christensen and Sverdrup-Jensen)

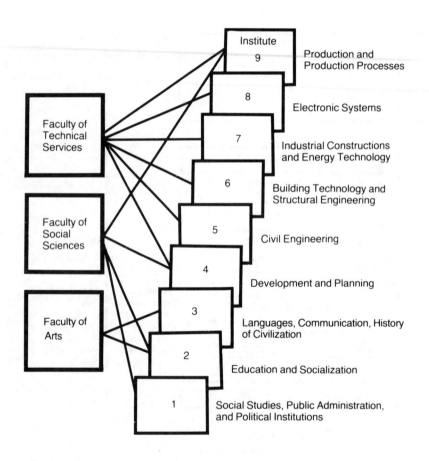

obvious differences between the societies they serve.
Both institutions, for instance, are consciously development oriented.   Perhaps Aalborg had an advantage in that
its region's problems are more easily identified through
research than were the problems Bu-Ali Sina confronted;
but both institutions committed themselves to interdisciplinary research and teaching, and both established
courses of varied lengths to satisfy different needs and
purposes.   Both institutions, furthermore, attempted to
identify and ameliorate local problems, each in its own
way. And finally, both experienced the teething problems
typical of any new university in the recruitment of
faculty and students in the quest for local and official
recognition, and in the identification of its appropriate
responsibilities and roles.   While in many respects
Aalborg and Bu-Ali Sina differed significantly, they
nevertheless illustrate two similar attitudes toward
institutional management, integrating the principles of
diversity and sensible planning as roads toward
innovation.

Soon after the Wingspread conference, revolution
broke out in Iran.   Bu-Ali Sina University ceased to
exist in the form which Riahi describes. He is no longer
associated with the university, and indeed has suffered
personal hardship because of his past association with
the university.   Riahi, and the university he
represented, were prime movers in developing the conference and in lending it vitality.   The suggestion that
managing change was difficult and even perilous was often
made at Wingspread. Few would have dreamed that the personal consequences could be as sad as they proved to be
for Farhad Riahi.   But had he been content to quietly
pursue his chosen field of physics at Tehran University,
his life and career would have been a great deal more
secure.   Hence, we have dedicated this book to him, a
brave man who gave everything he had for the ideals that
inspired it.

13
New Challenges,
New Responsibilities

The world of higher education has changed radically
in the last quarter of a century. The idea of the university as a major contributor to national purpose, which
first came to the fore in Britain and in the United
States during the Second World War, has since become
universal. Undoubtedly, universities have since their
inception been important components of society, both in
educating the young and in expanding the frontiers of
knowledge. But traditionally they held themselves apart
from the world of affairs. They tended to be quiet
havens of thought rather than launching pads for action.
The contribution the university made to the war effort,
from deciphering codes to developing the Manhattan
Project ended its relative isolation. Economic,
political, and demographic changes all over the world
since the war have pushed and pulled it into a larger
arena.

Current professional and public comment tends to
emphasize the troubles higher education is experiencing.
The picture presented is one of retrenchment in the face
of declining enrollments, of a return to basics in
response to falling student achievement, of declining
budgets, of disenchantment with the experiments of the
1960s and 1970s, of the students' rejection of liberal
learning in favor of a narrow career focus. No one at
Wingspread made light of such ills. Educators throughout
the world are aware of the problems they face.

Inevitably, the participants at Wingspread took a
positive view of the changes to which they have devoted
their careers. Any account of the proceedings is bound
to reflect this positive attitude, and reflect to an
uncomfortable degree criticisms which may justly be
leveled at many of the consequences of innovation. This
is an upbeat account of education produced at a time
when it is more fashionable to accentuate the downside.
But the conference showed that the lively experimentation
of the last two decades has not been fruitless.

Some innovations, undoubtedly, have fallen by the
wayside. Indeed, some of the universities described in
this study have suffered drastic change. Bu-Ali Sina
University in Iran is no more, and Paris-Vincennes has
been moved to a suburb of Paris, with profound effects
upon its previous character and mission. Other changes,
though, have taken root and are beginning to flourish.

The Wingspread conference raised questions as to how
much these changes will affect higher education as a
whole. The first question is whether significant change
is in fact occurring. Are the educators who participated
at Wingspread representative of a powerful current of
university reform, or are their efforts simply eddies in
an otherwise stagnant pool? Open universities and the
development university in the Third World seem to represent major changes. But open universities are themselves
only one manifestation of the move toward greatly widened
access to higher education, not only in terms of social
class and financial status of the student but also in
terms of their age. Vincennes and the University of
Wisconsin-Whitewater are only two examples of these
efforts to reach a broader category of students.

Similarly, the development university represents a
constellation of changes. The University of Zambia and
the University of Botswana have broken with a largely
colonial heritage through changes in entrance
requirements. In both cases, the change in admissions
led to curriculum changes to accommodate the different
level of preparation of the incoming students. At the
same time, the goals of the university have changed.
Instead of educating replacements for predominantly
expatriate civil servants, these African universities
seek to educate future leaders in all facets of national
life--business and engineering, science and medicine, as
well as government and administration. In addition, the
universities are focusing on indigenous culture as a
vehicle for transmitting social values and attitudes.

In India, for example, Mitra insists that faculty
returning from abroad to teach must combine the best of
the German, American, and British models with Indian traditions and circumstances, while Hamdan Tahir described
how the University of Science of Malaysia broke with
earlier university traditions in Malaysia. The institutions that are emerging are carving out a distinctive
role for themselves in their own societies.

Are they truly universities? During the conference,
James Perkins defined a university as:

> ...a place where the production of research, of
> learning and instruction, and application up to the
> point of implementation, are all integrated in one
> institution. A university is the only institution
> that tries to do all of these things. If it gets too

far into application, it is likely to get lost. And
if it forgets its research and instructional
function, it might just as well be a research
laboratory. The uniqueness of a university is that
it combines in a single organization, under a common
administrative approach, a preoccupation with the
interrelationships among these three primary functions without being the exclusive agent in any one of
them.

Perkins did not discuss the relative emphasis to be
placed on each function in all circumstances; implicit is
the expectation that such emphasis will vary. But all
the institutions represented at Wingspread did, in
varying degrees, conform to this definition, combining
research, teaching, and application.
     Of particular interest are those universities that
include all postsecondary school instruction, technical
as well as theoretical, in a comprehensive institution.
Examples that have been discussed are the University of
Botswana, Yarmouk University in Jordan, and the
University of Northern Kentucky in the United States.
Broadening the function of the university to include
training technicians is, in many cases, altering
radically the nature of the curriculum. For example,
general courses have traditionally preceded technical or
specialized education. But if technicians attend the
same classes as baccalaureate candidates, as in these
institutions they do, the order of subjects must change.
This mode of education meets a requirement suggested by
Whitehead[1] many years ago.

     There are three main methods which are required in a
     national system of education; namely, the literary
     curriculum, the scientific curriculum, the technical
     curriculum. But each of these curricula should
     include the other two. What I mean is that every
     form of education should give the pupil a technique,
     a science, an assortment of general ideas, an
     aesthetic appreciation, and that each of these sides
     of his training should be illuminated by the others.

Such experiments in comprehensive higher education, then,
may well prove as enriching and advantageous for the
student selecting a more traditional university curriculum as for those whose primary motivation is their desire
for technical training.
     The ends and means of the university overlap. The
drive for wider access to the university as a way for the
individual to acquire more of society's goods has had a
large impact on the self image of the university. At the
same time, the new goals the university has begun to set
for itself have in turn affected the kinds and number of

people who get in.   Universal access changes the nature
of the university.   New models are required to accommodate a new clientele.

Extending   access   to   new   groups   also   encourages
diversity--among institutions in large systems of education   and   within   an   institution   in   smaller   systems.
Single   institutions   such   as   the   University   of   the
Philippines at Los Baños must adopt a multitude of roles
to   accomplish   their   stated   purpose--the   promotion   of
national development.

As the goals of higher education expand, new kinds of
institutions will acquire respectability, attracting the
talented faculty that now tends to migrate to the prestigious institutions in the developed world.   Not all the
universities that have been described here will one day
be institutions of worldwide repute, although some are
likely to achieve major status.   But it seems clear that
Wingspread participants are on the cutting edge of
change.

The   message   that   emerged   from   Wingspread   is   as
optimistic as it is realistic: Tomorrow's universities
have healthy roots, both in the lessons of yesterday's
experience and in the courage demonstrated in today's
continuing innovation.

Notes

CHAPTER 1
ACCESS: WHO SHOULD GET IN?

1. Naomi E.S. McIntosh, "Access to Higher Education in England and Wales," in Robert M. Pike, Naomi E.S. McIntosh, Urban Dahllöf, INNOVATION IN ACCESS TO HIGHER EDUCATION: ONTARIO, CANADA; ENGLAND AND WALES; AND SWEDEN, International Council for Educational Development, New York, 1978, p. 180.

2. Guy Neave, "Patterns of Equality: The Influence of New Structures on European Higher Education Upon the Equality of Educational Opportunity," quoted in R. Premfors and B. Östergren, SYSTEMS OF HIGHER EDUCATION: SWEDEN, International Council for Educational Development, New York, 1978, p. 148.

3. "Report of the Committee of...Experts...on...Lifelong Education," UNESCO (December 1977), p. 12.

4. Farhad Riahi, "On the Role of the University in Developing Countries," Bu-Ali Sina University, Iran, 1978, p. 13.

5. INTERNATIONAL ENCYCLOPEDIA OF HIGHER EDUCATION, Vol. 2, Jossey-Bass Inc., San Francisco, 1977, p. 83.

6. Choh-Ming Li, "Emerging Patterns of Higher Education in Asia," Report, Institute of International Education, 1973.

7. Typology of Higher Educational Systems, adapted from Martin Trow, "Problems in Transition from Elite to Mass Higher Education," POLICIES FOR HIGHER EDUCATION, Organisation for Economic Cooperation and Development (OECD), Paris, 1974.

8. INTERNATIONAL ENCYCLOPEDIA, op.cit., p. 83.

9. "Standards Stir Debate in Colleges," NEW YORK TIMES, (December 5, 1975).

10. J.W. Burkett, "Higher Education's Growing Edge," EDUCATIONAL RECORD (58:3, Summer 1977), p. 268.

11. James A. Perkins and Barbara A. Burns, ACCESS TO HIGHER EDUCATION: TWO PERSPECTIVES: A COMPARATIVE STUDY OF THE FEDERAL REPUBLIC OF GERMANY AND THE UNITED STATES OF AMERICA, International Council for Educational Development, New York, 1978, p. 6.

12. Luis Garibay, "Innovations of Postsecondary Education in Mexico," Autonomous University of Guadalajara, Mexico, 1978, pp. 35ff.

13. Urban Dahllöf, "Strategies for a Broader Enrollment in Swedish Higher Education," in Robert M. Pike, Naomi E.S. McIntosh, and Urban Dahllöf, INNOVATION IN ACCESS TO HIGHER EDUCATION, op. cit., p. 303

14. Lillemor Kim, "Strategies for a Broader Enrollment in Swedish Higher Education: Two Case Studies," pp. 31-35.

15. Kenneth W. Thompson, Barbara R. Fogel, and H.E. Danner, HIGHER EDUCATION AND SOCIAL CHANGE: PROMISING EXPERIMENTS IN DEVELOPING COUNTRIES, Vol. 2, CASE STUDIES, Praeger Publishers, New York, 1977.

16. Kim, op. cit., p.36.

17. Dahllöf, op. cit., p. 309.

18. McIntosh, op. cit., p. 211.

19. Sir Walter Perry, "How to Save the Educational System," HUMAN NATURE (September 1978), p. 70.

20. Kenneth W. Thompson and Barbara R. Fogel, HIGHER EDUCATION AND SOCIAL CHANGE: PROMISING EXPERIMENTS IN DEVELOPING COUNTRIES, Vol. 1, REPORTS, Praeger Publishers, New York, 1976, p. 42.

21. Perry, op. cit., pp. 70-71.

22. Burton R. Clark, "The Insulated Americans: Five Lessons from Abroad," CHANGE (Vol. 10, November 1978), p. 28.

23. Ibid., p. 27.

24. McIntosh, op. cit., p. 181.

25. Report of the Committee of...Experts...on...Lifelong Education, op. cit., p. 6.

26. Tom Heneghan, "West Germany to Revise University Admission," THE CHRONICLE OF HIGHER EDUCATION (Vol. 15, September 26, 1977), p. 6.

27. INTERNATIONAL ENCYCLOPEDIA, op. cit., p. 88.

CHAPTER 2
RELEVANCE: WHAT SHOULD THEY LEARN?

1. Chitta Mitra, "Education for Self-Reliance," MODERN INDIA: HERITAGE AND ACHIEVEMENT (no date), p. 792.

2. Alan Pifer, "Introduction: Some Current Issues," SYSTEMS OF HIGHER EDUCATION: UNITED STATES, International Council for Educational Development, New York, 1978, p. 16.

3. John Millett, STRENGTHENING COMMUNITY IN HIGHER EDUCATION, Academy for Educational Development, Washington, D.C., 1975, p. 5.

4. Riahi, op. cit., pp. 7-8.

5. Ibid., pp. 12-13.

6. Puey Ungphakorn, quoted in Thompson and Fogel, op. cit., p. 36.

7. Jerome B. Wiesner, "Text of Remarks to the National Council of University Research Administrators," THE CHRONICLE OF HIGHER EDUCATION (Vol. 17, November 13, 1978), p. 14.

8. Sippanondha Ketudat in Banphot Virasai, ed., HIGHER EDUCATION IN SOUTHEAST ASIA IN THE NEXT DECADE, Regional Institute of Higher Education and Development, Singapore, 1977, p. 50.

9. Wiesner, op. cit., p. 17.

10. Mitra, op. cit., p. 796.

11. Nathan Glazer, "Theory and Practice in the Social Sciences," THE CHRONICLE OF HIGHER EDUCATION (Vol. 16, July 31, 1978), p. 28.

12. Sir Walter Perry, "Locked Into an Outdated Philosophy of Learning," THE CHRONICLE OF HIGHER EDUCATION (Vol. 17, November 27, 1978), p. 72.

13. Pifer, op. cit., p. 5.

14. Report of the Committee of Experts on Lifelong Learning, op. cit., p. 5.

15. Perry, op. cit., p. 72.

CHAPTER 3
FLEXIBILITY: WHERE DOES CHANGE TAKE HOLD?

1. THE MANAGEMENT OF INNOVATION IN HIGHER EDUCATION, Organisation for Economic Cooperation and Development (OECD), St. John's College, Cambridge, 1969, p. 16.

2. Riahi, op. cit., p. 15.

3. Mitra, op. cit., p. 793.

4. Lyman Glenny, "Effectiveness of the System," SYSTEMS OF HIGHER EDUCATION: UNITED STATES, International Council for Educational Development, New York, 1978, p. 97.

5. B. Williams, SYSTEMS OF HIGHER EDUCATION: AUSTRALIA, International Council for Educational Development, New York, 1978, p. 83.

6. Sippanondha, op. cit.

7. Janet E. Lieberman, "The Pathology of Innovation," LIBERAL EDUCATION (Vol. LXII, No. 3, October 1976), p. 382.

8. Tony Becher, Jack Embling, and Maurice Kogan, SYSTEMS OF HIGHER EDUCATION: UNITED KINGDOM, International Council for Educational Development, New York, 1977, p. 122.

9. A.M. Huberman, "Understanding Change in Education," UNESCO, Paris, 1973, p. 9.

10. Brian MacArthur, "Flexibility and Innovation," in Clark Kerr, John Millett, Burton Clark, Brian MacArthur, and Howard Bowen, TWELVE SYSTEMS OF HIGHER EDUCATION: SIX DECISIVE ISSUES, International Council for Educational Development, New York, 1978, pp. 118-119.

11. THE MANAGEMENT OF INNOVATION IN HIGHER EDUCATION, op. cit., p. 37.

12. Riahi, op. cit., p. 14.

13. Ibid, p. 15.

14. "The Learning Society," Report of the Commission on Postsecondary Education in Ontario, Toronto

15. Robert M. Pike, "Part-time Undergraduate Studies in Ontario," in Pike, McIntosh, and Dahllöf, op. cit., p. 104.

16. THE MANAGEMENT OF INNOVATION IN EDUCATION, op. cit., p. 5.

17. Clark, op. cit., p. 27.

18. Madras Development Seminar Bulletin (Vol. III, No. 10, October 1973) p. 652.

19. MacArthur, op. cit.

CHAPTER 4
EFFICIENCY: HOW DO WE SET A PRICE ON PROGRESS?

1. John Millett, "Challenges in Statewide Planning for the 1980s," HIGHER EDUCATION AND THE 1980s, Academy for Educational Development, Washington, D.C., 1978.

2. Clark, op. cit., pp. 24-25.

3. R. Premfors and B. Östergren, SYSTEMS OF HIGHER EDUCATION: SWEDEN, International Council for Educational Development, New York, 1978, pp. 181-186.

4. Alan Pifer, J. Shea, D. Henry, and L. Glenny, SYSTEMS OF HIGHER EDUCATION: UNITED STATES, International Council for Educational Development, New York, 1978, p. 15.

5. EDUCATIONAL DIRECTORY, COLLEGES AND UNIVERSITIES, 1977-78, National Center for Education Statistics, U.S. Government Printing Office, Washington, D.C., 1978, p. xxviii.

6. MacArthur, op. cit.

7. Premfors and Östergren, op. cit., p. 188.

198

8. "Teaching Policies Issued by the University Council of the University of Costa Rica" (no date), p. 8 (distributed at the Wingspread conference).

9. P.R. Christensen and S. Sverdrup-Jensen, "Aalborg University Center and the Region of North Jutland - An Educational Experiment in a Regional Development Area," Aalborg University Center, Denmark, p. 69.

10. Ibid., p. 2.

11. Howard Bowen, "Measurements of Efficiency," in Kerr, Millett, Clark, MacArthur, and Bowen, op. cit., p. 147

12. R.L. Jacobson, "Accreditors Urged to Shift Standards," THE CHRONICLE OF HIGHER EDUCATION (Vol. 17, October 10, 1978), p. 12.

13. Max Rowe, EVERYMAN'S UNIVERSITY: REPORT TO THE WORLD CONFERENCE ON INNOVATIVE HIGHER EDUCATION, Israel, June 1978, p. 11.

14. Christensen and Sverdrup-Jensen, op. cit., p. 60

15. Millett, op. cit.

16. Glenny, op. cit.

17. Bowen, op. cit.

CHAPTER 5
DELIVERY SYSTEMS

1. ECONOMIST, London (June, 1979).

2. J. Scupham, "The Open University of the United Kingdom," OPEN LEARNING, UNESCO, Paris, 1975.

3. Sir W. Perry, THE OPEN UNIVERSITY, Jossey-Bass, San Francisco, 1977.

4. Becher, Embling, and Kogan, op. cit.

5. Rowe, op. cit.

6. Perry, THE OPEN UNIVERSITY, op. cit.

7. Günther Dohmen, EXTERNAL STUDIES: INTERNATIONAL DEVELOPMENTS TOWARDS AN INTEGRATION OF EXTERNAL STUDIES INTO UNIVERSITY AND CONTINUING EDUCATION PROGRAMS, Vol. 12, Tübinger Beiträge zum Fernstudium, Weinheim und Basel, 1978.

8. Otto Peters, "The German Fernuniversität." Paper delivered at the Latin American and Caribbean meeting on New Forms of Postsecondary Education, Caracas, Venezuela, 1976.

9. M.S. Archer, SOCIAL ORIGINS OF EDUCATIONAL SYSTEMS, Athens, Ohio, Sage, 1979.

CHAPTER 6
NEW CLIENTELES

1. Archer, op. cit.

2. Ibid.

3. M. Debeauvais, L'UNIVERSITÉ OUVERTE: LES DOSSIERS DE VINCENNES, Universitaires de Grenoble Press, Grenoble, France, 1976.

4. Nicolas Domenach, "Université: Vincennes rentre à Saint-Denis," LE MATIN (17 November 1980).

5. K. Patricia Cross, et.al., THE ADULT LEARNER, CURRENT ISSUES IN HIGHER EDUCATION, American Association of Higher Education, Washington, D.C., 1978.

6. A. Tough, MAJOR LEARNING EFFORTS: RECENT RESEARCH AND FUTURE DIRECTIONS, Ontario Institute for Studies in Education, Toronto, 1978.

CHAPTER 7
INNOVATIONS IN THE LAND-GRANT TRADITION

1. L. Beale, PEOPLE TO PEOPLE: THE ROLE OF STATE AND LAND-GRANT UNIVERSITIES IN MODERN AMERICA, National Association of State Universities and Land-Grant Colleges, Washington, D. C. (no date).

2. Ibid.

3. THE MAKING OF A UNIVERSITY, The University of the Philippines at Los Baños Public Information Program.

4. Abelardo G. Samonte, "Innovation and Technology for Educational Reform," EDUCATIONAL QUARTERLY, College of Education, University of the Philippines (Vol. XXIII, No. 3, January-March 1977), p. 11.

5. Ibid.

6. Beale, op. cit.

7. Edward W. Weidner, "Interdisciplinarity and Higher Education" INTERNATIONAL JOURNAL OF ENVIRONMENTAL STUDIES (Vol. V, 1973), p. 205.

8. Edward W. Weidner, "The Problem-Oriented Department: The Experience at the University of Wisconsin-Green Bay," in Dean E. McHenry, et.al., ACADEMIC DEPARTMENTS: PROBLEMS, VARIATIONS, AND ALTERNATIVES, Jossey-Bass, San Francisco, 1977.

9. W. Werner Prange, "Interdisciplinary Ecological Research and Teaching at the University of Wisconsin-Green Bay," METODOLOGIE DI INTEGRAZIONE DELLE DISCIPLINE IMPLICATE NELLA ANALISI ECOLOGIA, Studium Parmense, Parma, 1976, pp. 106-118.

CHAPTER 8
COMPREHENSIVE HIGHER EDUCATION

1. Thompson and Fogel, op. cit.

2. A MIDEAST REPORT 30 (Spring, 1979), Mideast Educational and Training Services.

3. N.O.H. Setidisho, "The University for a Developing Society," unpublished.

4. W. Alexander, "Report on Higher Education Needs to the Government of Botswana."

CHAPTER 9
INTERDISCIPLINARITY AND PROBLEM FOCUS

1. J. Piaget, "The Epistemology of Interdisciplinarity," INTERDISCIPLINARITY: PROBLEMS OF TEACHING AND RESEARCH IN UNIVERSITIES, OECD, Paris, 1972.

2. H. Heckhausen, "Some Approaches to Interdisciplinarity," ibid.

3. Guy Berger, "Opinions and Facts," ibid.

4. E. Boning and K. Roeloffs, THREE GERMAN UNIVERSITIES, OECD, Paris, 1972.

5. Premfors and Östergren, op. cit.

6. Ibid.

7. Ibid.

8. THEMES: A NEW PATH FOR RESEARCH AT THE UNIVERSITY OF LINKÖPING, University of Linköping, 1977.

9. Thompson, Fogel, and Danner, op. cit.

10. HEALTH, HIGHER EDUCATION, AND THE COMMUNITY: TOWARDS A REGIONAL HEALTH UNIVERSITY, OECD, Paris, 1977.

11. Ibid.

CHAPTER 10
EXTENSION AND NATIONAL DEVELOPMENT

1. F.M. Rosentretter, THE BOUNDARIES OF THE CAMPUS, University of Wisconsin Press, Madison, Wisconsin, 1957.

2. Ibid.

3. Ibid.

4. BRITISH OPEN UNIVERSITY OCCASIONAL NEWSLETTER, New York (March 4, 1979).

5. Zeferino Vaz, "The Third Role of the University in Developing Nations: Direct Service to the Community." Paper distributed at the Wingspread conference.

6. Ibid.

7. "American Farming: A Survey," ECONOMIST, London (January 11, 1980).

8. C. Verner and J.S. Newberry, Jr., "The Nature of Adult Participation," ADULT EDUCATION (Summer 1958).

9. R.V. Scott, THE RELUCTANT FARMER, University of Illinois, Champaign-Urbana, Illinois, 1970.

10. T.J. Shannon and C.A. Schoenfield, UNIVERSITY EXTENSION, Center for Applied Research in Education, Inc., New York, 1965.

11. L.H. Watts and R. Weick, "A Commitment to Serve--Then, Now and Tomorrow," HERITAGE HORIZONS, Extension Journal, Inc., 1976.

12. Rosentretter, op. cit.

13. H.G. Dasslin and R.C. Scott, "Updating Staff for Specialized Agriculture," HERITAGE HORIZONS, Extension Journal, Inc., 1976.

14. Scott, op. cit.

15. Samonte, op. cit.

16. Ibid.

17. THE MAKING OF A UNIVERSITY, op. cit.

CHAPTER 11
RESEARCH

1. Becher, Embling, and Kogan, op. cit.

2. C.H. Schauer, "The Foundation-College Relationship" in S. Strickland, ed., SPONSORED RESEARCH IN AMERICAN COLLEGES AND UNIVERSITIES, American Council on Education, Washington, D.C., 1968.

3. D. Wolfle, THE HOME OF SCIENCE, McGraw-Hill, New York, 1972.

4. Ibid.

5. Prange, op. cit.

6. Christensen and Sverdrup-Jensen, op. cit.

7. "Griffith University--An Introduction for Prospective Staff," Griffith University, Brisbane, Australia.

8. Debeauvais, op. cit.

9. Mitra, op. cit.

10. L.P. Tembo, "University of Zambia: An Analysis of Some Major Issues," in T.M. Yesufu, ed., CREATING THE AFRICAN UNIVERSITY: EMERGING ISSUES IN THE 1970s, Oxford University Press, Oxford, 1973.

11. Ibid.

12. T.M. Yesufu, "Introduction," ibid.

13. Thompson, Fogel, and Danner, op. cit.

14. Thompson and Fogel, op. cit.

15. A.S.H. Ong, "Graduate Education In Relation to Social Needs," ASAIHL Seminar on Postgraduate Education in Southeast Asia, Hong Kong, 1978.

16. Jacob M. Mwanza, "The Role of the University." Unpublished/distributed at the Wingspread conference.

17. J. Ki-Zerbo, "Education and Development," THE BELLAGIO CONFERENCE PAPERS, Praeger Publishers, New York, 1974.

18. J. Ki-Zerbo, "Africanization of Higher Education Curricula," in Yesufu, CREATING THE AFRICAN UNIVERSITY, op. cit.

19. J.F.A. Ajayi, "Towards an African Academic Community," ibid.

20. A.C. Eurich, "Reflections on University Research Administration," in SPONSORED RESEARCH, op. cit.

21. Thompson and Fogel, op. cit.

22. Yesufu, op. cit.

CHAPTER 12
THE MANAGEMENT OF INNOVATION

1. Riahi, op. cit.

2. Christensen and Sverdrup-Jensen, op. cit.

CHAPTER 13
NEW CHALLENGES, NEW RESPONSIBILITIES

1. Alfred North Whitehead, THE AIMS OF EDUCATION, Macmillan, New York, 1957, pp. vi, 247.

The World Conference
on Innovative Higher Education

Convened by
Bu-Ali Sina University of Iran
Linköping University of Sweden
and the
University of Wisconsin-Green Bay (U.S.A.)
in cooperation with
The Johnson Foundation

May 31 - June 3, 1978

Conference Chairman: W. Werner Prange

Organizing Committee: Farhad Riahi
Hans Meijer
W. Werner Prange

Universities have historically fulfilled a dual role: to maintain, augment, and transmit the cultural heritage while simultaneously training professionals and administrators. They have characteristically asserted the former role while drawing societal support for incidentally achieving the latter.

However, several trends are converging which may augur a change of emphasis. The explosion of knowledge and rising social expectations are the catalysts for an expansion both of the tasks to be accomplished by the educated and of the type of work thought appropriate for them. Even as problems become more complex and acute, there exists rising confidence that solutions can only be found by applying the new learning. Concurrently, increasing numbers of people throughout the world are aspiring to work which is both psychologically and materially more rewarding, and they are expecting to achieve this goal through education.

Such aspirations can be met; indeed, must be met. If implemented humanistically, our burgeoning technology is capable of raising the intellectual and imaginative content of much work, while offering the prospect of higher productivity and increasing concern for the health and welfare of the worker. Such concern includes attention to the cultural as well as the physical well-being of the individual.

While the role of higher education as conservator of culture is not in doubt, both the way in which liberal education is presented to students and the extent to

which it should be balanced by practical training is
being questioned. The precise terms in which such
questions are formulated differ among nations. In the
United States there is a rise in the popularity of management studies and other forms of pre-professional
training among students, together with wide-spread alarm
that too many graduates are being produced. In Europe
concern is expressed that university education is still
too much confined to students of traditional age and
class, pursuing traditional fields of study, and who may
find it difficult to obtain suitable employment upon
graduation. Many nations face the problem of
unemployment or underemployment of graduates while
simultaneously grappling with a lack of trained manpower
in crucial sectors of the country or of the economy.

Our universities face problems which are different in
detail. Nevertheless, they share an underlying commonality of both challenge and response, and it is this that
makes it worthwhile to consider an exchange of views and
experiences.

For example, much attention is currently being given
to the concept of problem-oriented education. Here the
instructional process is predicated upon some subset of
perceived problems, and the curriculum is directed
towards understanding and ameliorating identifiable
social ills. Such education must incorporate the
cultural heritage in which all problems are embedded,
thus fulfilling the ancient function of the university.

Another example is interdisciplinarity. Some
educators claim that academic disciplines have each
developed a unique concept of the known, which is not
necessarily congruent with reality, but which they
impress upon their students wittingly or unwittingly.

Yet another approach has been to integrate work
experience and the educational process, either through
internships, by giving workers release time for
education, or by making work a prerequisite of admission.

This is by no means an exhaustive list of the
concepts under which innovations have been suggested or
implemented somewhere in the world. Furthermore, listing
such concepts does not assume that it is profitable to
subsume all the experience under a few common headings.
To do so may obscure rather than illuminate. Solutions,
as well as problems, must be viewed at least in part in a
local context. There is no reason why either solutions
or problems should be the same in Sweden, Tanzania, and
the United States. Nevertheless, all peoples have common
threads of interest and aspiration, and professional educators have common strands of experience and experiment.
An attempt to explore and share this commonality is especially appropriate at present, and might contribute
significantly both to further educational advance and to
international understanding.

Bu-Ali Sina Univerity of Iran, Linköping University of Sweden, and the University of Wisconsin-Green Bay are taking the initiative by organizing a worldwide conference of innovating universities which will attempt to identify and address this shared array of problems.

The purpose of the conference is to provide participants with an opportunity to exchange ideas and experiences with those in similar university-building roles. Simultaneously, through the cut and thrust of debate, it is hoped that new light might be thrown on common problems and new pathways of interinstitutional cooperation explored.

Conference Agenda

The following agenda is an attempt to define and organize
the type of questions which might profitably be
addressed.   It is intended to be neither exclusive nor
exhaustive.   It is presented as an approach to a conference where the emphasis will be upon exchange of
views, interaction, and synthesis, rather than formal
papers.

I. THE CULTURAL CONTEXT: James A. Perkins, Moderator

The excess of graduates which some observers claim
to detect, either present or prospectively, may in
actuality be an excess of the wrong kind of
graduates.   Possibly universities are simply failing
to produce graduates adequately prepared to face the
challenges of a developing world in the twenty-first
century.   The modern university must continually
reflect upon the needs of the society in which it
exists and from which it draws its sustenance.
Certainly, the contemplative role may still have its
place.   But training leaders, galvanizing technological advance, and stimulating social change
must also be achieved.

For these functions, the new university may well
find that interdisciplinarity and problem focus are
important organizing principles: problem focus
because it represents a positive response to the
needs of society; interdisciplinarity because it is
inherent in the nature of problems.

Traditional values will not be surrendered in the
search for relevance, although institutions may well
prove to be more diverse than in the past.   While
the University of Dar es Salaam might need to
respond in the immediate future to the needs of
agricultural village economy, Linköping or Sussex

209

might strive for a wider integration of education
and service to an industrial society. Valle in
Colombia might achieve success in community health
care, while Ngee Ann in Singapore declines university status to concentrate upon training adept technicians for its unique entrepôt economy. However, a
universal thrust toward creative problem solving may
well characterize many, if not most, new departures
in higher education. And while health care,
agriculture, industrial development, and career
development all have strong scientific and technical
components, success will demand a keen perception of
the social and cultural contexts in which change
occurs. Such perceptions are as likely to flow from
the traditional humanities--art, literature,
history, and language--as from the social sciences.
Culture, not sociology, is the touchstone and
lodestar of change. Consequently, the new role of
the university transmutes, rather than destroys, the
former role of cultural conservator.

The Need for New Departures in Higher Education

If traditional models are failing, in what sense are
they doing so?

Are the reasons for failure different in Europe,
Asia, Africa, America?

Are there common reasons as well as unique reasons
in each region? Should innovative models seek to
supplant or supplement traditional models?

Can we define a single path for innovation? A small
number of paths? Or must a thousand flowers bloom?

National Problems and Development Status as Determinants of Educational Strategy

To what extent do national or regional priorities
determine educational goals? Are these priorities
absolute, or do common goals exist? How can we help
each other achieve our goals?

Does the prestige of traditional models inhibit
needed innovation? In the North Atlantic littoral?
Elsewhere in the world?

The Need for Cross-Cultural Comparisons

If problems are perceived in a cultural context, to what extent must students be provided with cross-cultural comparisons? Can this be achieved? How can it best be achieved?

Can students understand large cultural transitions (e.g., U.S. to Tanzania, Tanzania to Brazil)?

Problem Orientation as an Organizing Principle

What is meant by problem orientation in education? How does it differ from professional or technical education?

Can problems be defined which will provide a lasting framework for organizations?

Do common problems exist which all universities should address?

Which problems are common to all, and which unique?

Does problem orientation provide an organizing principle? Are there alternative organizing principles?

The Identification and Definition of Appropriate Problem Sets

Can these be defined in broad terms (e.g., health, agriculture, environment)? Does such a definition provide a focus?

Must they be defined in narrow terms (e.g., rural health delivery, urban planning)? If so, how is this distinct from professional education?

Can problems be defined which last as problems?

How can the possibility of change of focus be incorporated into the system as previously perceived problems become obsolete?

II. THE EMERGING CURRICULUM: Edward W. Weidner, Moderator

The problems of development are legion, and know no bounds of nation or continent, of wealth or stage of industrialization. While in Europe the need for change may be expressed primarily in terms of a wider access to educational opportunity, this

problem is real in the Americas and Asia. While in
Africa or India the necessity of service to the
village, rather than the city, might appear
paramount, a parallel need exists for service to the
deprived urban and rural poor in the United States.
Asians might feel free to emphasize their traditional respect for learning for its own sake, but
Africans must seek to define and conserve their deep
cultural heritage as a topic of scholarship, lest it
be lost in the rush for development.

Meanwhile, all must seek ways to overcome the
inertia of faculty, staff, and students, enjoying as
they do the time-honored perquisites of the life
of the mind as practiced in the ancient university.

Furthermore, educational planning has a ridiculously
long lead time. It has correctly been pointed out
that the demands of a national five-year plan may
require responses in the educational system years
prior to university entrance. And the consequences
in terms of minds trained for a specific task persist
for years after graduation.

A very special responsibility is thus placed on
university administrators. Narrow specialization
cannot demand the sacrifice of broadly applicable
skills. Technical competence, however urgent the
need, cannot supplant a broadly informed
intelligence. The commitment to continued intellectual growth, however achieved, must be maintained.

Defining and Transmitting Problem-Solving Skills

Is it desirable to define some topics as skills
(e.g., mathematics, communication skills, accounting,
foreign languages)? Does it offend professional
susceptibilities to do so?

Are there universal skills?

Are some topics "skills" in one frame of reference,
but "topics" in their own right in another?

How can we cope with such a dichotomy?

Establishing a Conceptual Framework

Is there a duality between concept and skill (e.g.,
literature as opposed to language, mathematics as
opposed to computational skill)?

Can problems be solved outside a conceptual framework?

What are the culture-specific dimensions of the conceptual frame of a problem?

How are these to be communicated?

What is the role of social science in natural science-type problems, and vice versa? What is the role of the humanities and fine arts?

The Role of Interdisciplinarity

Are conventional disciplines restrictive? Or is it simply the professional organization of disciplines which makes them so?

How can we dispense with disciplines without losing rigor?

Does interdisciplinarity simply spawn new disciplines (e.g., biochemistry, social psychology, Latin American studies)? Is it a bad thing if they do? Can it be prevented?

Is interdisciplinarity vital to innovation? If so, how can it be fostered?

Experiential Learning

Is experience in a specific problem-solving role vital to learning?

At what educational level should it be provided? As an introduction or as a capstone? How can it be provided for all students? What portion of degree requirement should it fulfill? Can it be related to the entire education? Or should it relate only to a portion?

Is this only a problem of developed nations?

The Ephemeral Nature of Currently Perceived Problems

Do problems become outmoded? If not, do they become disciplines? If so, how do we ensure their replacement by more current problems?

How do we prepare students to move on to new problems as they grow older? To perceive a wider array of problems as their careers develop?

Do we need to worry about intellectual depth and breadth in innovative education?

III. THE SYSTEM OF DELIVERY: Mulugeta Wodajo, Moderator

Faculty and staff tend to be wedded to traditional divisions of subject matter, traditional concepts of excellence, and traditional modes of transmission. We must understand the nature of that commitment. It has served both the needs of society and of scholarship in the past, and what replaces it must possess equal merit. Furthermore, we must be wary of those who are eager to break with the old system because of their inability to cope effectively within it, or for ideological reasons which have little to do with the quality of education. And we must welcome contributions, both of ideas and effective personnel, from the noncollegiate sector. For example, at Monterrey in Mexico the impetus for the development of an effective program in technology and management came from industrialists, and a small group of concerned health practitioners were instrumental in the development of a community health program at Valle in Colombia.

Other areas of concern are important. Much experience is being accumulated indicating that flexibility in place and time of learning can and should be achieved. A notable example is the British Open University. Communications media continue to be underutilized in terms of their promise, but success has been achieved in Kenya and elsewhere using radio, television, and newspapers. And finally, the role of students, especially in relation to experiential learning, needs to be defined. Experience in Tanzania, in Ethiopia, and in Latin America indicates that an effective way to assist students in relinquishing their ideas of the cherished role of the intellectual and scholar is to involve them in the planning process--which is easier said than done.

Recruiting and Grouping an Effective Faculty

How can faculty be recruited who are sympathetic to the goals of innovative education? What reward structure is necessary to keep them sympathetic?

How can they best be grouped into productive teams? How are new organizational structures to be defined?

What constitutes a major of field of study? How are they to be defined?

How can faculty leadership and initiative be encouraged?

What is the role of faculty in experiential learning? How can it be defined and improved?

The Place and Time of Learning

What is the role of Open Education? Of Lifelong Learning? Of correspondence courses? Of refresher courses?

What can media offer to overcome problems of distance?

Is occasional contact with other students necessary? Is occasional contact with faculty essential?

How can practical or laboratory work be incorporated if necessary?

The Format of Instruction

Is the lecture/laboratory format outmoded? In part or in whole? In which part or which whole?

What is the role of seminars? Of programmed instruction, either in book, slide/tape, or computerized form?

What is the role of communications media?

Have all alternatives been adequately explored?

Student Initiative in Developing Programs of Study

To what extent should students participate in designing their own programs? Not all, U.S. cafeteria style, or total design of individual major?

If different circumstances dictate different answers, what circumstance and which answer?

What should the role of students be in experiential education? Can they help make it more effective and meaningful?

Cost Effectiveness

Ideal systems are easy to create; hard to deliver. What are the likely cost constraints on innovation? Are there any ways to avoid the worst of these?

216

Are there demonstrable costs of failure to innovate? Are there demonstrable benefits to offset costliness? Or is innovative education inherently cheaper sometimes (e.g., in training health professionals)?

Can it be made cheaper?

IV. THE ROLE OF RESEARCH: Hans Meijer, Moderator

Research is one of the most perplexing problems facing the innovative university. Traditionally, the university has tended to be defined by its original contributions to knowledge. But it is difficult to incorporate basic research into a problem-oriented curriculum. Applied research can, of course, be as challenging and satisfying as any other kind, but again the very process of innovation makes demands on personnel which often seem to preclude effective research; a problem often compounded by the demands of interdisciplinarity. Nevertheless, both for students and faculty, for reasons of professional pride and the maintenance of institutional stature, an active research involvement may be vital. Indeed, it seems desirable that students themselves should be involved in the process of inquiry as early and as fully as possible. If they are to become effective problem solvers, they cannot start on it too soon.

It has been suggested that the primary legacy of the major agricultural research institutes has been the production of trained professionals, rather than the Green Revolution itself. This may well indicate that the road to successful research involvement lies in the clear definition of problems and the incorporation of experiential learning into the curriculum. If research is separated from training, both will suffer. However, it is easier to prescribe such an approach than to implement it. Problems of funding and release time, of prestige, competence, and lack of enthusiasm need to be overcome.

The Determination of Research Priorities

What kind of research should be fostered? Is there a role for basic research? How can applied research problems be defined? Are broad or narrow definitions to be preferred?

Must the definition of research problems reflect the curricular organization? Or vice versa? Or should there be no relationship?

How can research teams best be put together?

Is there a role for the humanities?

Fostering Professional Development

How can professional status be maintained? How can elitism and subservience to conventional disciplinary structures be avoided?

Can applied research achieve status?

Can professional success be measured in new terms (e.g., consultancies or community service, rather than publication)?

Funding and Community Relations

How can funding be obtained in the absence of a place in the research power structure?

Can a social role be achieved without damaging community relationships? Without political entanglements?

Is there a role for the university in applied research, where more immediate pay-off attracts government or market-oriented organizations? If so, how can they be attracted?

Research and the Classroom

How can research results best be brought into the classroom? How can students become involved in research? To what extent should they be involved?

Research and University Relations

Can research catalyze relationships between innovative universities? If so, how can such relationships be fostered? How can they be funded?

Are faculty and student exchange feasible?

V. PROBLEMS OF ADMINISTRATION AND ARTICULATION: Farhad Riahi, Moderator

Any departure from the accepted organizational norm imposes severe demands on administrators. These can be exacerbated when newer institutions exercise less of the power and prestige than the old; when they are smaller and infinitely less glamorous. And if the institution is in a remote location, if the community to be served is both diffuse and politically and socially impotent, then all these problems are compounded. There is little incentive for an able administrator in mid-career to leave the security of an established order and the comforts of a place close to the seats of power, and to promote energetically the new and innovative in the face of an indolent establishment, a hostile professional structure and an indifferent populace.

Special problems are presented in overcoming faculty and student inertia and in building and maintaining a social role for both in the larger society. Student internships served in distant provinces can be a continual source of difficulty. Political relationships can be troublesome, especially when the administrator may have strong relationships with the government itself and may, in fact, alternate between government and academic appointments. Government can make demands which conflict with educational needs because of the shorter planning cycle in which it operates. Problem focus demands that the larger society be embraced. Maintaining the role of the university as social critic and source of new insights demands that it be kept at arm's length. Is an embrace at arm's length conceivable? Administrative problems are sometimes the most underestimated in institutional building, perhaps because they seem so mundane in the glow of intellectual promise. But administrative success is the sine qua non, whether building new institutions or maintaining old ones.

Recruiting a Sympathetic Staff

What are the problems faced by the staff of innovating institutions? Do they derive from lack of prestige, remote location, the unique nature of the curriculum, or the characteristics of the student body?

Are there any staff functions which give particular problems (e.g., recruitment, registration, scheduling, advising, placement)?

Do some functions require special emphasis or special skills?

Relationships with Conventional Institutions

What special problems does the administration face in establishing an innovative university in the presence of a conventional educational establishment? Do they derive from lack of prestige, inadequate funding, different student body, or other factors?

What steps can be taken to resolve such problems?

Establishing an Appropriate Reward Structure

Is international transfer or promotion within an institution the best vehicle for professional growth and reward? Is interinstitutional transfer precluded by identification with an innovative institution?

What other components of reward can be established?

Do we need to promote professional growth through travel or sabbaticals at similar institutions? How can this be achieved?

If staff is successfully encouraged to grow, are they lost to better opportunities elsewhere? How can this be avoided?

What internal reward systems are successful and appropriate?

Fostering a Sense of Excellence in Students, Faculty, and Staff

Is there a problem with innovative institutions being labeled as second best? What is the source of such problems?

If innovative institutions are more responsive to the real needs of society, how can a sense of mission be fostered? Of institutional pride?

Can we ensure that the benefits of innovative education trickle down to the population at large? How can we make society aware of such benefits?

Placement of Graduates

Are there unique problems in placing graduates of innovative universities? What are the causes of

such problems?   Do solutions lie in curricular
structure, in academic advising, in placement
services?   Or do they derive from lack of status
vis-a-vis conventional institutions?   Or from the
novel curriculum?

Are there particular tasks for which graduates are
especially suited?   What are they?   Are they
recognized as such?

How can we improve this situation?

Conference Participants

J.F.M.C. Aarts
Director, Department of
  Education
Katholieke Universiteit
  Nijmegen-Holland
Erasmuslaan 4
Nijmegen, Holland

Jane M. Alden
Acting Chief
Academic Relations Division
Educational & Cultural Affairs
International Communication
  Agency
Rm 4802, New State Dept. Bldg.
Washington, D.C.   20520

H.R. Arakeri
Vice Chancellor
University of Agricultural
  Sciences
P.O. Box 2477
Bangalore, Karnataka State
India

Adnan Badran
President
Yarmouk University
P.O. Box 20184
Amman, Jordan

Albert Y. Badre
President
Beirut University College
P.O. Box 4080
Beirut, Lebanon

Guy Berger
Professor, Head of Dept. of
  Science & Education
Vice President
Committee on Instruction
Université de Paris-Vincennes
Route de la Tourelle
75571 Paris Cedex 12
France

Varaphorn Bovornsiri
National Education
  Commission
Sukhothai Road
Bangkok 3, Thailand

Sven Caspersen
Rektor
Aalborg
  Universitetscenter
9100 Aalborg, Denmark

Kenneth Fleurant
Associate Professor
Humanism & Cultural
  Change
University of Wisconsin-
  Green Bay
Green Bay, Wis. 54302

Barbara R. Fogel
Director
School Programs
Academy for Educational
  Development, Inc.
680 Fifth Avenue
New York, New York 10019

Luis G. Garibay
President
Universidad Autonoma de
  Guadalajara
P.O. Box 1-440
Guadalajara JAL, Mexico

Eduardo González-Reyes
Executive Secretary for
  Education, Science &
  Culture
Organization of American
  States
17th St. & Constitution
  Avenue, N.W.
Washington, D.C. 20006

221

Siegfried Grosse
Former Rector
Ruhr-Universität Bochum
Head, Wissenschaftliches
  Sekretariat für die
  Studienreform
463 Bochum
Unterfeldstrasse 13
D4630 Bochum, Germany

Claudio Gutiérrez
Rector
Universidad de Costa Rica
Apartado No. 37
San Jose, Costa Rica

Rose Hayden
Director
International Education Project
American Council on Education
One Dupont Circle
Washington, D.C. 20036

Osmo Ikola
Rector and Professor
University of Turku
Turun Yliopisto
20500 Turku 50, Finland

Joan H. Joshi
Vice President
Educational Services
Institute of International
  Education
809 United Nations Plaza
New York, New York 10017

David Jowett
Professor
Science & Environmental Change
University of Wisconsin-
  Green Bay
Green Bay, Wis. 54302

Everett Kleinjans
President
The East-West Center
1777 East-West Road
Honolulu, Hawaii 96848

William Kuepper
Associate Professor
Regional Analysis
University of Wisconsin-
  Green Bay
Green Bay, Wis. 54302

Yngvar Løchen
Rector and Professor
University of Tromsö
Postboks 635
9000 Tromsö, Norway

Nicolaas Luykx
Deputy Director
Office of Title XII
Coordination & University
  Relations
Agency for International
  Development
DS/DA
Rm. 520 B, AS/18
Washington, D.C. 20523

Hans Meijer
Rector
Linköping University
S-581 83 Linköping
Sweden

Pierre Merlin
President
Université de Paris-
  Vincennes
Route de la Tourelle
75571 Paris Cedex 12
France

Chitta R. Mitra
Director
Birla Institute of
  Technology & Science
Pilani 333031 Rajasthan
India

Stephen Fisher Moseley
Senior Vice President and
  Director
International Operations Div.
Academy for Educational
  Development, Inc.
1414   22nd Street, N.W.
Washington, D.C. 20037

Lewis K. Mughogho
Principal
Bunda College of Agriculture
University of Malawi
P.O. Box 214
Malawi, S.E. Africa (on leave)
Professor
St. John's College
Cambridge, CB2-ITP, England

Juan Jacobo Muñoz
Rector
University of the Andes
Apartado aereo 4976
Bogotá, D.E., Colombia

Jacob M. Mwanza
Vice Chancellor
University of Zambia
P.O. Box 2379
Lusaka, Zambia

James A. Perkins
Director
International Council for
  Educational Development
680 Fifth Avenue
New York, New York 10019

Phasook Kullavanijaya
Rector
Prince of Songkla University
Haad-Yi, Thailand

W. Werner Prange
Professor and Director
Urban Corridor Consortium of
  Universities
Former Vice Chancellor
University of Wisconsin-
  Green Bay
Green Bay, Wis. 54302

Lorman A. Ratner
Vice Chancellor/Dean of
  Faculty
University of Wisconsin-
  Parkside
Kenosha, Wis. 53141

Farhad Riahi
Chancellor
Bu-Ali Sina University
Hamadan, Iran

Max Rowe
Vice Chancellor
Everyman's University of
  Israel
16 Klausner Street,
  Ramat Aviv
P.O. Box 39328
Tel Aviv, Israel

George Rupp
Dean for Academic Affairs
University of Wisconsin-
  Green Bay
Green Bay, Wis. 54302

Abelardo Samonte
Chancellor
University of the
  Philippines at
  Los Baños
College, Laguna,
Philippines

N.O.H. Setidisho
Rector
University of Botswana
  and Swaziland
University College,
  Botswana
P.O. Box 0022
Gaborone, Botswana

Edwin G. Speir, Jr.
Vice Chancellor/Dean of
  Faculty
University of Wisconsin-
  Whitewater
Whitewater, Wis. 53190

Richard Straus
Director
Academic Programs
Educational & Cultural Affairs
International Communication
  Agency (ICA/ECA/A)--Rm. 719
1750 Pennsylvania Ave., N.W.
Washington, D.C. 20547

Y.V. Tan Sri Datuk Haji Hamdan
  Sheikh Tahir
Vice Chancellor
Universiti Sains Malaysia
Minden, Pulau Pinang, Malaysia

Francisco Thoumi
Chief
Social Studies Section
Economic & Social Development
  Department
Inter-American Development Bank
808 17th Street, N.W.
Washington, D.C. 20577

James Turner
Council Member, Overseas
  Liaison Committee
American Council on Education
Director, Africana Studies and
  Research Center
Cornell University
310 Triphammer Road
Ithaca, New York 14850

Zeferino Vaz
Professor and Rector
Universidade Estadual de
  Campinas
Caixa Postal 1170
13,100 Campinas
São Paulo, Brazil

Charles A. Wedemeyer
William H. Lighty Professor of
  Education Emeritus
University of Wisconsin-Madison
2 Blue Spruce Trail
Madison, Wis. 53717

Edward W. Weidner
Chancellor
University of Wisconsin-
  Green Bay
Green Bay, Wis. 54302

F. John Willett
Vice Chancellor
Griffith University
Nathan, Brisbane,
  Queensland 4111
Australia

Mulugeta Wodajo
Former Vice President
  Addis Ababa University
Senior Educator
Education Department
The World Bank
1818 H Street, N.W.
Washington, D.C. 20433

Yayehyirad Kitaw
Commissioner for Higher
  Education
P.O. Box 30747
Addis Ababa, Ethiopia

Mohamed Zayyan Omar
Dean
King Abdul Aziz
  University
P.O. Box 1540
Jedda, Saudi Arabia

Johnson Foundation Staff

Leslie Paffrath
President

Henry Halsted
Vice President-Program

Rita Goodman
Vice President-Area Programs

Richard Kinch
Program Associate

Pamela Smith
Program Associate

Kay Mauer
Conference Coordinator

University of Wisconsin-Green Bay Staff

Sharon Bisely

Index

Cooperative extension service, 133-138; methods used by, 128, 135-136

Cornell University: School of Agriculture, a model of land-grant concept, 84; early difficulties of extension at, 133-134

Cost effectiveness: of Open University, 52-53; of Everyman's, 52; of open universities, 65-66

Cow college, 134

Credit-course system: at Open University, 60; at Everyman's, 64; enhances diversity and equal opportunity, 177

Cross, K. Patricia, 80-81

Culture in education. See Humanities and social science, role of

Czechoslovakia, planning in, 179

Dahrendorf, Rolf, 114

Delivery systems, alternate, 59-71. See also Open university

Deutsches Institut für Fernstudien, 68

Distance learning: described, 65; perspectives on, 65-71. See also Open university

Diversity: advantages of, 49; in Wisconsin, 49-50; less possible in developing countries, 50; kinds of educational, 93; forced upon us by diverse needs, 93, 176; allows access, 175-176; and planning, 175-176, 179; in American education, 176; in British education, 176

Dohmen, Günther, 67

Domenach, Nicolas, 79

Dossiers de Vincennes, Les, 77

Drucker, Peter, 167

East-West Center, The, 40

Education, continuing. See Adult education, New learner, Extension

Education in developing countries, 96; reflects different development concerns, 101; must be part of the development process, 110

Education in France: history of, 74-76; Grandes Écoles, 75; Instituts Universitaires de Technologie, 75; Units of Teaching and Research, 76; achieving multidisciplinarity in, 76. See also University of Paris-Vincennes

Education in Great Britain: compared to U.S. education, 61-62

Garibay, Luis, 25, 26, 67, 144-145; describes continuing education in Mexico, 9; describes innovations of Universidad Autonoma, 120-122

Glazer, Nathan, 29

Glenny, Lyman, 33, 57

Goals: of education vary with social climate, 43; important in evaluation of innovation, 58; of society determine success of education, 71

González-Reyes, Eduardo, 13, 43, 66, 67; discusses planning, 178-179

Grandes Écoles, 75

Greek and Latin, study of: in England, 41; in African universities, 164

Green Revolution, 160; an example of developing related innovations simultaneously, 160

Griffith University, 13, 39, 114, 150; admissions procedures, 3; curriculum design, 20; mission, 40; governing structure, 48; Center for the Advancement of Learning and Teaching, 55; described, 112-113; focus and significance of, 113

Grosse, Siegfried, 7, 22, 26, 46, 57, 67, 73, 103, 114; describes research at Bochum, 150-151

Gutiérrez, Claudio, 8, 12, 59, 93, 176, 178

Haceteppe University, 124-125; interdisciplinary throughout, 124

Hatch Act of 1887, 83

Heckhausen, J., 104

Huberman, A.M., 36

Humanities and social science, role of, 163-167; at the University of Zambia, 163-164; in the African university, 164-165; vital in rural development, 165-166

Illinois Industrial University, 134

Ikola, Osmo, 27, 47, 152

Innovation: not always successful, 32; requires internal impetus, 35; may become orthodoxy, 42; must reflect reality, 109; essential to Green Revolution, 139; works well in combination with other innovation, 139; management of, 175-187. See also Change

Instituts Universitaires de Technologie, 75; fill technical training role in France, 93

Interdisciplinarity: emphasized at Universidad Autonoma de Guadalajara, 25-26, 121; need for, 103; and problem focus, 103-125; required for progress, 104; answers educational obsolescence, 104; criticisms of, 105, 108-109; at Universiti Sains Malaysia, 106, 110; in developing countries, 108; in higher education, 109, 125; aims

Organisation for Economic
Cooperation and
Development, 32, 38, 40

Östergren, Bertil, 49, 50,
116; diagram of Swedish
university structure,
Figure 1.2

Outreach programs: as part
of problem solving, 25-
26. See also Adult edu-
cation, Extension

Perkins, James A., 50,
175-176; defines
"university," 84,
190-191

Perry, Walter, 11, 12, 29,
30, 61, 67

Peters, Otto, 68

Phasook, Kullavanijaya,
13, 20, 33, 39, 51-52,
166-167, 172

Piaget, Jean, 104

Pifer, Alan, 18, 29, 49

Planning: essential for
higher education, 178;
limited ability for, 178-
179; in Czechoslovakia,
179; needs right people
to implement effectively,
179

Pliny, 156

Prange, W. Werner, 147

Premfors, R., 116-117

PRIMOPS program, 122-124

Problem focus: defined, 104;
an approach to interdisciplinarity, 104; in voca-
tional and nonvocational
education, 104-105; a means
for problem-solving, 107;
an objective of interdisciplinarity, 112; at
Griffith, 112-113; in
Sweden, 117, 119, 120;
emphasized at Universidad
Autonoma, 121

Problem-focused education:
at UPLB, 87; elements of,
91; at UWGB, 91-92

Problem orientation: vs.
project orientation, 21;
two kinds, defined, 21,
107; a nonprescriptive
approach, 23, 108; develops
alternatives, 108; at
Linköping, 119

Problem solving, 23-26; role
of university in, 23-24; in
developing nations, 24-26

Project orientation, 21

Reber, Louis, 128-129

Relevance, 17-30; need for,
18; in research, 26; may
lessen as university be-
comes development tool, 28-
29; important for
university, 110

Research, 143-173; at
Linköping, 21, 149-150;
problems in, 26-27; at
UPLB, 87, 138-140;
strengthened if integrated
with extension and teach-
ing, 130, 172; distin-
guishes university from
other institutions, 143;
role of, 144, 168; valuable
for students and institu-
tion, 144, 168, 172-173

238

in educational develop-
ment research, 158;
cultural problems at,
158-159; must contribute
to cultural development,
163; subjected to
Western culture, 164-
165. See also Ahmadu
Bello University,
University of Botswana,
University of Zambia

University, traditional:
structure and manage-
ment of, 45-46;
compared to inter-
disciplinary university,
110-111, Table 1.1

Vaz, Zeferino, 25, 129-
133; describes functions
of UNICAMP, 104;
describes role of
UNICAMP, 129-131

Von Neumann, John, 155

Watts, L.H., 135

Wedemeyer, Charles A., 13,
70; describes cost-
benefit analysis of
open universities, 52-
53, 66; discusses life-
long learning, 81

Weick, R., 135

Weidner, Edward W., 21, 23,
36, 38, 42, 50, 53, 55,
84, 103, 146; describes
UWGB, 88-89; discusses
strength of problem-
oriented approach, 107-
108

Whitehead, Alfred North,
191

Wiesner, Jerome B., 27

Willett, F. John, 3, 13, 23,
34, 38-40, 42, 47, 55, 104;
describes Griffith, 112-113

Wisconsin Idea: extended to
all disciplines, 80

Wodajo, Mulugeta, 42, 46, 51

Wolfle, D., 143, 146

World Bank, The: study of
Everyman's, 52, 55, 65

Yarmouk University, 37, 191;
admissions practices, 5;
provides comprehensive
higher education, 48-49,
96; goals and history of,
95-97; compared to
University of Botswana,
101; research at, 169-170;
collaboration with Georgia
Tech, 169-170

Yesufu, T.M., 173

Mohamed Zayyan Omar, 20, 22,
51; describes open program
of King Abdul Aziz
University, 68-69